D1598038

The Anatomy & Development of the Formula One Racing Car from 1975

Sal Incandela

To Lilian Beatrice

ISBN 0 85429 320 5

© Haynes Publishing Group &
Sal Incandela 1982

All rights reserved. No part of this book may be reproduced or transmitted in any form or by any means, electronic or mechanical, including photocopying, recording or by an information storage or retrieval system, without permission of the copyright holder.

Published by:
Haynes Publishing Group
Sparkford, Yeovil, Somerset BA22 7JJ,
England

Distributed in North America by:
Haynes Publications Inc.
861 Lawrence Drive, Newbury Park,
California 91320 USA

Editor: Ian Bamsey

Cover design: Rowland Smith

Cover pictures: (front) Renault RE30, courtesy Renault Sport; (rear) typical 'ground effect' front suspension and rear aerofoil section, courtesy Giorgio Piola, plus illustration of tyre slip angle.

Printed in England, by: J. H. Haynes & Co. Ltd.

Contents

Forewords

In their continued striving for greater performance, designers of Grand Prix cars have placed these machines at the forefront of automotive technology. The rate of development over the last few racing seasons has been greater than ever before, with an emphasis on aerodynamics and to a lesser extent, engines.

Because the evolution of a Formula One vehicle is so secretive, so rapid and because the industry involves such a small number of people, very little is written about the technical side of the sport. The author is one of the small group of people who have been intimately involved with the technical development of current Formula One cars.

This book is a unique, behind the scenes look at the recent technical development of Grand Prix cars and engine. It will appeal to those who take more than a transient interest in the technical side of Formula One racing and it offers a good grounding in chassis and engine set up, but more importantly, it provides a well documented and interesting record of the incredibly rapid evolution of the Grand Prix machine over the past few seasons.

Gordon Murray – FI Designer, Team Brabham

In motor racing, there exists a very special and unique group of people who don't always receive the credit they justly deserve. They spend days and nights on end taking apart and rebuilding those fantastic pieces of equipment. Their dedication is the same regardless of winning or losing. They are far away from the glory, the glamour, the celebrity, and yet without their endless sacrifice and devotion to their mechanical vocation, the great thrills that motor racing brings to each and every one of us would be non-existent.

Racing drivers put their lives in the hands of these people, and the trust and respect that develop as a result often creates longlasting friendships.

I have known Sal for many years now and have teamed with him during two full G.P. seasons. I felt assured that he would put as much heart and effort into his book as he did in preparing his racing car. Every aspect and detail concerning a modern Formula One car is covered here, described and analysed by a person directly involved in the construction of these sophisticated machines. I think it a real success... Well done Sal, you've won this one on your own .

Patrick Tambay – FI Driver

Introduction & Acknowledgements

This book is for all enthusiasts who wish to understand the anatomy and workings of a modern Formula One car in all its technical aspects, and has been written in a simple yet concise way so that engineering knowledge isn't required.

Readers should appreciate that, although the five cars detailed are now "retired", they represent a constant and fast technical evolution during a very short time. By the same token, they show the different approaches in design between five top constructors. As for the engines, these are explained in basic terms since some builders don't wish to divulge figures or details relating to their units.

The remaining chapters cover other areas equally important to a Formula One car which should give a better overall view of the highest level of Motor Racing.

I would like to express my sincere thanks to the following people for all their assistance and encouragement, be it a large or small contribution, in my quest to write this book.

Ernie Awad
Bert Baldwin
Dave Baldwin
Gerard Baras
Christoph Berns
Winston Bush
Rory Byrne
Jean Damon
John Gentry
Maurice Hamilton
Graham Lewin
Franco Lini
Claude Lobo
Giorgio Piola
Marcel Ryser
Eric Vuagnat
Glen Waters
Chris Witty
Catherine & Daniel Simonet
N. D. Anderson of BBC Crown Boveri (U.K. & Switzerland)
Simon Arkless of A. P. Lockheed
P. F. Bonser of Salisbury Transmission
P. G. Carter of Garrett AiResearch

Francois Castaing, Marie-Claude Beaumont } of Equipe Renault Sport

Gerard Ducarouge – Ex Team Manager Equipe Ligier
Keith Duckworth of Cosworth Engineering

Mauro Forghieri, Claudio Degoli } Scuderia Ferrari

Mr. Harten of KKK Germany
Patrick Head of Williams Team

Mike Hewland, Jim Bus } Hewland Engineering

Georges Martin, Jean-Francois Robin, Bruno Vincent } Engins Matra

Gordon Murray of Brabham Team
Mo Nunn of Ensign Team
Dave Wass of Arrows Team
Derek Williams of Goodyear

Ted Toleman, Alex Hawkridge } Toleman Group Motorsport

Sal Incandela

F.I.A. – F.I.S.A. – F.O.C.A

The *F.I.A. – Federation Internationale de l'Automobile* – is based in Paris and is an international organisation representing automobile clubs from all over the world which work together in order to carry out activities embracing touring and motorsport. Before 1978 the F.I.A. was known as the C.S.I. – *Commission Sportive Internationale.*

The *F.I.S.A. – Federation International du Sport Automobile* – is the sporting arm of the F.I.A. and governs motorsport on an international level on behalf of the F.I.A. Its activities include the development and revision of the International Sporting Code (rules, regulations, calendar etc.).

The *F.O.C.A. – Formula One Constructors Association* – is, as its name implies, an independent organisation of Formula One constructors and is composed of the majority of teams, with the notable exception of most continental teams. It looks after the interests of its largely British, Cosworth D.F.V. equipped member teams and looks after the financial dealings with Grand Prix organisers on behalf of all the participating teams.

Chapter 1

Evolution of the Formula One Car

Formula One designs have changed rapidly in recent years and the pace is still accelerating.

The beginning of the end for "conventional" rear engined Formula One cars was the introduction of the Lotus 78, the first "wing car".

The Lotus 78 was introduced in 1976 and missed the 1977 World Title by only a few points due to mechanical problems, notably caused by the transmission. By then it was evident that aerodynamics were going to be the major factor in Formula 1 design and that drastic changes in tyres, suspension and aerodynamics designs were going to be necessary.

Strangely enough, the opposition reacted very slowly to the new Lotus invention, partly because ground effect design was unknown and perplexity led to uncertainty. It was a question of whether to improve the existing "conventional" ideas or whether to design a totally new car which required deeper knowledge in the field of aerodynamics, and a new approach from the designer. For many teams the hesitation in doing this, the "wait and see what happens" philosophy, led to their downfall. A good example was McLaren, pioneers of conventional Formula One engineering. Change *was* necessary and the struggle of McLaren started in 1978 and lasted until the end of 1980, when things started to get a little better.

While the Lotus 78 was still in its "development" stage, a new design was on the drawing board, the Lotus 79 which destroyed the opposition with an insolent ease. At that time a few teams had a go at ground effect while others modified their existing cars by fitting side pods "a la Lotus", in order to try to do something about it. The Lotus 79 took the 1978 World Championship in the hands of Mario Andretti, the late Ronnie Peterson finishing second. From then on it was time for opposition to get back to the drawing office.

Going back to the mid to late '70's, conventional cars presented interesting variations on chassis, suspension, aerodynamics, etc. A particularly successful car in the mid '70's was the McLaren M23.
In 1977, after winning its second World Title with the M23, McLaren organisation entered the same car for the new season, for its new M26 was still under construction. The M23 was a typical robust McLaren design which had been introduced at the beginning of 1973 and ended in a museum in mid 1977.

During its life, the M23 received various changes in order to keep it competitive. The last version of the M23 was a full monocoque car with steel front bulkhead. The fuel cells were located behind the driver, alongside the monocoque. The water and oil radiators were placed at the back of

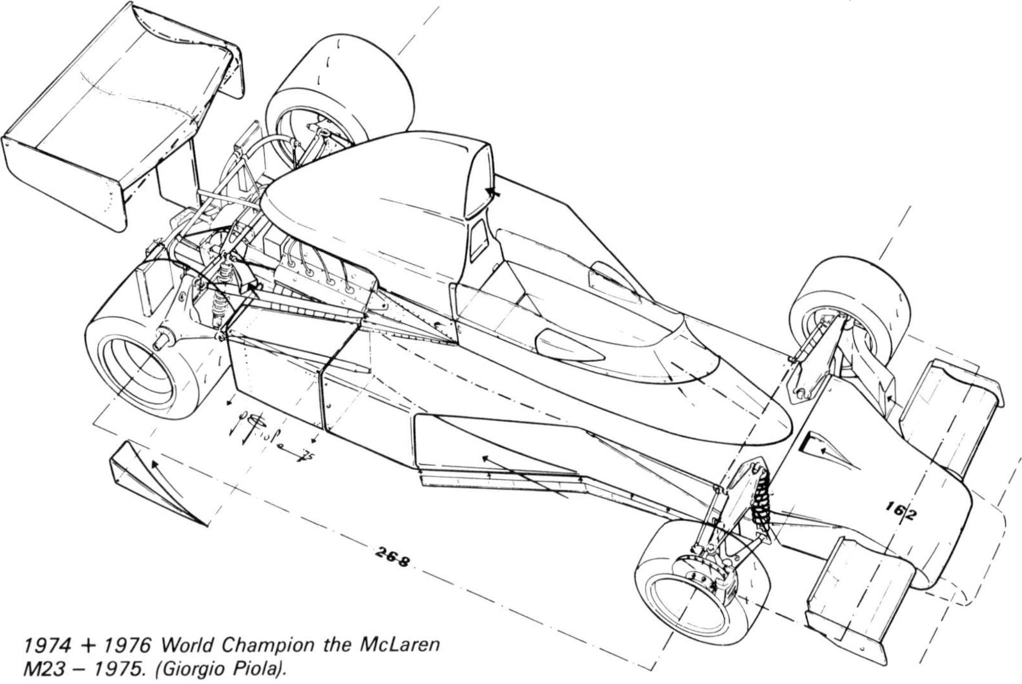

1974 + 1976 World Champion the McLaren M23 – 1975. (Giorgio Piola).

the chassis, in front of the rear wheel, forming a fairly large chassis area.

At the rear, transmission was by a Hewland FG400, modified from 5 to 6 speed ratios. Large titanium drive shafts with Glenzer-Spicer cross joints were utilised and brakes were located inboard, next to the final drive unit. The suspension was simple with cross member, top link and bottom wishbone, the wishbone attached to the gearbox. The uprights were cast magnesium, moving on the axles.

The whole rear suspension package was guided by double radius rods attached at the back. This concept was kept on further creations such as the M26, M28, M29 and M29 Mk 1, Mk 2, etc. The rear wing was supported by an arrangement of drilled aluminium plates allowing for different combinations of wing angles and positions.

The front end was even simpler, with top rockers acting directly on spring/damper combination units and lower wishbones anchored to the cast magnesium uprights. The steering rack and pinion was supported by a cast magnesium box fixed to the top section of the chassis, and was operated by a simple steering column and detachable steering wheel. The brakes were mounted outboard at the front and were single caliper, as at the rear. The nose and its wings rested on a titanium frame which often cracked.

The dashboard was reduced to simplicity and was supported by a titanium over loop. Safety was ensured by Willans seat belts, two fire extinguishers located under the driver's knees and a life bottle on the top of the central fuel tank area, underneath the titanium roll over bar.

The Ford Cosworth DFV engine was started by an air powered starter mounted to the left of the gearbox and activated from outside by one of the mechanics, a system pioneered by McLaren. With this system the car carried a bottle of highly compressed air which permitted the driver to restart the engine about six times before the bottle ran out of air.

This bottle was made of light alloy and was reduced to the size of a Coca-Cola can. Nowadays the system is fitted as standard on the majority of Formula One cars. On the M23 the entire fibre glass bodywork including cockpit, nose and air box was removable. A feature that most cars appeared with at the time was a plastic rubbing strip, bolted just in front of water radiator scoop, as well as underneath, starting from the front end of the chassis, and joined to the lateral strips, forming a 'V' shape. The purpose of this was to create a vacuum under the car, consequently increasing the down force, which gradually disappeared as the strips wore down.

In the same year, innovations appeared in the field of new materials, for honeycomb was used on the top section of the chassis which was further reinforced by a honeycomb box dashboard area. Bodywork was made with the same material, saving a fair amount of weight.

The M26 borrowed many features of the M23, but had better weight distribution close to the centre of gravity thanks to a narrowing of the overall chassis width. The water radiators were positioned closer to the engine, oil coolers mounted under the rear wing were discarded, and a simple oil cooler appeared on the front nose. After a little struggle with the handling, the car won its last Grand Prix, the Japanese.

In terms of suspension geometry and tyre development, nothing exciting had happened. Rising-rate geometry was still strongly applied on the Surtees TS19, Brabham BT46 and Ensign N176, while the Ferrari T2 used the same principle by putting the front damper-spring combination in a very open angle.

The principle of rising-rate is to help to minimise ride height changes with load and pitch amplitude variations under acceleration, and braking, its main disadvantage being complication in design. An attempt by Ferrari to use the antique De Dion system was made without success.

In the aerodynamics department, many different versions and shapes of front and rear wings and things, as well as air-boxes, appeared from time to time.

Research in this area was obvious on the Ligier-Matra JS7 where the quantity of bodywork was well above average, but nevertheless the car appeared to be a strong contender in the team's second year of Formula One, winning the Swedish Grand Prix and scoring at many other races.

Engine-wise, Alfa Romeo had entered the Formula One scene the previous year, supplying the Brabham team. Its powerful flat 12 was designed to lower the centre of gravity and stayed in that configuration until the end of the 1978 season. The association did not produce a great deal of success due to the unreliability of the power unit. A major feature of Formula One at the time was the uncompetitiveness of the Regie Renault Sport with their V6 1500cc turbocharged engine powered, Michelin shod, car. Their adventure of going turbo in Formula One was subject to a great deal of criticism. Nevertheless, appreciating the difficulties faced by such a radical new approach, and the competitiveness of the opposition, Renault Sport carried on to make progress at the expense of a lot of engine blow-ups, putting Michelin in difficulty in their tyre development at the same time.

Another innovation of the 1977 season was the Tyrrell P34 6 wheeler, which produced very good results at the hands of the late Patrick Depailler, (see Tyrrell P34 chapter).

In Italy things were going strong for the Ferrari organisation. The new T2 series was a typical Ferrari design, monocoque and steel frame forming the full chassis. The fuel was distributed around the driver in the large and strong chassis. However, the weight distribution was not the best, since the width of the flat 12 engine governed the general layout of the car. Water radiator, oil coolers and tank had to be located somewhere, which resulted in very large bodywork. Front and rear suspension geometry were "standard" with tubular bottom wishbone, and top rocker acting on an angular positioned spring damper combination at the front. The rear end suspension featured bottom wishbones guided by a single link and anchored to the gearbox. At the top, a usual link connected with a single radius rod to an enormous magnesium upright. Front and rear anti roll

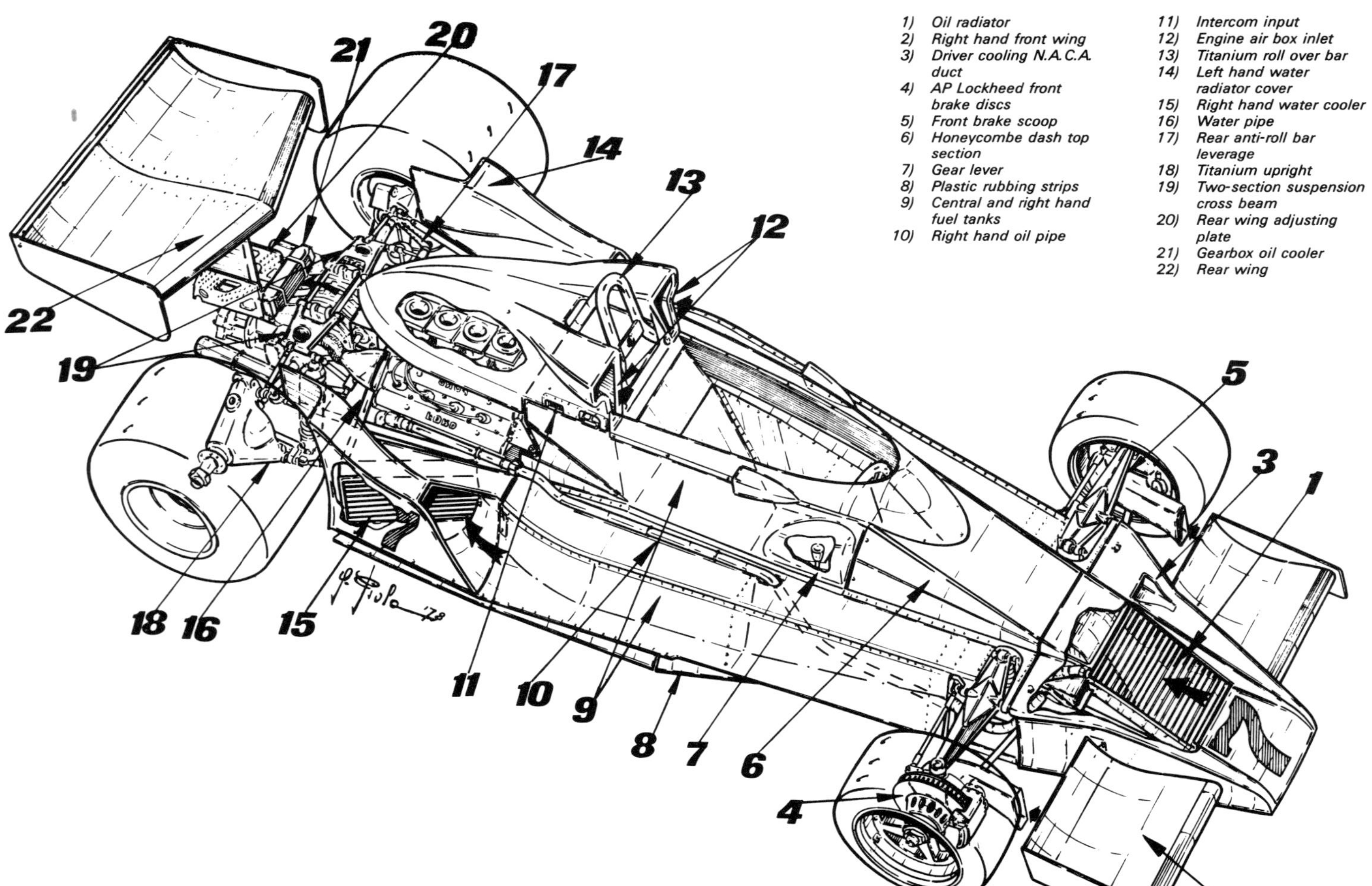

The McLaren M26. (Giorgio Piola).

The first modern Renault Formula One car RE01. (Courtesy Renault Sport).

bars were supported in a magnesium cast support. The transmission was composed of a complicated transverse gearbox with Lobro joints and steel drive shaft. The braking system arrangement included ventilated inboard discs at the rear and outboard discs at the front and massive single calipers all around. Added to this was a Ferrari brake anti-lock device located at the front end of the chassis. Aerodynamics being a subject of constant research, the massive bodywork clothed the car up to the rear of the engine.

The large N.A.C.A. ducts incorporated within the bodywork to the front of the cockpit area fed the engine. Downforce was provided by a single and large front wing and, at the rear, a choice of wing section mounted in a cast magnesium frame. The superb flat 12 engine and the ability of Niki Lauda gave Ferrari another World Title despite the Lotus 78 demonstration.

Lotus 78

Although the 78 came into service in 1977, it was a few years before that Team Lotus thought the answer might be a "wing car" (technically called "ground effect" car). After much thinking and debating, the decision was made to use the car's own form to produce aerodynamic downforce, in addition front and rear wings. The idea was apparently taken from a second World War British bomber's inner wings. The idea was that the whole section mounted alongside the chassis which had water coolers buried in it would provide negative lift, in addition to that produced by the conventional front and rear wings.

In order to get maximum side wing area, the monocoque was slim, the tub having a central fuel tank behind the driver's shoulders and one on each side, and a structural honeycomb panel in the front section, providing extra stiffness, and at the same time, lightness. The dash roll over bar was part of the chassis, and the rear roll over bar was made of steel, riveted to the top of the central fuel tank.

Twin side mounted copper water radiators were connected to the Ford DFV

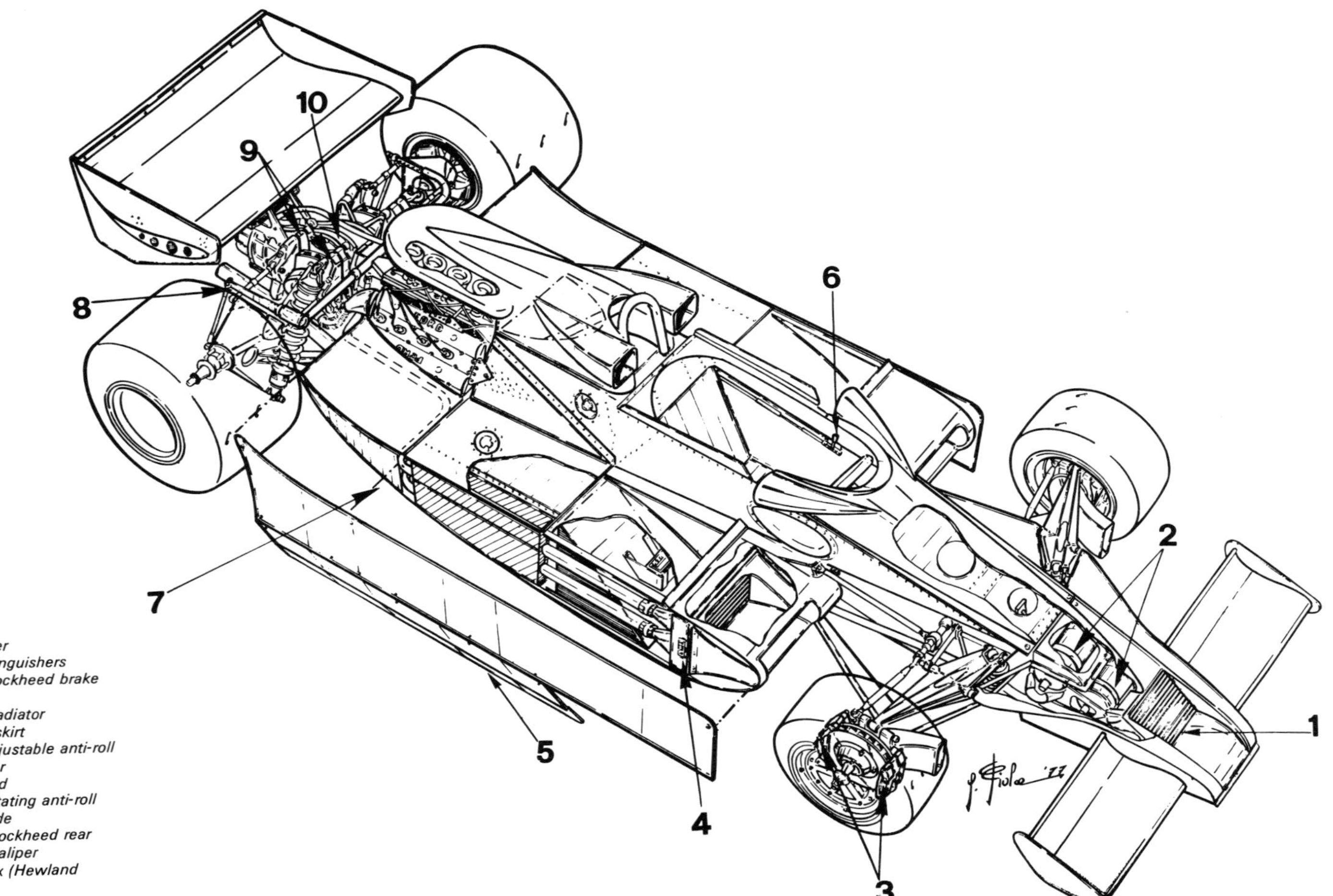

1) *Oil cooler*
2) *Fire extinguishers*
3) *Lotus/Lockheed brake calipers*
4) *Water radiator*
5) *Plastic skirt*
6) *Rear adjustable anti-roll bar lever*
7) *Side pod*
8) *Rear rotating anti-roll bar blade*
9) *Lotus/Lockheed rear brake caliper*
10) *Gearbox (Hewland FG400)*

Lotus 78. (Giorgio Piola).

engine with aluminium pipes buried in oil cooler had Aeroquip and aluminium pipes running to the engine and the oil tank was incorporated in the bell housing between the clutch and gearbox. A Hewland FG400 gearbox with special side plate was used to mount the twin inboard brake discs twin calipers and served also to pick-up the twin parallel suspension links. At the bottom large fabricated wishbones were attached to the gearbox and also to the fabricated steel uprights, which were guided by a single radius rod on either side and were dampened by spring damper units with Koni shock absorbers which were mounted on the forward brake calipers.

At the front, fabricated alloy upper rocker arms operated inboard spring/damper units and very wide based lower wishbone attached to the magnesium uprights with large bearings supporting the outboard brakes. The brakes were disc with twin calipers, and the steering was a rack and pinion arrangement. The car had a wide front track for better airflow under and over the side pods.

The transmission was geared by the faithful Hewland FG400, Lotus drive shafts and Lobro joints. A self-locking differential helped to cure wheel spin for better traction and handling since the Lotus 78 had a preferential fuel drainage system from the same source. This unique fuel system was used to allow the drivers to select which tank to empty first in order to maintain a weight distribution bias within the car as the race progressed. The balance of the car could be further influenced by an adjustable rear anti roll bar worked by the driver. The fuel drainage system and adjustable anti roll bar concepts were innovations for Formula One in 1977 but the ideas were borrowed from American U.S.A.C. cars.

As for the "secret" of this first ground effect car, it was in the side wings. Made of fibreglass, these were bolted alongside the chassis. The water radiators were housed close to the leading edge air intake and hot air exhausted through duct-ramps placed on the topside. The undersides curved upwards towards the rear of the monocoque to an inverted wing section. The section was closed-off by a side plate placed between the front and rear wheels and sealed to the ground with brushes in order to seal the air under the car (those brushes were to be called skirts). This obtained two distinct air flow regimes and the difference between air speed under and over the wing section created a downforce which "sucked" the car down to the track, the downforce created through the chassis being transferred to the tyres through spring-damper combinations. In comparison to a "conventional Formula One car", the downforce from the sidewings enormously increased the tyres' grip, thus raising cornering speed. All the way through the 1977 season the car's aerodynamics and suspension geometries were subject to modifications to improve cornering capabilities, straight line speed and other areas such as traction.

At the end of the 1977 season Lotus finished second to Ferrari in the Formula One Car Constructors Championship, having scored 5 wins, 1 by the late Gunnar Nilsson and 4 by Andretti, while winner Lauda and runner-up Jody Scheckter in the World Drivers Championship had only three wins each. From that year onwards the new Championship points system was rewarding consistency, not the number of wins, but the Lotus 78 had demonstrated the potential of ground effect design.

It was obvious that ground effect was the trend to follow and a further demonstration of the concept was held by Lotus the following year. 1977 was also notable as the second and last season of the Tyrrell P34 6 wheeler, which was interesting in terms of aerodynamics. The basic idea was to reduce the frontal area of the car for a greater straight line speed by using four small front wheels. However, the car never showed a convincing potential despite some very good results at the hands of top drivers such as Jody Scheckter and the late Patrick Depailler.

1978

The 1978 Grand Prix season saw the unexpected move of Michelin to the

Scuderia Ferrari. With their radial tyres fitted to the new Ferrari T3, which was an improved version of its predecessor, the 1977 World Championship winning 312T2. With Renault and Ferrari, Michelin had two strong teams to challenge the Goodyear stronghold and it is from then that rubber development made an interesting turning point.

In the ground effect department, the Wolf Team was one of the first to realise its potential and came up with a new concept in the form of its WR5. This dark blue creation could be differentiated from other cars by a big oil cooler mounted on the top of the dashboard area, short nose and simple front wing "a la Ferrari". The side pods were sealed by rigid honeycomb skirts which rubbed constantly on the ground to keep the air passing underside from spilling out for a maximum ground effect.

Because the wing section gradually tapered up at the back of the car, the exhaust system was formed so that it was level to the engine cylinder head and its tail pipes ran on top of the gearbox to finish under the rear wing which was supported by two huge side plates bolted to a large size tube section, itself fixed at the back of the gearbox. The idea of the big tube was to reduce drag under the rear wing. Front and rear suspension geometry were quite conventional. In all, the car was bulky but very nicely designed and its general outlook gave an idea of what "ground effect" F1 cars were going to look like.

The new "Arrows" contender entered the scene with a totally different design of ground effect system by using two double wing sections bolted onto the side of a very narrow chassis, to get maximum wing section area. Originally the car appeared with fixed skirts but later sliding skirts were introduced. Suspension layout was such that spring damper combinations were mounted on the top of the gearbox in order to let the air extract from the side wing freely. At the front, the suspension had inboard spring/dampers to allow maximum air penetration to the side wings. Braking was inboard at the back and outboard at the front with twin brake calipers on each wheel. This disposition featured on most cars at the time. Lack of room, or a consideration of weight distribution forced Arrows' designers to locate a single oil cooler right at the front, in the nose area. The car was peculiar with a different approach to the ground effect concept yet it certainly became quite competitive as its development progressed.

The Brabham BT46, created by the brilliant Gordon Murray, was still running with the "conventional" bunch. The chassis was designed around surface cooling, with two side panels for the water and oil, so that is why a triangular shape was chosen. It was built entirely in aluminium with a titanium bulkhead for the pedal frame and an aluminium based honeycomb dash area for stiffness and driver safety reasons. The back section was wide because of the width of its Alfa Romeo, including crown wheel of its Alfa Romeo flat 12 engine. Gearbox casting and special side plates were by Brabham-Alfa Romeo, including crown wheel and pinion output flanges, oil system driver shafts etc. The rest of the gearing was Hewland made, the actual bell housing was cast within the main gearbox casing for extra rigidity. At the rear were top and bottom link, parallel links machined from an aluminium block, conventional cast magnesium uprights guided by a single short radius rod and an outboard spring/damper arrangement.

The front suspension had a spring rate arrangement with spring/damper unit semi-outboard, bottom machined aluminium wishbones, and steel fabricated wishbone at the top. The steering box was riveted to the monocoque and took all the main cornering loads from the front suspension. The car did not have a nose frame as such, in fact the structural radiators were located inside a wing shaped cowling and the aerodynamic load was taken by the water radiators. The oil coolers were mounted parallel alongside the engine and built into the chassis, the oil tank coping with the engine's half-a-dozen different oil pumps. The chassis carried no less than four fuel cells and the system was as complicated as the Italian flat 12 engine.

The stopping power was provided by

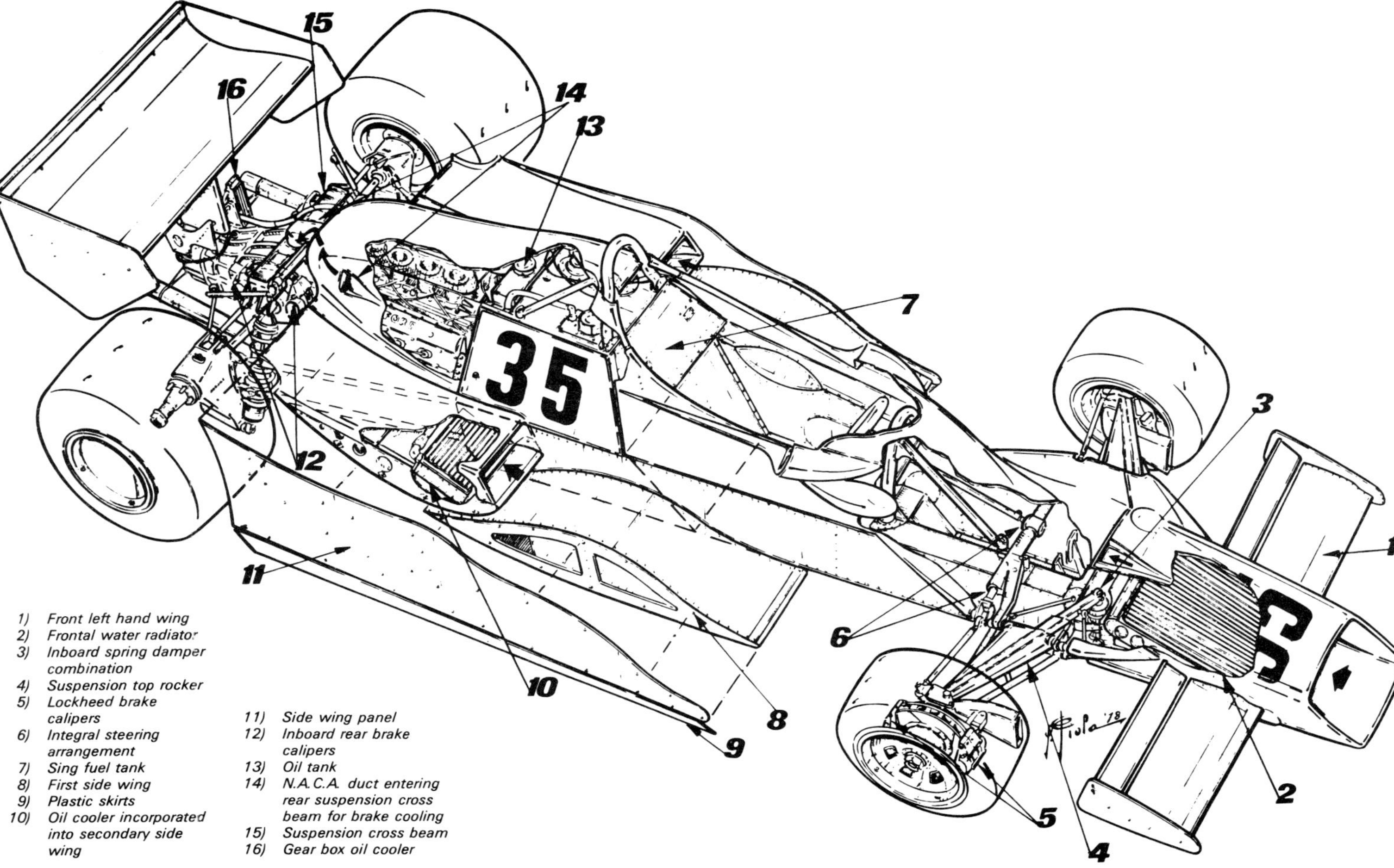

1) Front left hand wing
2) Frontal water radiator
3) Inboard spring damper combination
4) Suspension top rocker
5) Lockheed brake calipers
6) Integral steering arrangement
7) Sing fuel tank
8) First side wing
9) Plastic skirts
10) Oil cooler incorporated into secondary side wing
11) Side wing panel
12) Inboard rear brake calipers
13) Oil tank
14) N.A.C.A. duct entering rear suspension cross beam for brake cooling
15) Suspension cross beam
16) Gear box oil cooler

The Arrows A1. (Giorgio Piola).

Brabham BT46 fan car. (Giorgio Piola).

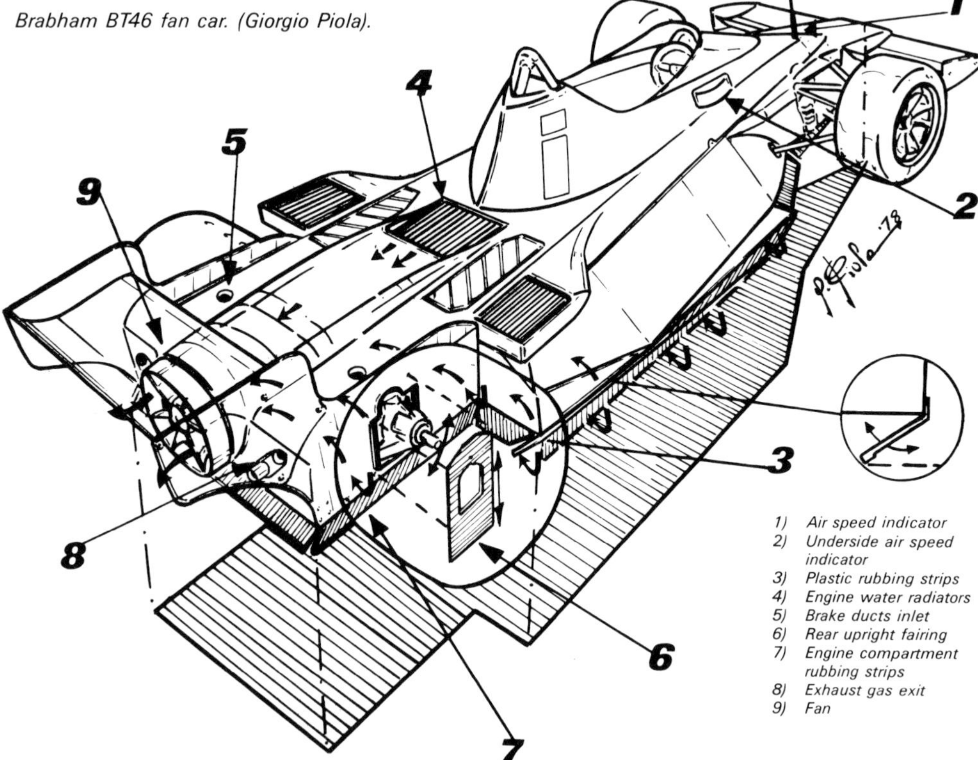

inboard discs at the rear, single caliper, and the same arrangement at the front, but outboard. Brabham was the first Formula One Team to try carbon fibre brake discs. Heat and inconsistency problems were encountered but nevertheless the system was retained and development continued. At the front brake cooling was arranged with the wheel rims forming centrifugal fans which had been developed originally for the carbon fibre brakes, in order to get rid of some of the intensive heat generated. The cooling of the rear brakes was "standard" with glass fibre ducts, and was activated by small centrifugal fans mounted on the inner CV joint and turning at the same speed as the drive-shafts. All these ideas were retained and further developed on the later Brabham Formula One cars. The Brabham team pushed its "fan-mania" even further by creating a "fan car". The principle was to have a large fan mounted at the back of the car, near the gearbox, and to seal off the underside of the chassis. The primary function of the fan idea was said to be to cool the engine but it also created an aerodynamic downforce, so it was really a different approach to ground effect design.

At the end of practice for the Swedish Grand Prix, the new Brabham became the centre of a blazing argument, despite the fact that the sport's governing body had given the car permission to run weeks before and that their representatives confirmed that the car was within the regulations. At first the car was a source of amusement but that did not last long for the two cars entered ended up on the first two rows of the starting grid. It was then that complaints were raised by other teams. Complaints were also made by the other drivers since the air being blown out of the back of the fan had picked up "debris" from the track and this was being blown straight into their faces. The car won the race in front of the amazing Lotus 79 but it was subsequently banned from racing.

The "French connection" was still "comme ci - comme ca" with the conventional single turbo Michelin shod Renault which was slowly improving its engine reliability.

1978 was the last year of the Ligier-Matra association. Once again Matra Sport retired from racing activities, this time for financial reason. However l'Equipe Ligier managed to finish 14 out of 16 Grand Prix races, showing overall reliability and consistency. The car was a conventional design and the powerful V12 a bit old fashioned. The Team was left with no other option but a Cosworth DFV power unit for 1979. The JS7/9 and the Matra V12 are described in separate chapters.

The third French connection was the entry into the circus of Automobiles Martini with its antiquated and uncompetitive first ever Formula One car, the MK23. After a few races the Team pulled out altogether. Back in England, Team Surtees sadly also packed up due to financial difficulties, as well as lack of competitive drivers. The car was a rather complicated conventional Formula One car.

The 1978 season was totally dominated by Team Lotus. The Lotus 78 was used up to mid-season and replaced by the new 79. The 8 wins, 12 pole positions and 7 lap records notched up by the two designs confirmed that ground effect was the way to go, despite a strong opposition by Ferrari which took four wins. The rest of the conventional field shared what was left, Brabham taking two wins and the new Tyrrell 007 (replacing the P34) taking one win. Good performances were given by the Williams team, steadily coming out of the dark with the neat FW06 designed by Patrick Head and driven by Alan Jones. In contrast the McLaren team was in decline with an old fashioned 'M26' design.

Ground effect principles had really originated many years before with the Chaparral Can Am Sucker cars, but the Lotus 79 did not extract air from under the car with fan, but used the underbody airflow. The Lotus 79 was another step further for that concept, which was destined to be copied by all Formula One teams in the year to come. The Lotus 79 was the first ever real ground effect car and it is described in a separate chapter.

1979

Inevitably everybody appeared in Argentina for the start of the 1979 season with ground effect interpretations. From now on Formula One design became a "hit or miss" affair since it was believed that this new use of aerodynamics needed to be exploited in order to do better than Lotus.

One of the biggest hits was the new, Cosworth-powered Ligier JS11. The car had a different appearance to its rivals. The most distinctive aspect was its outer side pod panels which looked like shark fins. This was the result of a winter-time of work undertaken in a wind tunnel. The idea was not to make the car look different or pretty, but to improve the air flow passing underneath the car, by abruptly "lifting" the upper external part of the side pod to the level of the rear wheel tops. As one third of the tyre width section was still in the low speed air path, the high rotation of the wheel extracted the air a lot quicker, acting as an "air extractor". This seemed to be quite efficient and as usual a few teams didn't hesitate to copy, in most cases without being thoroughly sure of its effects. (See photo, page 114).

In addition, for Ligier, the general approach in aerodynamics, a very good chassis, good tyres, competitive drivers and A1 preparation made it possible to make a sparkling start to the season, winning the first two races, Argentina and Brazil. Unfortunately, Ligier subsequently lost control of the situation, first by having one of their drivers hospitalised due to a mishap which occurred during his leisure time, secondly to the difficulties of adapting the car to certain European circuits. However Ligier managed to pick things up again toward the end of the season, but it was too late to cause any concern to Ferrari in the chase for the Championship Title.

In the Ferrari camp, the T4 replaced the T3 and was conceived as a better ground effect car. The main problem in accommodating the sidepod sections was the extra wide flat 12 engine and gearbox but nevertheless Ferrari managed to get around it and produced a very effective weapon which came into play at the South African Grand Prix. The T4 took a series of five victories and "runner-up" places.This was the result, perhaps not of the best chassis around, but of a powerful engine, competitive tyres, fast drivers and above all an astonishing reliability and consistency. It was enough to give Ferrari another World Title for F1 Constructors. The 1979 winner is described in a separate chapter.

Undoubtedly *the* car of 1979 was the Williams FW07, inspired by the Lotus 79, as well as many other cars more, or less, competitive. The 07's amazing superiority from the second part of the season clearly showed that simplicity in design can be a winning approach. The difficulty to understand why the car was so quick, since it didn't feature anything special, caused perplexity among the opposition. It can be suggested that a marginal superiority came from its closeness to the minimum weight limit, and its better exploitation of aerodynamics, an optimum compromise between lack of drag for maximum straight line speed and the right amount of down force for maximum cornering power. Although these are the points that everyone is aiming for, it seemed that Williams hit the "bulls eye" almost right away. The car won more races (six) than any other car in 1979, but the title still went to Ferrari's T4.

Renault's gamble finally paid off at the French G.P.,where it took its first win, while several pole positions and fastest race laps proved that their turbocharged car was very competitive indeed. Although the 1.5 litre turbocharged engine's reliability was far off that of the DFV or 312 Ferrari boxer, tremendous progress had been achieved. However, more work had to be done in order to achieve a greater reliability.

It was clear from Renault's performance that the turbocharged 1500cc V6 engine was at least equal, and probably superior, in power to the normally aspirated 3000cc V8/V12. Renault's performance had started to concern rival teams. The fear of being dominated by a turbocharged engine resulted in unofficial suggestions for imposing a much tighter fuel load limit. Following that, Mr Keith Duckworth (creator of the DFV Cosworth engine) took the opportunity to introduce a device to limit the maximum fuel flow to 27cc per second. This would in effect limit the maximum available power and thus make F1 racing much more equal, while making the engine design challenge that of obtaining the most power from a given amount of fuel. Engine capacity would be free. Perhaps in his proposition, Duckworth was above all concerned about the continuity of his own engine in F1, but one must recognise that the idea is most valuable and should be seriously considered as a means of bringing racing engines performance to a more equal level and contributing at the same time at a lower level of fuel consumption in the interests of energy conservation research. Unfortunately, nobody seemed to take notice of that; instead Ferrari, Alfa Romeo, B.M.W., to name a few, undertook to develop their own versions of turbocharged engines under the 1966 C.S.I's equivalence factor of ½ (1500cc supercharged engine equating to a 3000cc normally aspirated engine). In the meantime the DFV was still going on winning races.

In terms of aerodynamics and chassis designs, some unusual interpretations were seen in 1979. As an example, the Fittipaldi F6 used very short side pods but total coverage of engine and gearbox by the bodywork to improve airflow at the back of the car. The Arrows A2 pushed the ground effect theme even further by creating a car which seen in perspective formed a single wing section. This was achieved by tipping up the engine and rear axle by 4° and by a complex side pod sealing, with extra skirts mounted right under the nose frame section. Good intentions were there, but the car didn't live up to its expectations and never showed competitiveness during the season.

Brabham, whilst running amongst the leaders, were for three years hampered by unreliable V12/flat 12 Alfa Romeo engines. Enough was enough and eventually, late in the season, the DFV Cosworth replaced the Italian units. The BT48 was one of the first F1 cars to have outboard brakes all around (Williams also had them), this to allow a better air circulation under the car. Other interesting features were included items such as a rising rate suspension system, the use of carbon fibre panels in certain areas of the chassis, while development of carbon fibre brake discs was still going on. As a whole, the car appeared to be a very strong contender for 1980.

Up to the beginning of the European season, the Lotus had been good enough to amass points for its team. Unfortunately, Lotus' 1978 performance was quickly overshadowed in 1979 by Ligier, Williams and some others. While waiting for the new Lotus 80, attempts to improve the "old" 79 with alterations such as different suspension geometry, different venturi sections and rear outboard brakes did not ease the situation. The new 80 was introduced officially at the Spanish G.P. Its exciting new approach to ground effect proved to be a major disappointment.

Conscious of having to retain their lead in ground effect design over the opposition, Lotus created the 80, and carried out tests prior to the Spanish G.P. at the Jarama circuit. Amazement was expressed at the complexity but beauty of the car. Never had people seen such a superb racing car, both as regards its general line and, above all, its mechanical layout. The revolutionary and inventive minds of the Lotus people had, at first sight, created something to cause the opposition some concern. The large nose was devoid of front wings and the outer curve of the large side pods ended up inside the rear wheels. The nose had a small oil-radiator which took in air via a small opening in the front. The rear wing was mounted on large end plates, as on the 79, and was situated very low, but what attracted most attention was the shape of the skirts, starting at the front end of the nose and going as far as the rear wheels, blending in with the rounded shape of the side pods. The rear end assembly was completely enveloped, joining up with the rear of the body and providing a general shape resembling that of a whole aircraft wing. The complex construction, advanced mechanical elements (all-titanium suspension arms for example) and above all the way in which the skirts functioned, appeared to be a step forward. However, the air circulation underneath the car was complex, and it was difficult to keep control of it. From this fact it appears that the air underneath the car was trapped, forming a cushion of air, and consequently the venturi effect was reduced to a minimum (see aerodynamics).

From that point onwards, Team Lotus plunged downhill, accompanied by a series of compromises that in the end led to the car looking little like it did when first introduced. Perhaps Lotus should have retained the venturi effect obtained on the 79 by developing that concept further. Quite apart from this, mechanical troubles forced Lotus to withdraw the car from the track for the remainder of the season, after which the team was obliged to revert to the 79, without success. At the end of the season, the new, conventional "81" ground effect car took shape, ready for the 1980 season.

In the field of the "disasters", the McLaren M28 was another example. Unlike the Lotus 80, the M28 did not create amazement, but deception in terms of aerodynamics as a whole and the fundamental concept that a Formula One car should be as small and light as possible, given the imposed weight limit. The cumbersome McLaren creation used an all honeycomb chassis containing three large fuel cells and the positioning of various "heavy" elements did not help weight distribution either, because the honeycomb chassis configurations could not be altered. The car never responded to changes in suspension and aerodynamics. Added to this were problems of lack of traction, excess weight of around 100lbs and a low straight line speed. McLaren joined the people at the back of the grid. In mid-season, the new M29 took over, using this time a conventional (single fuel cell) chassis. Overall, the M29 was an appreciable improvement on the M28, but that one didn't hit the headlines either.

1980

Passing to the 1980 season, nothing drastic

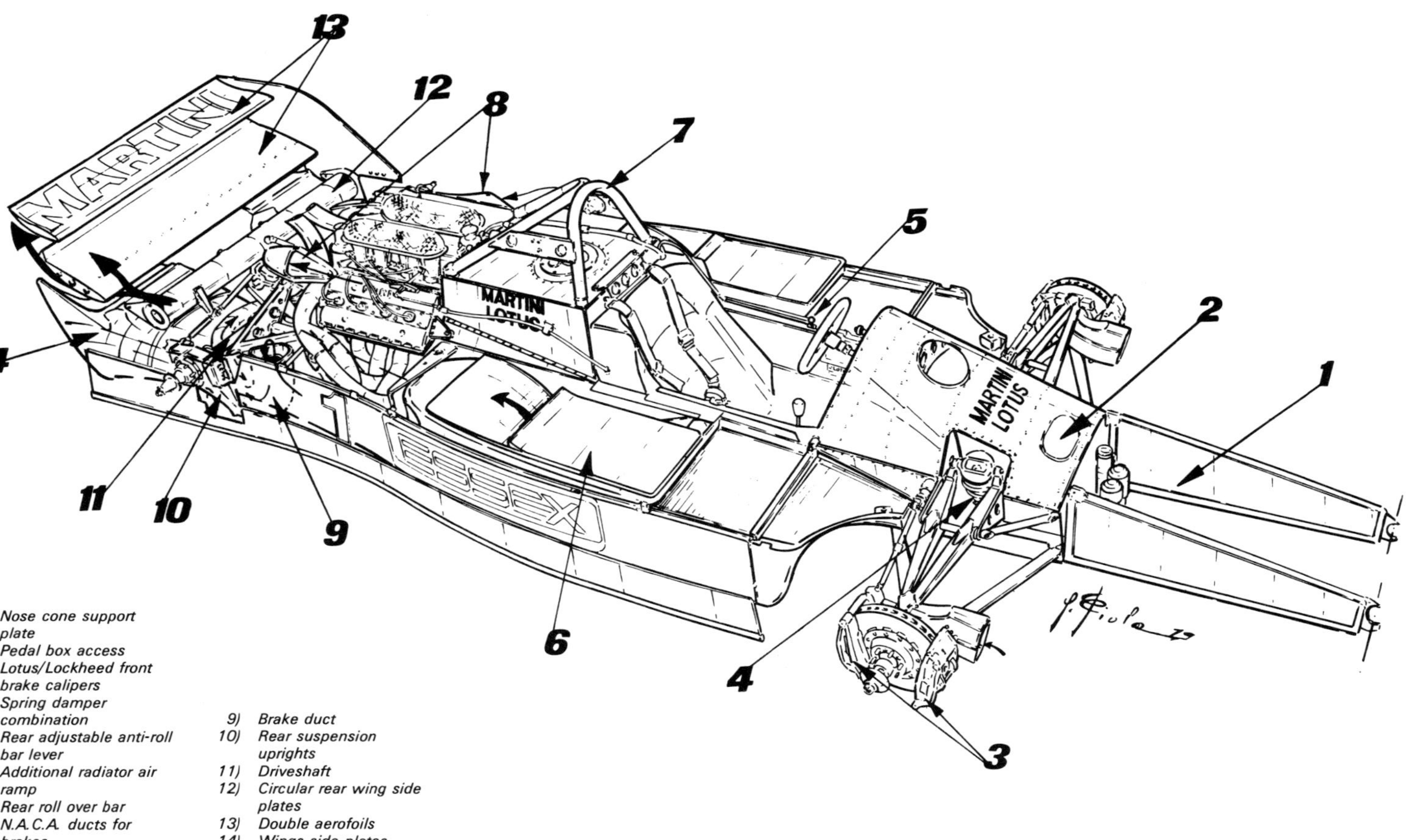

1) Nose cone support plate
2) Pedal box access
3) Lotus/Lockheed front brake calipers
4) Spring damper combination
5) Rear adjustable anti-roll bar lever
6) Additional radiator air ramp
7) Rear roll over bar
8) N.A.C.A. ducts for brakes
9) Brake duct
10) Rear suspension uprights
11) Driveshaft
12) Circular rear wing side plates
13) Double aerofoils
14) Wings side plates

The Lotus 80. (Giorgio Piola).

1) Kevlar nose
2) Chassis front bulkhead
3) Steering rack
4) Suspension rocker clearance hole
5) Front suspension rocker pick-up beam
6) Suspension rocker
7) Sliding skirt
8) Engine oil cooler
9) Water radiator
10) Honeycombe under wing side panel and Kevlar top bodywork section
11) Titanium rear roll over hoop
12) Inboard spring damper combination
13) Engine exhaust primary pipes
14) Rear suspension cast magnesium upright
15) Air box
16) Integral rear wing side plates
17) Exhaust trail pipes ramp
a) Top and bottom facing skins
b) Honeycombe core
c) Film adhesives

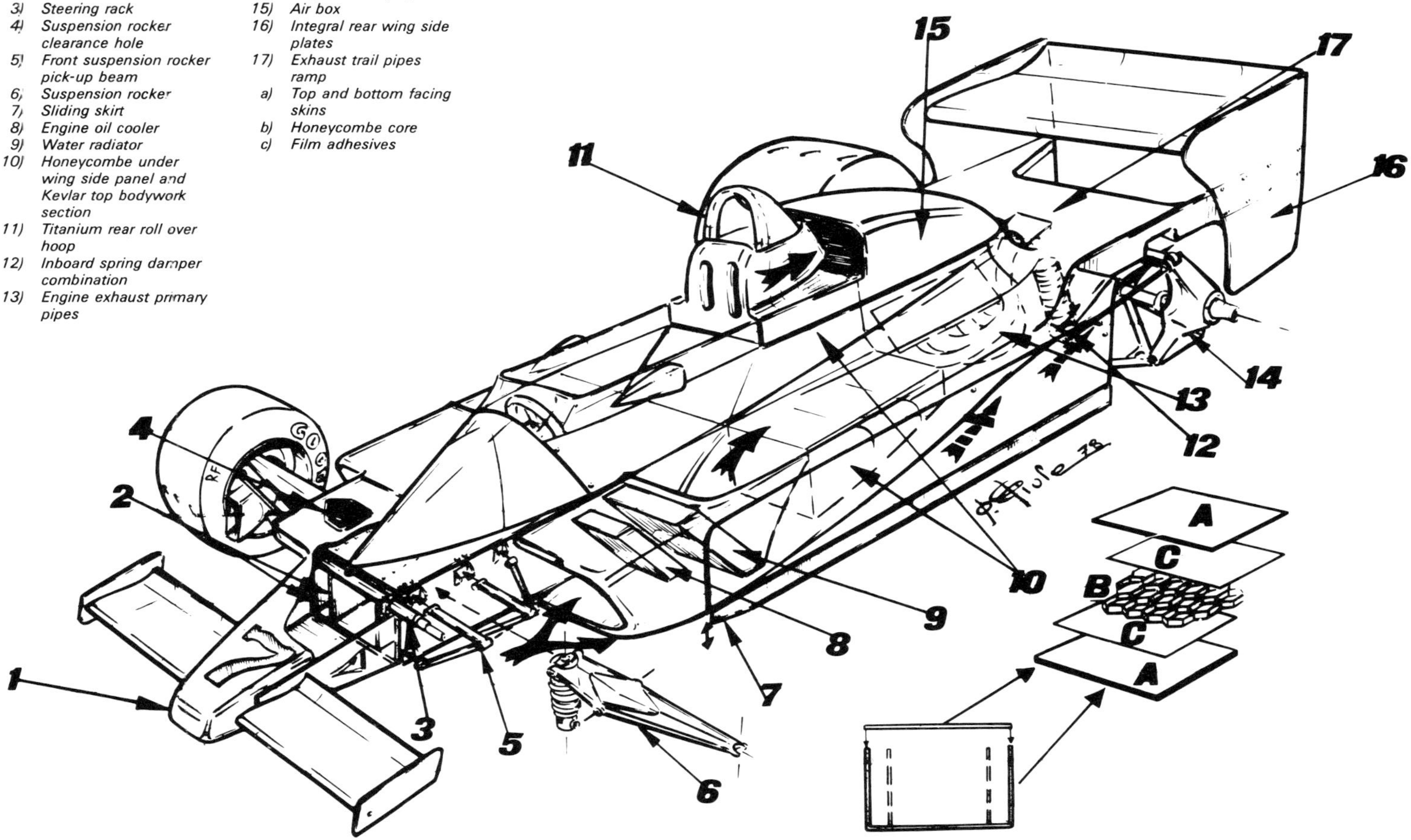

Honeycomb chassis McLaren M28. (Giorgio Piola).

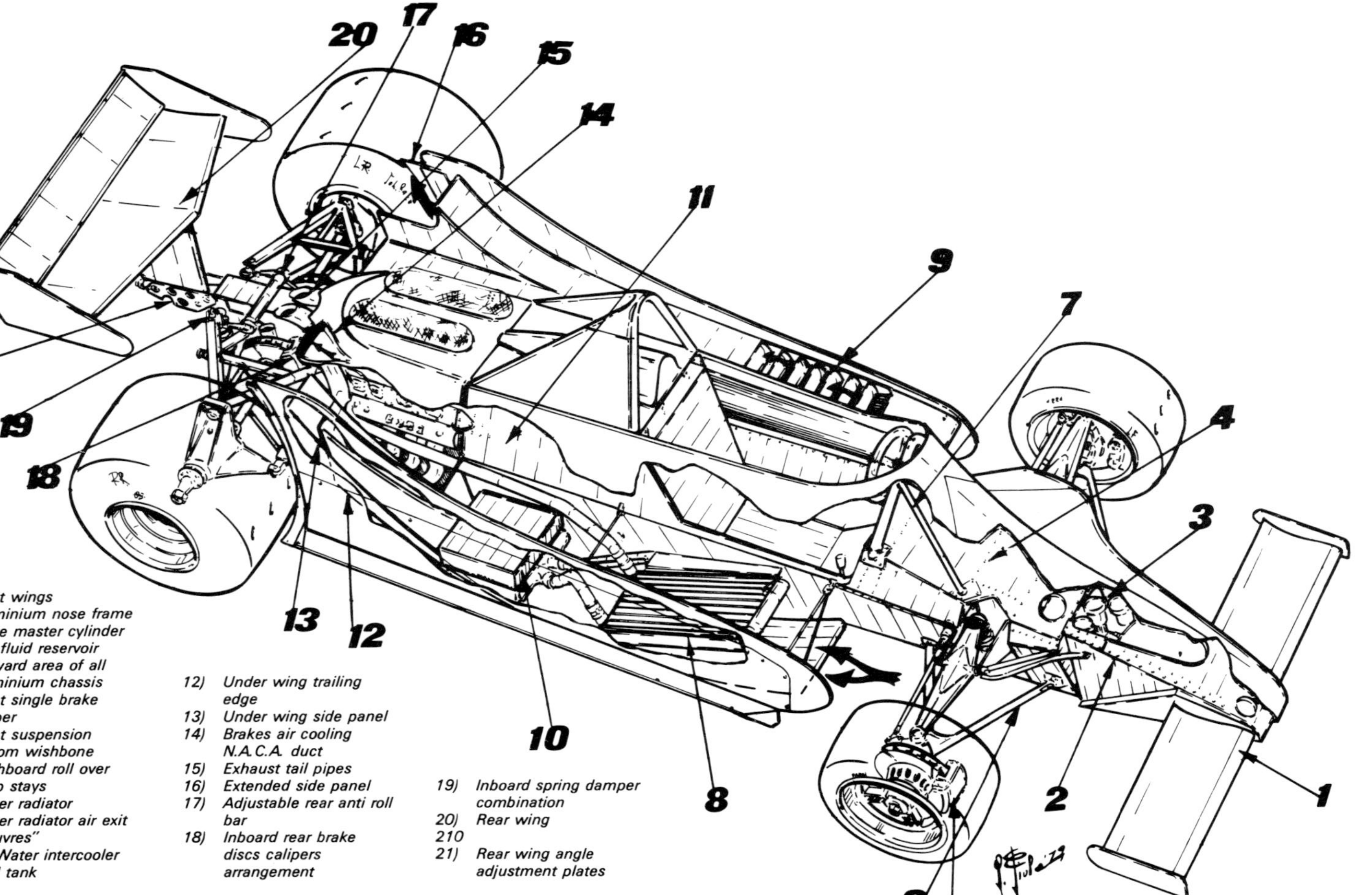

1) Front wings
2) Aluminium nose frame
3) brake master cylinder and fluid reservoir
4) Forward area of all aluminium chassis
5) Front single brake caliper
6) Front suspension bottom wishbone
7) Dashboard roll over hoop stays
8) Water radiator
9) Water radiator air exit "Louvres"
10) Oil-Water intercooler
11) Fuel tank
12) Under wing trailing edge
13) Under wing side panel
14) Brakes air cooling N.A.C.A. duct
15) Exhaust tail pipes
16) Extended side panel
17) Adjustable rear anti roll bar
18) Inboard rear brake discs calipers arrangement
19) Inboard spring damper combination
20) Rear wing
210
21) Rear wing angle adjustment plates

The Mclaren M29. (Giorgio Piola).

happened. The ground effect theme seemed well established and everybody started with an "up-to-date" car, the main efforts being orientated around better exploitation of aerodynamics in general. The season was again to be dominated by four teams: Williams, Brabham, Ligier and Renault.

This time, Williams were soon well under way, winning the first G.P. of the season. That was followed by five other victories. For its second consecutive year, the FW07 chassis, with minor changes, demonstrated an astonishing superiority that only the Brabham BT49 was able to challenge.

The BT49's reliability was equally impressive. It scored three wins and many other runner-up places. In the team's second car, a Weismann gearbox replaced the traditional Hewland FGB in a bid to improve the airflow at the back of the car, as the American unit is a lot slimmer and taller than the British one. Otherwise the car was kept basically as it had been the previous year.

In the French camp, Ligier continued to improve the JS11/15, but again the results were on a "see-saw" and Ligier had to be content with only two wins. Unfortunate circumstances prevented them scoring other wins.

As for Renault, their turbocharged V6 engine proved to be more and more reliable. If the engine and tyres caused less concern than in previous years, this year persistent failures occurred in the transmission. Three wins plus several pole positions and lap records were sufficient to cause a deeper concern about turbocharged engines and that's what Alfa Romeo and Ferrari were preparing for the coming year.

Ferrari had a disastrous 1980 season with its T5 car, largely due to unusual engine failures. It was clear to Ferrari that its 312 Boxer engine was at its limit of performance and the team's new 126c turbocharged car undertook its first practice sessions at the Italian G.P., by way of a trial. At the end of the season, the T5 ended up in the museum, the team concentrating on the development of its new design.

The 1980 season saw the official entry of Alfa Romeo with its own version of the ground effect concept, in the form of the bulky 179 which was improved as races went by and which in the end appeared to be a serious challenger for the coming season.

At the last 2 rounds of the 1980 championship, the competitiveness of the Williams FW07 and the sheer driving ability of Alan Jones simultaneously took the Formula One Constructors and Drivers World Titles.

1981

Interesting innovations were to be seen in this new season, despite the new F.I.S.A. rules aimed at reducing ground effect. The inventive minds of some designers were capable of turning the situation to their advantage.

Although Williams dominated the first race of the season in South Africa, still with sliding skirts, in Argentina Brabham found a way round the newly introduced skirt ban to produce the much loved downforce by means of a jacking hydraulic suspension system, which soon was to be reproduced on all other Formula One cars. Team Lotus meanwhile was battling to introduce its 88 creation, but without success. (See Lotus 88 story). On the grounds of decreasing cornering speed by diminishing ground effect, F.I.S.A. had banned sliding skirts as from the Long Beach Grand Prix. The new rules stated that "at any time all suspended parts of the car must be no less than 6cm from the ground". The hydraulic syspension system itself wasn't defying the rules as there was no regulation to say that hydraulic or variable suspension was illegal, but by lowering the car at speed it was breaking the 6cm rule. However, scrutineers could only measure the 6cm gap when the car was stationary, in the pits.

The easy win of Nelson Piquet in Argentina caused a furore of protest from other teams against the supposed illegality of Brabham's hydraulic system, (some teams had tried a similar idea during winter testing). As it appeared to be a relatively

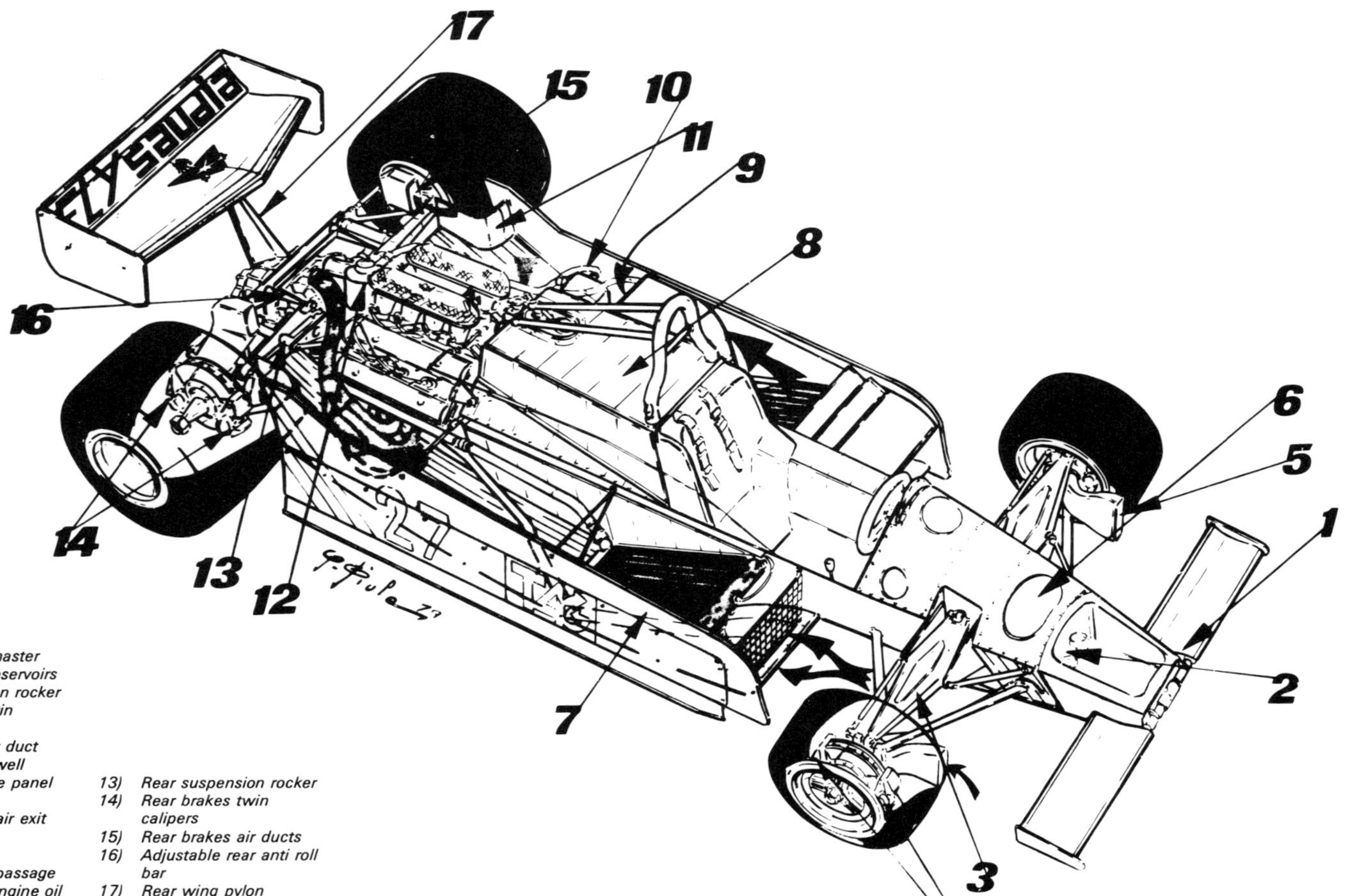

1) Front wings
2) Brakes clutch master cylinders and reservoirs
3) Front suspension rocker
4) Front brakes twin calipers
5) Front brakes air duct
6) Pedals access well
7) Under wing side panel
8) Fuel tank area
9) Water radiator air exit ramp
10) Inter cooler
11) Integral wheel passage
12) Bellhousing – engine oil tank
13) Rear suspension rocker
14) Rear brakes twin calipers
15) Rear brakes air ducts
16) Adjustable rear anti roll bar
17) Rear wing pylon

1980 World Champion the Williams FW07. (Giorgio Piola).

The Brabham-Ford BT49.

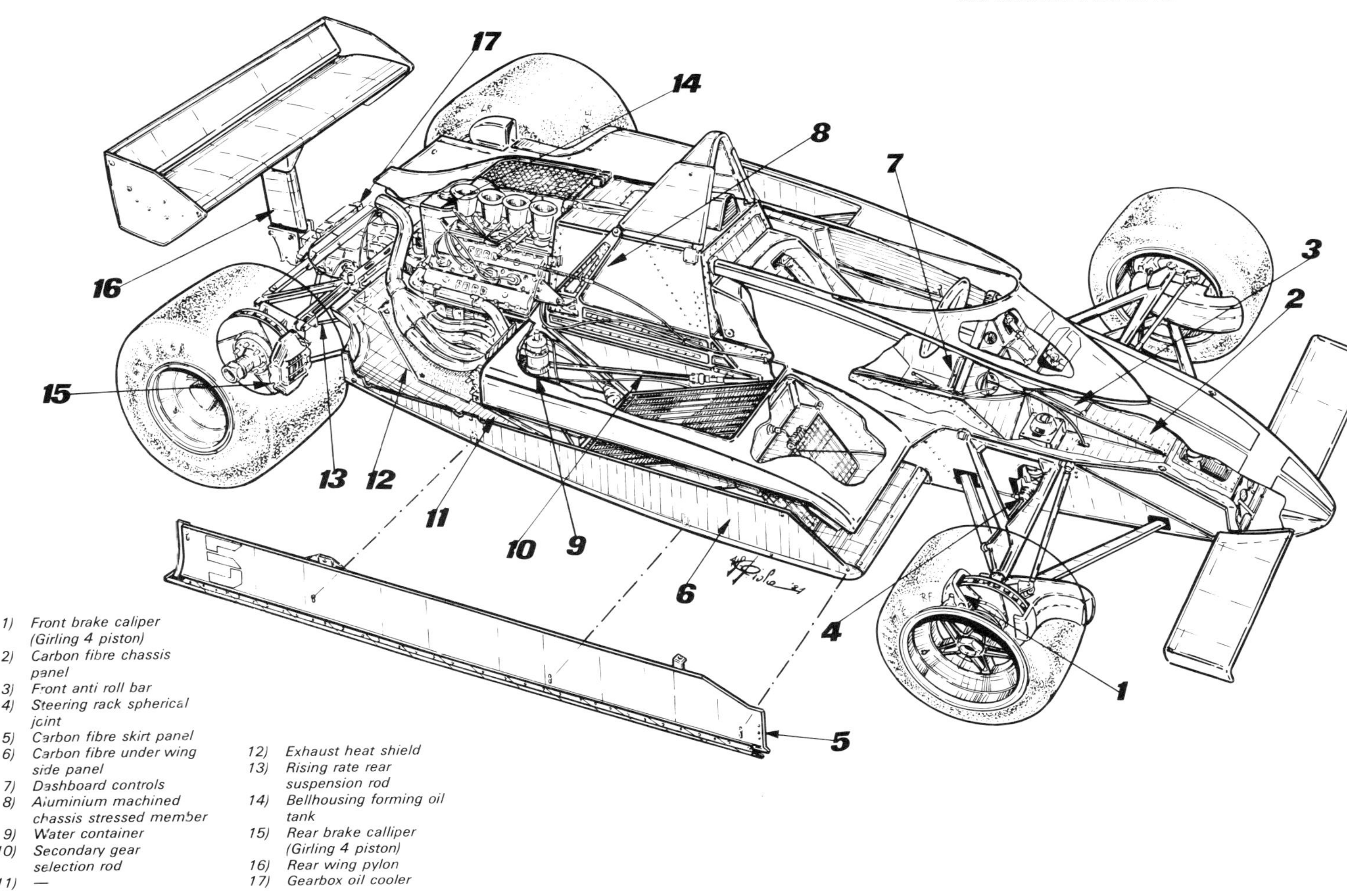

1) Front brake caliper (Girling 4 piston)
2) Carbon fibre chassis panel
3) Front anti roll bar
4) Steering rack spherical joint
5) Carbon fibre skirt panel
6) Carbon fibre under wing side panel
7) Dashboard controls
8) Aluminium machined chassis stressed member
9) Water container
10) Secondary gear selection rod
11) —
12) Exhaust heat shield
13) Rising rate rear suspension rod
14) Bellhousing forming oil tank
15) Rear brake calliper (Girling 4 piston)
16) Rear wing pylon
17) Gearbox oil cooler

1) Front wing pick-up points
2) Brake master cylinder
3) Front suspension tab fairing
4) Pedal box
5) Brake scoop
6) Single Girling caliper
7) Wheel stub axle
8) Additional aluminium brake scoop
9) Driver's knee bridge
10) Oil cooler
11) Water cooler
12) Skirt
13) Radiator air exit louvres
14) Water port
15) Fuel pumps protection shield
16) Side pod support frames
17) Medical air bottle
18) Water pipe
19) Fuel tank trap
20) Cockpit/bodywork section
21) Under side wing section
22) Rear wheel fairing
23) Fuel tank bay
24) Engine top pick-up plate
25) Exhaust system
26) Side pod side plate
27) Bodywork engine cover section
28) Left hand exhaust tail pipe
29) Bellhousing
30) Brake ducts
31) Twin brake calipers (Girling)
32) Inboard spring damper combination
33) Suspension cross beams
34) Rear wing

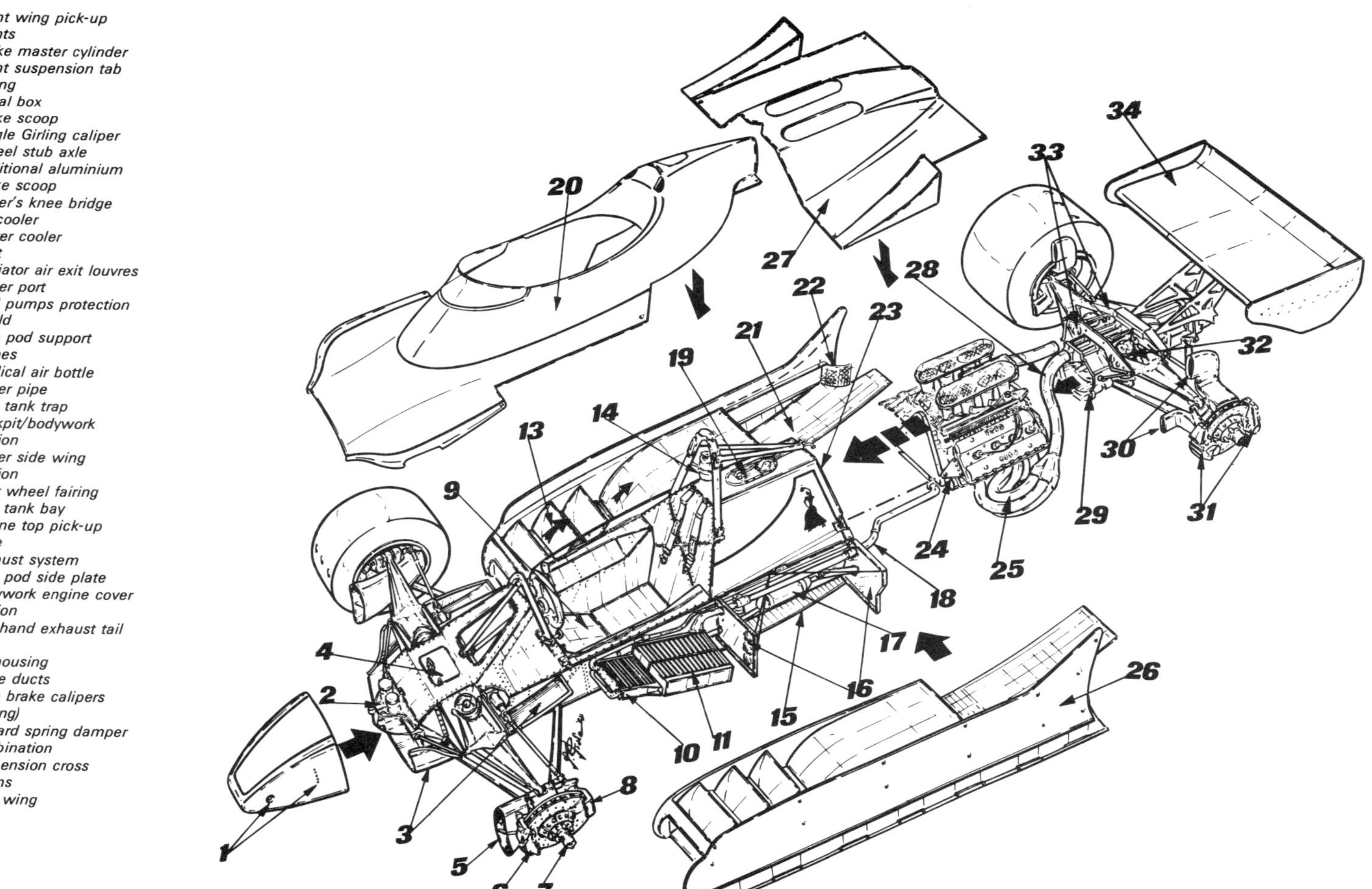

The Ligier-Ford JS15. (Giorgio Piola).

easy concept to reproduce, in a short time the opposition dropped their protests. After all, this innovation was the best way of recovering the loss of ground effect. As the system had been accepted as legal (F.I.S.A. had no choice), work was concentrated on finding the ideal type of flexible plastic rubbing strip to attach to the lowest part of the bodywork side pods. The design of the hydraulic system as a whole and the evolution in search of more ground effect led to the use of heavy suspension spring rating, up to 4,000 lbs per inch. Consequently the cars became "suspension-less", which was widely publicised by the drivers as a dangerous situation. This declaration could be supported by the fact that a sudden loss of ground effect (while riding a chicane or a sudden irregularity of the track) could be disastrous.

The jacking suspension system can be quite simple, consisting of a sealed cylinder-piston combination mounted directly between the lower part of the shock absorber and the spring. (Shorter springs are fitted to compensate the cylinder-piston height). Inside the left or right side pod is a pressurised reservoir filled with air to provide the necessary force to work the jacks which are fed by means of flexible pipes (similar to brake lines) through a mechanically or electrically governed one-way valve. When the valve is activated from the dashboard, pressurised air fills the jacks which in turn automatically lift the whole chassis, so that it conforms to the 6cm rule. As the car leaves the pit road the driver closes the valve (by electric switch or leverage arrangement), letting the air contained in the jacks into the atmosphere. The weight of the car immediately pushes the piston back down, lowering the whole chassis to a desired and well defined level. Consequently the plastic rubbing strips can be touching the ground, recovering full the ground effect. (Unlike the switch device the Brabham was activated by the downforce created according to the car's speed).

Before entering the pit road the action was reversed; the car's chassis was jacked up and rolled onto a flat area where the 6cm gap was checked by the scrutineers of the Grand Prix in question. The whole operation was simply a farce. As from 1982 new F.I.S.A. rules increased the height of the rubbing strips to 10cm, and by doing so the jacking suspension system became unnecessary, which makes things a lot easier for everybody.

The '81 season saw Matra re-enter Formula One, supplying Ligier with a revised V12 to comply with ground effect requirements. Like many other teams, Ligier started the season poorly, on one hand due to engine trouble and on the other, losing out until ground effect was recovered with the jacking suspension system. Their JS17 rapidly became more and more competitive as the Grand Prix went by, three wins and many runner-up placings bringing some hope for the final round of the Championship which, in the end, was a repetition of previous records and situations. in the end, was a repetition of previous records and situations.

As expected Ferrari turned up at Long Beach with the new 126c turbocharged V6 engine with a choice of Comprex and KKK turbos, but the Comprex system was quickly put aside due to a constant breakage of the cell wheel driving shaft (see Comprex). Consequently the team concentrated their effort on the KKK version. Two consecutive wins (Villeneuve) confirmed the potential of turbocharging in Formula One but the rest of the season was hampered by engine trouble, accidents and bad handling.

With Williams maintaining competitive-ness for a third year, the team proved that ground effect was well under its control. Once again the logical concept of the FW07, beautifully driven by Jones and Reutemann, made the point of versatility and reliability, both drivers sharing the wins. Leading the Championship from the start, Reutemann's, at one stage, commanding position became unpredictable in the last few races for Piquet closed the gap until just one point separated the two of them. The final round at Las Vegas found both with difficulties, Reutemann with gear selection problems, which for a driver of his experience really shouldn't have slowed him down to the extent that it did, while Piquet

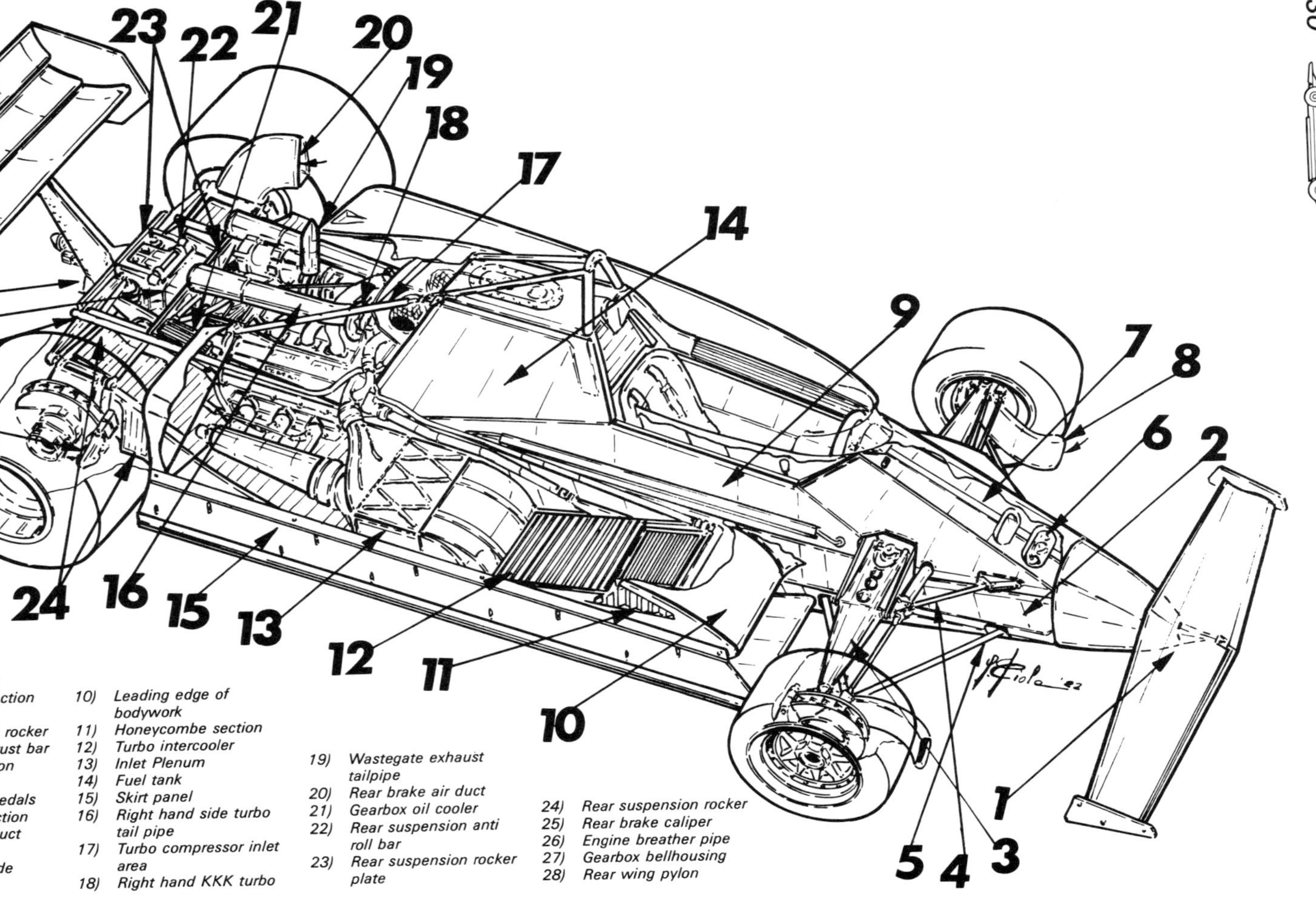

1) Single front wing
2) Drivers foot protection area
3)m Front suspension rocker
4) Rocker plates thrust bar
5) Bottom suspension wishbone
6) Access hole to pedals
7) Chassis front section
8) Front brake air duct
9) Chassis cockpit reinforcement side panels
10) Leading edge of bodywork
11) Honeycombe section
12) Turbo intercooler
13) Inlet Plenum
14) Fuel tank
15) Skirt panel
16) Right hand side turbo tail pipe
17) Turbo compressor inlet area
18) Right hand KKK turbo
19) Wastegate exhaust tailpipe
20) Rear brake air duct
21) Gearbox oil cooler
22) Rear suspension anti roll bar
23) Rear suspension rocker plate
24) Rear suspension rocker
25) Rear brake caliper
26) Engine breather pipe
27) Gearbox bellhousing
28) Rear wing pylon

The early version of the 1981 Ferrari 126C. (Giorgio Piola).

had problems of the physical kind, but his determination to win that Championship kept him going to finish fifth, enough to take the title by a one point margin. As for Jones, he led his last race majestically from start to finish with the insolent domination of a great Champion and retired from racing to return to his native country.

Piquet's title should be greatly attributed to Gordon Murray's superb machinery as well as its preparation and the hard work in developing the car to a winning pitch. The Team introduced its own version of a turbocharged Formula One car from the start of 1982. This new creation, called BT50, is powered by an in-line four cylinder BMW (KKK turbo) engine, bringing the number of teams using turbo engines to five.

In the McLaren clan, the whole approach to the business had been changed for the better through an amalgamation with Ron Dennis' team, Project Four, the new operation referred to as McLaren International. The extensive use of carbon fibre on the new Marlboro (McLaren) MP4 commanded a lot of attention in the paddocks. Engineering wise its design was simply magnificent, meticulous attention to details as well as its approach to aerodynamics making a large number of other Formula One cars look like war tanks. But above all, this carbon fibre chassis should set a new pattern in the near future (The Brabham BT49, BT50, Lotus 88, 87 and 91 chassis are partly or fully built with carbon fibre).

Many critics of carbon fibre advanced the idea that the new material wouldn't necessarily offer the rigidity required in a Formula One chassis, and expressed concern about a possible lack of driver protection. This allegation was quickly proven wrong as McLaren International's second driver, Andrea de Cesaris, demonstrated many times the qualities of carbon fibre in massive shunts during the '81 season. His teammate John Watson won the British Grand Prix and scored on many other occasions, showing the competitiveness and reliability of the MP4. In 1982 Niki Lauda returned to Formula One in the seat of an MP4, and the team is planning to go turbocharged in the near future with a Porsche V6. Proper use of carbon fibre requires a vast amount of specialized knowledge and construction can only be carried out by highly trained personnel.

In the Renault camp continuous development and research with their turbocharged V6 car in the field of engines, aerodynamics and handling, proved that the Regie could be at home on any kind of circuit and engine reliability became remarkable. Their demonstrations in 1981 proved the worth of the turbocharged solution as the RE30 became a strong threat in Formula One Alain Prost took three convincing wins and lost quite a few others only due to minor mechanical failures.

Entering Formula One for the first time in 81 was Toleman Group Motorsport, the 1980 European Formula Two Champion. The Toleman Group is a private group of companies in the U.K. The Group's Chairman is Ted Toleman, himself a world top rated off-shore power boat pilot, having won the 1979 British Class 1 Championship and the following year, having become European off-shore power boat Champion. Toleman Group Motorsport was created by the Group's Managing Director Alex Hawkridge, himself a former racing driver. He introduced the Company to motor racing in the early '70's, initially in a very small way with saloon cars. Toleman has progressed each year through the echelons of the sport until in 1978 it was decided to promote the Company's wider interest through motor racing at an international level. Commercial experience has shown that self sufficiency can play a major role in success, so it was decided to form a Toleman Racing Team that could directly apply proven commercial practices to a racing division. 1978 saw the first step into Formula Two with the running of a privately entered March which caused many people in the establishment to take note of this new competitive force. 1979 produced an expanded Team with a works supported Ralt car resulting in a high competitive season.

1980 proved that the decision to produce a brand new Toleman Formula Two

The 1982 Marlboro McLaren Int'l MP4.

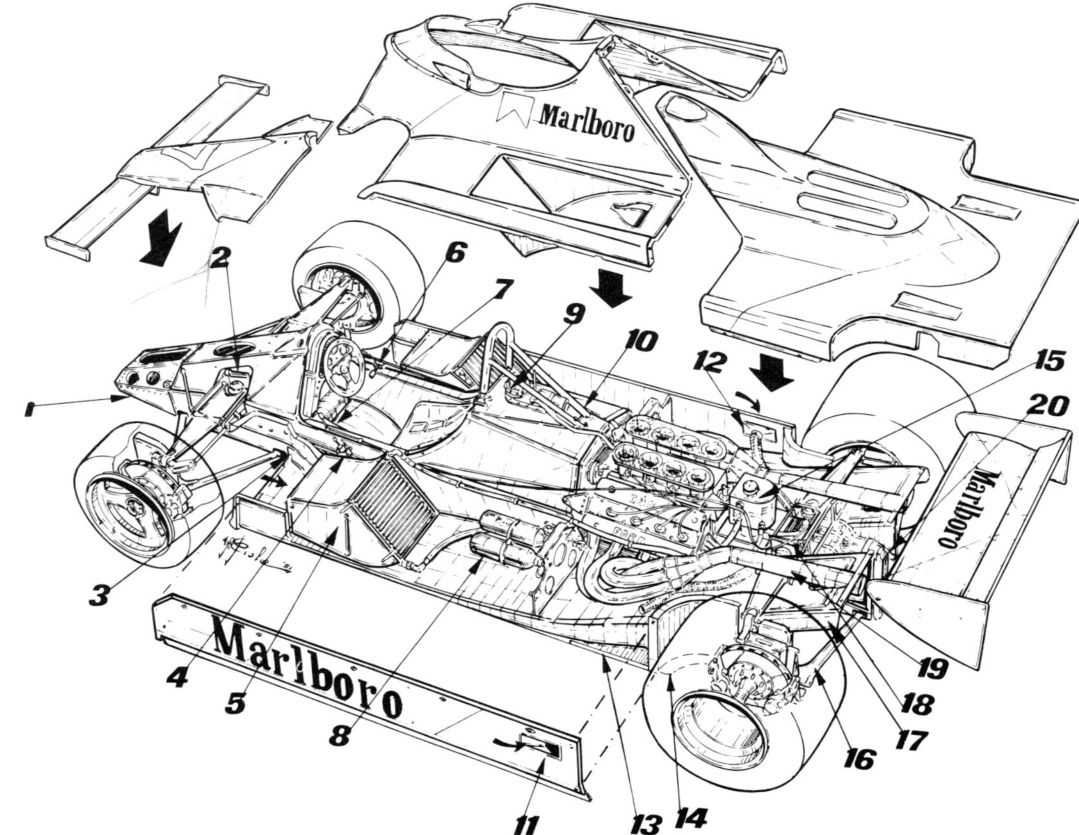

1) Aluminium chassis nose section
2) Front anti roll bar blade
3) Bottom suspension wishbone, rear leg inboard pick-up point
4) Air starter action lever
5) Honeycombe oil radiator air duct
6) Gearlever
7) Rear anti roll bar stiffness adjusting lever
8) Air starter bottles
9) Fuel tank quick filler
10) Titanium chassis roll bar
11) Left hand rear shock absorber cooling duct
12) Right hand rear shock absorber cooling duct
13) Carbon fibre under wing
14) Rear wheel sealing to under wing
15) Engine oil filler and catch tank
16) Rear suspension fabricated steel bottom wishbone
17) Under wing extension to the back end of car
18) Adjustable rear anti roll bar
19) Left hand exhaust tail pipe
20) Gearbox oil tank

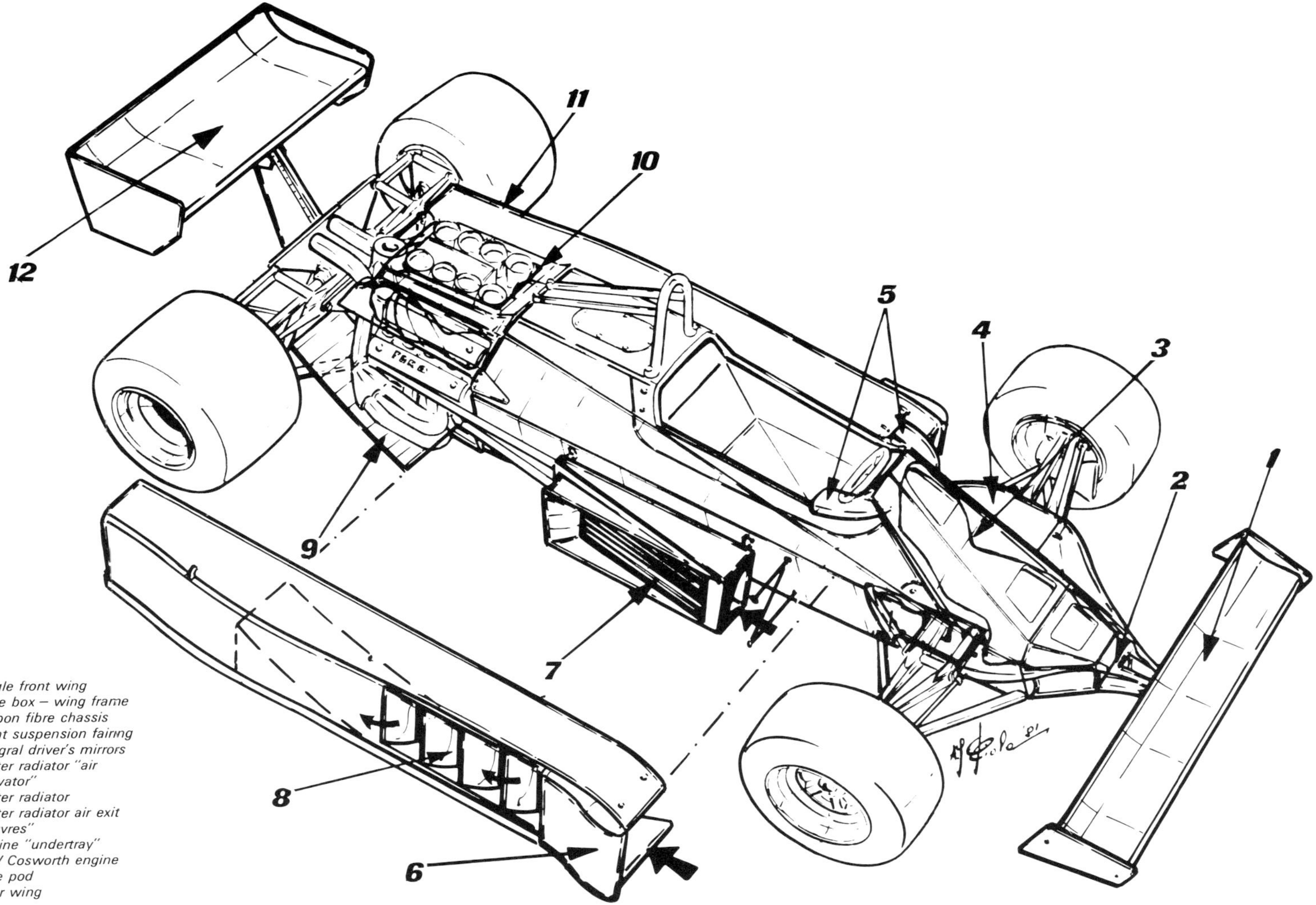

1) Single front wing
2) Nose box – wing frame
3) Carbon fibre chassis
4) Front suspension fairing
5) Integral driver's mirrors
6) Water radiator "air activator"
7) Water radiator
8) Water radiator air exit "louvres"
9) Engine "undertray"
10) DFV Cosworth engine
11) Side pod
12) Rear wing

The carbon fibre Lotus 87. (Giorgio Piola).

The Candy-Toleman-Hart turbo TG181. (Courtesy Toleman Group Motorsport).

car was right. The Pirelli shod, B.P. backed and superbly prepared TG280 dominated the whole season enabling Brian Henton to take the European Championship with Derek Warwick runner-up.

In the autumn of that season work started in earnest on a radical new Formula One car, the Candy Toleman TG181. This much criticised new package featured an all honeycomb chassis, Hart 1500cc turbocharged engine and tyres supplied by Pirelli (a newcomer to modern Formula One). Toleman chose the most difficult path to tread that any Formula One team could for its first attempt at Formula One.

As expected, numerous problems arose, mainly with the engine lacking obvious power. However, air charge temperature and turbo lag, a typical phenomenon of turbocharging, didn't ease things either and at the same time the problems put Pirelli in difficulty in developing its rubber. In the middle of the European season Brian Hart introduced a monobloc engine (the cylinder block and cylinder head were cast and machined in one piece) and a secondary water cooling system, designed only to assist the air charge termperature. This improved the response, which altogether slightly improved the general situation. Unfortunately, the saga continued up to the end of the season where after 10 attempts Toleman finally made the grid at Monza (Brian Henton) and Las Vegas (Derek Warwick).

At the traditional winter testing in the South of France another improved version of the 415T engine and new Pirelli tyres surprisingly shot the TG181's lap times among those of the establishment.

Having been a member of the team, the author can say that at Toleman there is no shortage of ability and enthusiasm so perhaps with a little more practical design approach the team might run among the front runners before expected.

From now on it looks as though Formula One evolution will be concentrated on aerodynamics, exotic materials (with an emphasis on carbon fibre), honeycomb chassis construction, tyres, but above all turbocharging, which should make the technical side of Formula One ever more interesting.

Chapter 2

Tyres

To transmit power under acceleration, to maintain grip under centrifugal cornering force, just four points of contact must grip the road surface. These four relatively small areas of rubber connect the racing car with the road: all else in the design of the car, such as aerodynamic devices and suspension geometry, is subsidiary and intended to assist these points of contact to do whatever is asked of them . . .

Each point of contact must be of sufficient size in relation to its vertical and lateral loading to provide enough traction for the required performance: in motor racing this traction is more commonly called "grip". Even in straight-line acceleration, where there is no lateral loading, the point of contact of each tyre is still important in that it must have sufficient area in contact with the surface of the track to transfer the tyre's force input to the road. Traction can be increased by the employment of mechanical means such as a locking differential (see transmission).

The forces acting on a car during cornering may be understood from the simple example shown in the drawing, which shows the forces acting on a ball being whirled around on the end of a piece of string. The centrifugal force generated goes in a straight line from the hand and through to the ball's centre of gravity. The opposing force, which prevents the ball leaving the circle it is describing, and flying off out of control, is the string. In this example the ball represents the car, whilst the string represents the car's tyres in their role of containing opposing forces. If the grip of the four tyres is equal to the centrifugal force generated by the car going round a corner, then the car will remain on its chosen path. But, should the centrifugal force become greater than the grip of the tyres, the result will be exactly like the string holding the ball breaking: the car will leave the circle, out of control, under the influence of centrifugal force.

Slip Angle

In cornering the manner in which the rubber elements of the tyre resist centrifugal side force (GF) is a combination of flexing and scrubbing action. Under centrifugal force each contact patch progresses along the track surface at an angle to the plane of the wheel, this angle is called "slip angle".

The amount of slip angle will be determined by the size of the tyre, its compound mixture, construction, inflation and the weight of the car aerodynamic downforce acting on the contact patch.

Tyre slip angle is the key to automobile behaviour, and is used throughout the analysis of racing car dynamics and cornering ability.

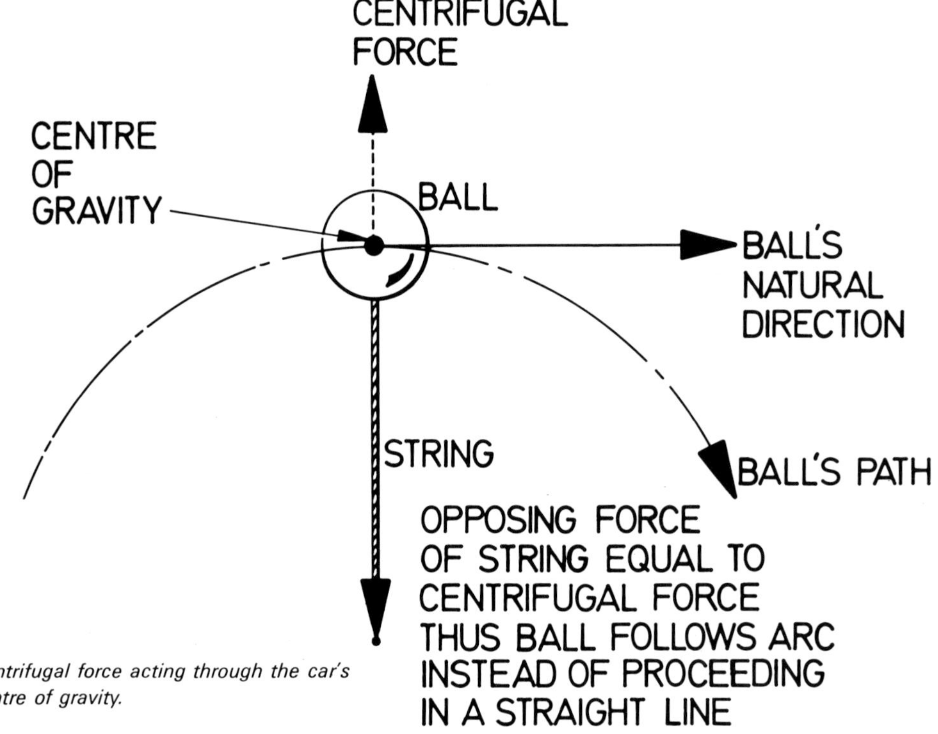

Centrifugal force acting through the car's centre of gravity.

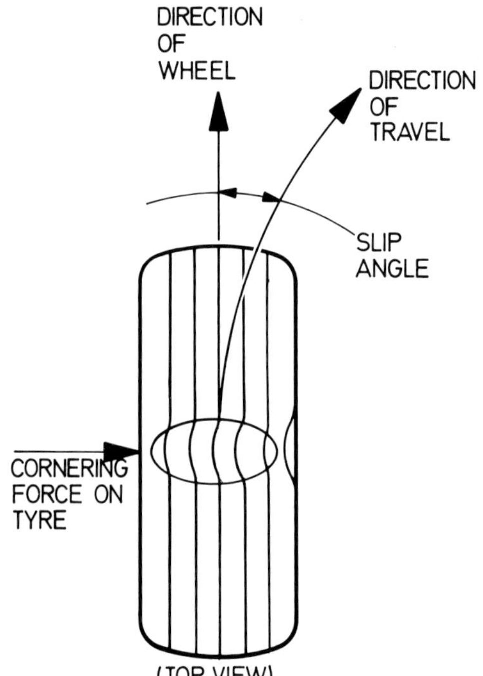

Tyre slip angle viewed from the top.

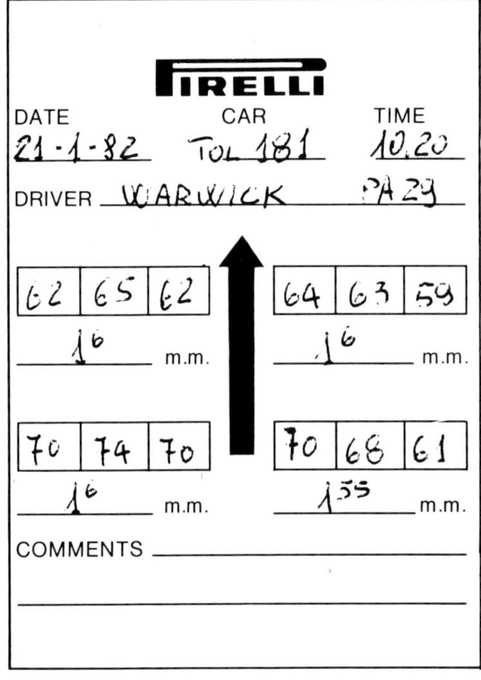

PIRELLI

DATE 21-1-82 CAR TOL 181 TIME 10.20

DRIVER WARWICK PA 29

62	65	62

16 m.m.

64	63	59

16 m.m.

70	74	70

16 m.m.

70	68	61

155 m.m.

COMMENTS

A tyre temperature sheet showing temperature in three locations on all four types during a Grand Prix practice session.

Temperature

Friction generates heat and is therefore a major consideration with respect to racing tyres is the temperature of the composition under working conditions. Some of the heat produced is dissipated into the airstream until a thermal balance is attained. Tyre temperature is affected by the weight of the car, cornering capability at speed, tyre pressure, tyre composition and construction, the temperature of the surrounding air and the temperature of the track. As regards the weight of the car, nothing much can be done, since the car is designed with care to meet the minimum weight limit imposed by the regulations.

Track and air temperatures are impossible to change, cornering speed depends on the car's handling, and the driver's experience and ability. The composition and construction are the responsibility of the tyre engineer. Running temperature is about 270°F maximum during a hot day.

Camber Thrust

Cornering power or tyre grip may vary considerably with wheel camber angle relative to the surface of the track as governed by the movement of the chassis. An initial amount of negative camber is applied when statically setting suspension geometry according to the expected chassis roll in cornering, so that the outside wheels reach an ideal position in terms of camber at around 0°. Camber thrust occurs when a wheel runs at a camber angle. Drawing a line around the circumference of the tyre at the centre of the tread forms an ellipse when looking down at it (assuming some degree of camber is present). As the tyre and point of contact with the road, this ellipse represents the direction of travel of the tyre when it is rolling, and it intersects a line drawn through the centre of the point of contact in the direction of travel. As the tread rolls through the point of contact, it attempts to follow the ellipse but the scrub induced by the rolling pulls the tyre and forces it to follow the linear direction of travel. The deformation of the tyre creates forces, which operate at the point of contact of the tyre.

When the wheel is set with negative camber angle, the camber thrust acts in the direction of the centre of the curvature, slightly increasing cornering power. With positive wheel camber angle, opposite effect will occur. No matter how much downward force is produced by aerodynamic devices, the deflection of the tyre on cornering depends on its characteristics as well as on the pressure. The change in camber is provoked by the chassis roll and is controlled with springs and anti roll bars. Nowadays the stiffness of the anti roll bars may even be altered by the driver from the cockpit.

Construction

"Conventional" racing tyres are of crossply construction. Crossplies for Formula One use are supplied by Goodyear. The entire casing is constructed of crossply nylon (nylon cords) and every ply, or layer, of the tyre possesses about 25 to 30 cords per inch, having these arranged in four-ply fashion. The cords are all enveloped in rubber. This stops them rubbing together which would create friction. They are laid at an angle to give maximum braking strength. There is a wire in the bead to hold the tyre to the rim, and this wire is the strongest part of the tyre. On top of the carcass is a thin skin of rubber, which is about two-tenths of an inch thick, the thinnest part being the centre line. The shoulder is about 0.32 inch thick.

The tyres are made in sections and these sections are then assembled. There is the carcass already described, then there is the tread which is drawn through a die to a pre-determined shape. It all comes together on a tyre building machine. The beads are inserted in a setting-ring on the outside of a drum. The plys all run onto this drum, some at an angle towards the right, others at an angle towards the left, then the beads are brought together against the drum. As the plys are turned up around the bead this causes the bead to be secured to the carcass, then two more plys are applied, at angles, to the right and left. In this way the plys are eventually wrapped and sealed inside the bead, and finally the tread is applied.

Compound

The compound is made up of over 25 different ingredients and only a chemist would be able to put a name to them all. Polymers of various types, synthetic and natural (the most commonly used is styrene-butadiene-rubber) are the main ingredients. The Polymers used should have good resistance to abrasion, combine well with the cords and have good energy absorbing characteristics. Another important ingredient is the carbon-black used for improving tensile strength and wear properties. Other materials are added, such as sulphur, zinc oxide, certain waxes, oils, oil derivatives etc. This list of ingredients is completed by further chemicals added to improve the vulcanising process. The composition is rendered softer or harder by the amount of oil used and the manner in which the composition is mixed.

The reason why there are differences in tyres is that some have the same tread and fabric composition but a different construction (that is to say, the side walls are made more rigid or softer) and furthermore, the surface of the tread may be of harder or softer composition to suit different circuits.

Qualifying Tyres

It is known that qualifying tyres contain more "oil" than other types of tyre. Qualifying tyres are the softest available. They are produced in limited quantities and are carefully distributed to the teams. Because of their softness, qualifying tyres have a greater adhesion to the track than other types of tyre and are therefore faster. Unfortunately, they last for relatively few laps, then they must be thrown away. Qualifying tyres have no stamina at all, because they contain so many oils. They blister as they get hot. The hotter they get the softer they become, up to a point, then they lose performance rapidly.

Generally, qualifying tyres are fitted on the car when the initial handling balance of the car is "satisfactory". New rules drawn up at the beginning of 1981 allow: "The use of 2 sets (2x4) of qualifying tyres per practice session". Each set of tyres are marked with the car's number and checked by scrutineers during official timed practice session only.

Pressure

Tyre pressure affects the co-efficient of friction, therefore modifying the performance of the tyres. The ideal pressure is difficult to determine, because it varies from car to car and from circuit to circuit and, of course, according to the characteristics of the tyre. Minimum pressure will provide the maximum area of contact and absorb some of the shocks. On the other hand the pressure should be high enough to minimize the heat generated by the deformation of the tyre. Pressure may vary during the race, depending on which tyre or tyres is/are working the hardest on a particular type of circuit. Cars occasionally start a race with different types of compound on the right and left hand sides of the car. In Formula One tyre pressures range from 14 to 18 PSI at operating temperature.

Slicks

The reason for using slicks is that the tread patterns generate heat. What happens is that the tyre "squirms" on the track and the greater the "squirming" the greater the heat generated. This makes it difficult for the compound to work at an ideal temperature. Slick tyres allow a softer compound to be used and also apply more rubber to the road in order to obtain better grip. Small slots may be seen cut into the surface, these enabling the depth of rubber remaining on the tyre to be measured.

Widths

Formula One tyres are so wide because of the amount of power they have to cope with, and this power won't be significantly reduced, unless the regulations are subjected to extreme change. A large tyre width also provides better stopping power, because of the extra area of contact. On the other hand, the width of a tyre is able to affect the moment of turning into the corner. It is also worth noting that tyres have evolved according to the regulations.

The width of the tyre is determined, basically, by what is allowed for the width of the rear wheel. The width of the rear tyre in turn determines what the width of the front tyre will be: it is a question of balance. The front tyres will have a construction that is compatible to that of the rear tyres.

Size

Tyre size is dependant on a number of factors. A tall tyre will have greater flex around its circumference and on a fast circuit it could be a disadvantage because the car will lean on the sidewalls and lose stability. However it can prove an advantage on a slower circuit, because it allows the carcass to wind up and thus provides more traction out of slow corners. The larger the tyre the softer the compound that can be run on it, because there is a longer area of contact and thus one revolution covers a longer distance, hence each one square inch of the tyre performs less work.

Stagger

Stagger is the name given to a difference in tyre diameter which causes imbalance between left and right hand cornering. Some drivers prefer to have some rear tyre stagger, with the bias, left or right, suiting the car.

Tyre stagger arises through inaccuracies at the construction stage. The smaller the tyre compared to the bead diameter, the more accurate the diameter is likely to be. The higher the side wall, the more chance there is of a difference occurring in circumference. When the tyre is placed in the mould it drops over a bladder. This bladder is inflated to the right shape, the mould closes over that shape and the amount of stretch taking place depends on the pressure inside the bladder. There are many variables including the fabric itself which can vary in elasticity, and this is referred to as a case factor. Some fabrics are more flexible than others, but all are processed through a large machine called a tensioning machine; everything is pre-tensioned as closely as possible, but there is a variation within tolerances.

Stagger is easily able to unbalance a Formula One car. Any difference in tyre diameter upsets the static cornering weight and transfers the main weight when power is applied.

Sometimes right hand and left hand tyres are switched over in order to cure a certain peculiarity in the behaviour of a car.

Tyres are usually selected and fitted in sets of four. These sets may have different compounds, constructions and characteristics, which have to be tried out in practice and finally a set has to be selected for the race and another set has to be kept as spares in case of punctures. Before any attempt is made to put a set of tyres on the car, pressures are checked, stagger is checked with a tape measure and then tyres are chosen so that they match in size. Usually stagger occurs after the tyres have been running for a while and it may be corrected by inflation or deflation, depending on what sort of pressure exists when the tyres are hot. This is not the ideal solution, but there is no alternative and a compromise has to be reached.

Wet Tyres

Wet tyres are made of a soft compound and designed so that water is channelled away. The channels are incorporated in a tread pattern which is cut by hand, in the form of circumferential drainage channels. The idea

Pirelli P7 wet tyre (rear) with its drainage channels.

is to give the water room to run away so that it does not get trapped between the surface of the track and the area of the tyre in contact with the track.

The total area of rubber in contact with the track is reduced by cutting the grooves, but there is no alternative. The channels are cut approximately ½ inch wide and ⅜ inch deep. About ⅓rd of the area of the tyre in contact with the track forces the water into the channels, the central ⅓rd squeezes the contact area dry and the ⅓rd on the trailing edge provides grip.

The construction of slick and wet tyres is basically the same. Tyre manufacturers come up with different tread designs but, although they do a fair amount of testing, wet racing conditions are needed for the development of a wet tyre. Generally the suspension is softened for wet conditions, in order to give a softer ride, to transmit the power as smoothly as possible and to allow for the smooth driving that should go with the conditions. Needless to say, drivers are aware of this, but some drivers are more skilled than others under these special conditions. It is possible that in wet conditions, radial tyres may have a certain advantage over crossply tyres.

Tyre Life

The maximum efficiency of the tyre is reached, initially when it reaches its optimum temperature. But then it goes through a slight change in structure, which means that the tyre becomes harder and loses some of its efficiency. Because the choice of compound and construction are related to the circuit in question, tyres tend to lose grip after about 250 miles. In Formula One many sets of tyres are run during the five hours of practice before a set is finally chosen for the race.

The main worries for manufacturers of racing tyres are punctures and blow outs, as these cause bad publicity. Blow outs are an instant puncture at high speed, but sometimes punctures are caused by debris or sharp objects, such as small stones on the track, working their way through the tread and cutting into the fabric. Generally the cause has nothing to do with the way in which the tyre has been produced.

More often, problems arise with "grain" on the outer surface, this indicates that the

Water spray created during bad weather conditions.

compound is not strong enough. Generally graining occurs on abrasive circuits or when a car's handling characteristics are poor. What happens is that the tyre is dragged over a coarse surface and rubber is sheared off in layers. Graining is generally cured by doing a few gentle laps. Tyre "blisters" occur when a tyre runs hotter than its optimum temperature. Blisters appear most commonly on soft compounds, especially on qualifying tyres if a driver does more laps than they should. Blisters cause vibrations but are quickly felt. A driver can spot blistering if, when the steering wheel is turned, he is able to discern a circular black strip. Under these circumstances a tyre change is obviously called for.

Radial Tyres

Radial tyres have cords running at almost 90° to the direction of travel. In other words, the cords run from one bead to another at a very low angle (23°) across the tread. On top of this, radial tyres have a steel band under the surface of the tread, which is sealed in by means of a coating of rubber. Then a tread is placed on top of that. From then on the assembly procedure is similar to that for crossply tyres.

Due to its construction, in theory the radial tyre provides greater flexibility and straight line stability, greater cornering force, greater traction out of corners and better braking.

A characteristic of the radial tyre is less tread distortion under load but more side wall distortion. The side walls are more flexible than those of cross ply tyres and the time required for the development of a slip angle is different. Because of their characteristics, radial tyres require more change of camber in suspension geometry. Wheel camber angle is set statically to within the region of 1° or more negative. Radials have a different construction and compounds and have to be selected and matched according to the circuit in question.

In 1981 Pirelli re-entered Formula One racing following an absence of 23 years from the Grand Prix tracks of the world. Initially, they supplied their P7 racing radial ply tyres solely to the Toleman Formula One team, following joint experience gained during Toleman's successful 1980 Formula Two campaign. The P7s featured an asymmetrical tread profile, meaning that the inside shoulder of the tyre is more rounded than the outside one, this maintaining the "square cut" look that is typical of a radial racing tyre.

Pirelli engineers have calculated that the cars of the top competitors in Formula One exert 23.8 bhp per square inch on their tyres. However, the World Endurance Championship winning turbocharged Lancia Monte Carlo Coupes produced 28.6 bhp per square inch, so racing P7s are clearly capable of standing up to severe loads for events which can last six hours.

For 1981 Pirelli Formula One involvement was of an experimental nature. Pirelli officially withdrew from Formula One motor racing in 1956, but the 1957 Championship was still won on Pirelli tyres, Fangio clinching the World Formula One title driving a Pirelli shod Maserati 250F. The last Formula One race won on Pirelli was the 1957 Italian Grand Prix at Monza won by Stirling Moss.

Michelin, like Pirelli, has made its name manufacturing radial tyres for road cars, and as far as they are concerned any racing tyre they make has to be radial. Radial tyres will run cooler and do not "squirm" about on the track, so softer compounds can be used. But in practice Goodyear cross plies have been just as successful as Michelin radials in Formula One.

Grand Prix Meetings

At each Grand Prix, tyres have to be fitted and balanced precisely by the supplier before the meeting begins. Most teams take their cars to Grand Prix meetings on dummy wheels, use wet tyres, or put on some of the spare tyres from previous meetings. These tyres are taken temporarily to the tyre fitting area for replacement. Normally each team has one or two members responsible

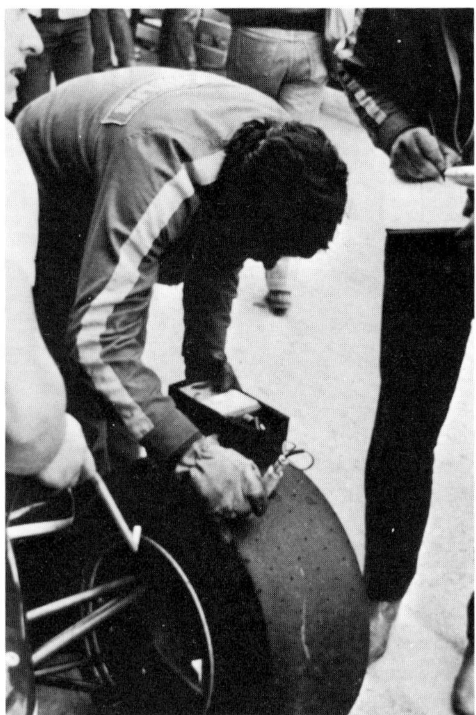

Checking tyre temperature.

for tyres. Their job is to match sets, constantly check pressures, check tyre diameter for stagger, check running temperature, look after storing the tyres, etc.

Usually in Formula One, one tyre engineer looks after two teams.

Racing tyres and racing car development is still a compromise, but the engineers try to reduce this compromise as much as possible. The main problem is that a tyre cannot be designed for each particular car.

Chapter 3

Suspension and Steering

Ground effects on Formula One cars dramatically changed all suspension requirements. The suspension geometry layout of a Formula One car is a very complex and specialized subject. Even with experience and theoretical knowledge suspension design becomes a difficult task with many conflicting problems such as the influence of tyres and aerodynamics.

Suspension tuning or modifications on any racing car can be costly, without a guarantee of improved performance, and constant suspension design trade-offs makes the subject difficult to interpret in depth. However, the basic principles of suspension geometry remain the same. The key is to make the tyre path one of maximum contact with the track, bearing in mind that the maximum road holding capacity of a racing car can be defined as the highest degree to which cornering forces can be developed without the driver losing control. Suspension layout must consider: chassis rigidity, amount of downforce (ground effect combined with other aerodynamic devices), tyre characteristics, overall weight and weight transfer, springs and dampers, track, wheelbase, etc. All these factors work together but do not necessarily function harmoniously and in fact the set up of any racing car put on the starting grid after many hours of practice is the result of the best compromise.

We are in the computer age and not surprisingly computers are used by major firms such as Renault and Ferrari, but these mathematical marvels aren't always a necessity since the results they produce are based on simplifying assumptions when feeding in information. Nevertheless, they can save valuable time. During private testing sessions some cars have been equipped with a mini-computer, recording on a little cassette every suspension and chassis movement. The system as used by Renault has been complicated over the years by adding a camber change mechanism governed by the system according to chassis, suspension movements, which feed a "black box". The drawback is that the system does not say what to adjust or modify, leaving this to the engineer, of course.

The handling of a racing car is influenced by a large number of factors, the basics of which we are going to review. Note that to keep it simple there is no mathematics.

Centre of Gravity

The centre of gravity is the centre at which the sum of the masses are considered to be concentrated when the action of gravity or other forces are applied to the whole car.

A Formula One car is made of hundreds

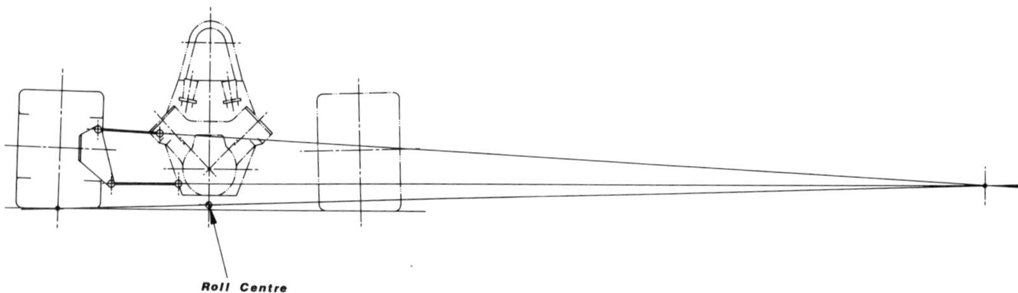

Roll centre.

of separate components, big and small, and their position about the centre of gravity can influence the cars' road-holding. Centre of gravity often brings to mind thoughts of a solid object in space. Its position in a racing car can be determined in height above the ground and in position fore and aft.

When we are considering the inertia of an object under a rapid rotation or angular rotation about its centre of gravity, the disposition of masses about the "C.G." becomes important.

The weight of the car is carried by the four tyres and divided among them by the location of the centre of gravity. Under braking and cornering, the distance between the "C.G." and the track causes pitching, rolling of the car and a change in the tyre loading caused by the weight transfer. The "C.G." should be as low as possible to minimise this weight transfer, thus reducing the problem of suspension design.

The rather technical term "polar moment of inertia" has been mentioned many times in specialised press without a straightforward and simple explanation. All it means is that you want to get as much weight of the car as possible close to the centre of gravity so that during cornerning, if the car starts to spin, the forces exerted by friction on the wheels will slow the car down. Assuming the car is like a dumb bell, the closer the masses to the centre of gravity of the car, the less likely it is to spin and the easier it is to control once it starts to spin.

The more weight close to the "C.G.", the less break-away moment the car will have. Obviously the designer is aware of this, so when laying out the car on the drawing board, he concentrates the masses as close as possible to the "C.G.", including the driver's weight. Having said that, with ground effect cars little choice is then left as to where to put this and that component because of the already crowded and slim chassis.

Roll Centre

Roll centre is the point in the transverse plane of the rear and front contact tyre patches about which the chassis will rotate under any disturbing force, such as in cornering.

In addition, with the downforce of ground effect Formula One cars, other suspension definitions and tyre specifications lower roll centre should load the tyres more equally with the chassis roll under centrifugal force and at the same time the roll becomes easier to control. Lower roll centre at the rear will have the same performance effect with lower roll centre at the front.

The roll centre of a suspension system is considered both sideways and vertically with the wheel travel.

As the roll centre is determined by the top and bottom wishbone, or rocker angle, the roll centre can be found by extending the centre line of the wishbone and joining each point of convergence to the tyre contact centre line.

Roll Axis – Stiffness

The car has separate roll centres for the front and rear suspension. In cornering under centrifugal force, the mass of the car is concentrated around the centre of gravity; it rolls or leans about these points, called roll axis. This roll movement, which acts on the springs, is provoked by the centrifugal force and the position of the centre of gravity. There is always a transitional phase when the car enters a corner when the chassis has not yet reached its maximum roll angle and a transitional phase when the car is coming out of a corner. Under these varying centrifugal forces the behaviour of the car is very much influenced by weight distribution and the amount of roll angle taken by the chassis. Roll stiffness is the resistance of the sprung mass, or chassis, rolling about the roll axis, against the spring and anti-roll bar.

Roll stiffness is measured in foot pounds per degree. It is the foot pound, or torque, required to roll the car about its roll axis by one degree. The overall roll stiffness of a car will be affected by the spring rates, the front and rear suspension linkage which determines the roll centre, the front and rear track, therefore the length of top rockers and its leverage ratio, between the pivot and damper attachments separated by its swinging point on chassis and of course by the anti roll bar.

Weight Distribution and Transfer

Modern fully adjustable Formula One cars can be set to achieve all sorts of behaviour, from understeer to oversteer, through neutral steer, none of these being an ideal behaviour. A tyre has to have slip angle in order to develop a cornering force. If the rear tyres have a larger slip angle than the front, then the car will want to spin; this is known as oversteer. On the other hand, if the front tyres have a larger slip angle than the rear, the car will want to go straight ahead rather than around the corner; this is known as understeer. A third possibility is neutral steer, a situation in which neither of the above conditions is created, which is in theory the quickest way to go around a corner. However, some drivers prefer their car sliding from the back or the front end, and that can prove as quick or quicker than going around "on rails", depending upon the driver's ability.

Weight distribution will initially determine both the lateral and vertical loadings on the wheels and will therefore influence handling characteristics. Formula One ground effect cars have a weight distribution in the region of 55% on the rear and 45% on the front. Weight distribution is a summation of all the moments of the weight above the ground divided by the total weight, and this will determine the height of the centre of gravity above the ground. The location of the car's enormous fuel cell, containing up to 38 gallons is nowadays behind the driver. Recently the height of the fuel cell has tended to be reduced, and the driver has been positioned ever further forward and the chassis kept as narrow as possible.

Large sizes of front tyre have been introduced to cope better with the weight transfer. Because fewer revolutions are made for the same speed, a more acceptable temperature and thus better tyre wear and improved grip are achieved with the larger tyres. However the use of larger or smaller tyres affects handling and may be influenced by a driver's preference.

Theoretical advantages in reducing unsprung weight have been forgotten now that brake discs and calipers are mounted on the upright inside the wheels. This is in order to narrow the back end for a better air flow under the side wings. As for the cooling system, the aluminium made water radiators are mounted alongside the chassis, just behind the front wheels and inside the open wing side, which means that the length and weight of the necessary plumbing is quite considerable.

The fire extinguishers and life bottles are located either under the driver's knees or in the nose frame while the air starter system is placed "about" the engine and gearbox. The engine oil coolers are mounted on top of the existing water cooling system.

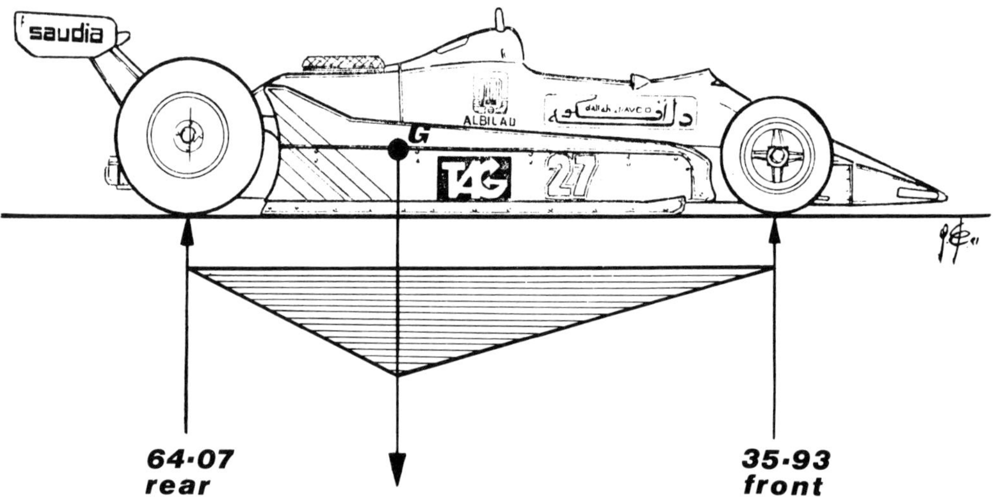

Weight distribution front and rear around the centre of gravity – Williams FW07. (Giorgio Piola).

Although it's not always possible, the idea is to bring the masses close to the cars' centre of gravity.

In cornering, lateral weight transfer is caused by centrifugal force, acting through the centre of gravity, which is resisted by the adhesion of the tyres and this results in a lifting force in the inside wheel and an increase in weight on the outside wheel, thanks to body roll. The more force the tyres can resist, the greater will be the cornering force, but the quicker the car goes around a corner, the greater the "G" force will be. The "G" force is counteracted by springs, roll bars, tyre characteristics and aerodynamic devices which have to be precisely chosen.

Weight transfer also takes place under acceleration and braking. Under acceleration a torque is applied to the rear driving wheels which in turn creates a forward thrust between the tyre contact patches and the road surface. This creates a weight transfer from the front to the rear, developing a movement of lift at the front and squatting at the rear. A few years ago anti-squat devices were used in order to reduce this weight transfer, thus avoiding possible disturbances to the handling. Now with ground effect cars, because of the downforce and consequent use of very high rate springs, the movement of the suspension and chassis is very limited. However, the motion of the car under acceleration can be seen on "Mickey Mouse" circuits like Monaco or Long Beach.

Under braking, the braking forces do not act through the centre of gravity of the car, hence there is a weight transfer from the rear to the front wheels which alters the load distribution at the wheels, creating a nose dive motion, or pitching, and consequently the rear end lifts.

The amount of disturbance under braking is governed basically by the location of static masses and varies depending on the amount of braking force applied. In cornering, the centrifugal force provokes weight transfer on the outside wheels and added to this braking and acceleration can happen also while cornering, which loads the tyres even more.

Castor

Castor is a factor which provides a vehicle

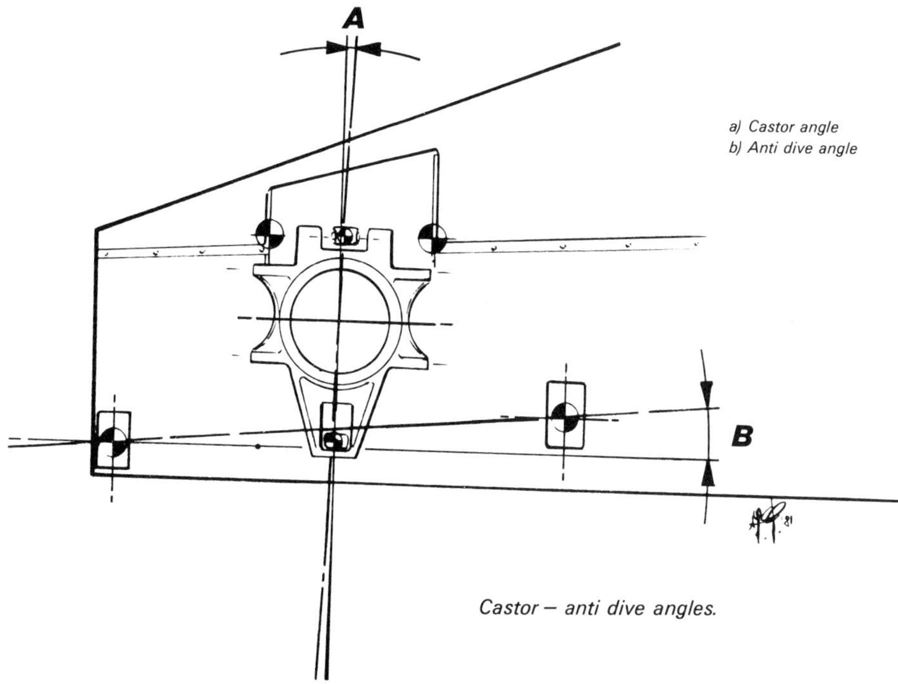

Castor – anti dive angles.

with directional stability and is inter-related with another stability factor, king pin inclination. Looking at the front suspension system from the side, the castor angle is defined as the backward tilt of the king pin (this being positive castor). Castor moves the point at which the king pin line intersects with the ground at a point forward of the centre of the tyre contact patch. The distance between the intersection and the centre of the patch is called trail distance.

The castor angle creates a torque movement from the king pin axis to the centre of the tyre contact patch. When steering or changing direction of travel, this torque movement acts around the king pin axis, creating a force that tends to bring the wheel back in a straight line position. The more castor angle, the more effort needed to turn the steering wheel.

In motor racing, positive castor angle is employed. This angle is carefully measured and is determined during previous testing or by previous experience. During cornering, a positive castor angle will add negative camber to the outside front wheel and therefore a compromise must be reached so that the camber changes created by the castor angle and the suspension geometry in roll are compatible. Nowadays with ground effect cars, the great speed reached in cornering makes the steering very heavy because of the load applied to the tyres, so most Formula One cars run with little castor angle; around 2° maximum. The castor angle can be changed by moving the top rocker or bottom wishbone backward or forward and is easily measured with a castor gauge.

King Pin Offset (Inclination – KPI)

Another factor which goes along with the steering axis is the king pin angle distance, determined between the centre line of the tyre contact patch and the steering axis line, when projected to the ground. This distance varies depending on the outside wheel offset and the steering axis angle.

King pin angle is necessary to give the steering a feel from the tyres. On road cars excessive steering axis is used and therefore the small king pin offset will cause the wheel to take positive camber, when turning the wheels, reducing tyre contact patch, but this excessive camber change can be absorbed by rounded tread and high diameter tyres. With the wide tyres used in Formula One, king pin angle and king pin offset is considerably reduced in order to avoid undesirable camber change. High king pin offset also produces heavy steering. When turning the wheels, little angle also avoids the torque applied to the tyres when the wheels travel forward, giving a tendency of toe-in or toe-out.

In race cars both toe-in and toe-out of both front wheels can be neutralised by the position of the track rod on the upright, rack clevis, length of rack clevis or simply in the position of the complete steering rack. All this is included in the steering geometry design. As for the rear wheels, the ups and downs of the suspension geometry gives a variation of toe-in or toe-out and this can also be neutralised simply by changing the position longitudinally of the top rockers or bottom wishbone, which results in a certain amount of upright angle, which is known as castor.

Steering Axis

The steering axis is the line drawn from the upper pick-up point and lower pick-up point of the upright, the amount of steering axis is the angle between the steering axis and the vehicle line where the steering axis line hits the ground. With the castor, the steering axis angle helps for directional stability, but mainly to distribute the weight of the vehicle evenly on spindle and bearings through the tyres.

The steering axis angle cannot be changed unless a redesign of the upright and suspension geometry is carried out. Current ground effect cars use as little angle as 1½°.

Wheel Camber

Wheel camber is inclination of the central plane of the wheel to the vertical plane of the chassis.

Camber is used to achieve the maximum contact patch with the road during suspension movement and chassis roll, since maximum cornering speed is achieved with maximum tyre grip. The tyre grip is influenced by its characteristics, by the contact patch temperature, the layout of the suspension geometry, including springs, dampers and anti roll bar, weight transfer, and, of course, by the amount of downforce provided by the ground effect as a whole, and, finally, track conditions. A lot of attention is concentrated on setting wheel camber adjustment, and radial tyres are very sensitive to camber angle.

Initially, when a suspension geometry is designed, a designer knows how much camber change will be needed according to the chassis roll, tyre specifications and other components which affect tyre patch and temperature, in order to gain maximum cornering power. As camber is governed by chassis movement, cars running with "conventional" tyre construction have little camber change, but on the other hand, cars equipped with radial tyres need more camber change, mainly because of the extra deflection of radial tyres. In any case, the tyre temperature must be kept in control, and this is achieved through many different mechanical and aerodynamic adjustments. The camber angle can easily be altered by changing the length of the bottom or top point on the wishbone or rockers.

Steering Geometry

Steering geometry is the term applied to the arrangement of the steering system. The layout determines the amount of input required at the steering wheel to achieve a given amount of turning motion at the front wheels, and, in effect, how much each wheel should turn to negotiate a corner.

In motor racing the rack and pinion system is widely used and without exception all Formula One cars use it. Its construction – small, light and compact – is far less complex than other types of steering arrangement and it is easy to locate at the front end of the chassis. The

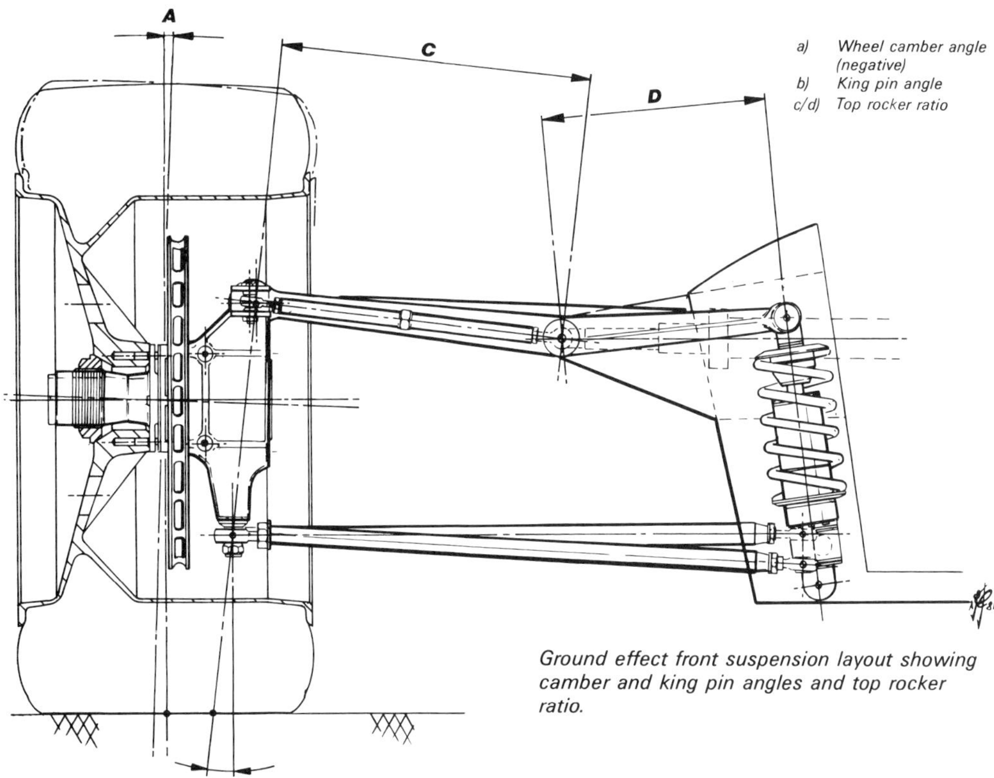

Ground effect front suspension layout showing camber and king pin angles and top rocker ratio.

system includes a cast magnesium box, (machined after casting), and bolted to the chassis. This centre piece supports the pinions, ball bearings, retaining washers and circlip and rubber seals to keep the rack lubricating grease inside the box. A spring loaded bush presses against a flat surface of the rack in order to keep it against the pinion teeth, this device also serving to eliminate any play which can occur. The extremities of the rack are supported by bronze bushes pressed.

The rack itself is accurately machined from a circular rod of steel. The middle section is cut to form a number of teeth (trapezoidal shape or straight cut). Underneath the same section, a flat surface takes the pressure from a spring loaded bush. Each end of the rack is threaded externally or internally to take a clevis locked to it by a nut.

The pinion is machined to match the teeth of the rack. The pinion is supported by bearings and is splined to take the steering column.

The difference between the number of teeth on the rack and the number of teeth on the pinion determines the steering ratio.

To carry on towards the wheels, at each end of the rack, a track rod mounted with rose joints is connected to a pick-up point on the upright. These rose joints are left and right threaded, so the toe-in or toe-out can be adjusted by lengthening or shortening the overall length of the track rods.

The steering column is a simple "tube" having one extremity splined to cover the "tail" of the pinion to which it is secured by a nut and bolt. The whole steering column can be divided in two pieces, joined by a universal joint or similar component, and is supported by bearings. The steering wheel is bolted on a flat flange welded to the steering tube.

The layout varies in design and construction from car to car, but the working order and the principles remain the same.

When a car is cornering, it usually

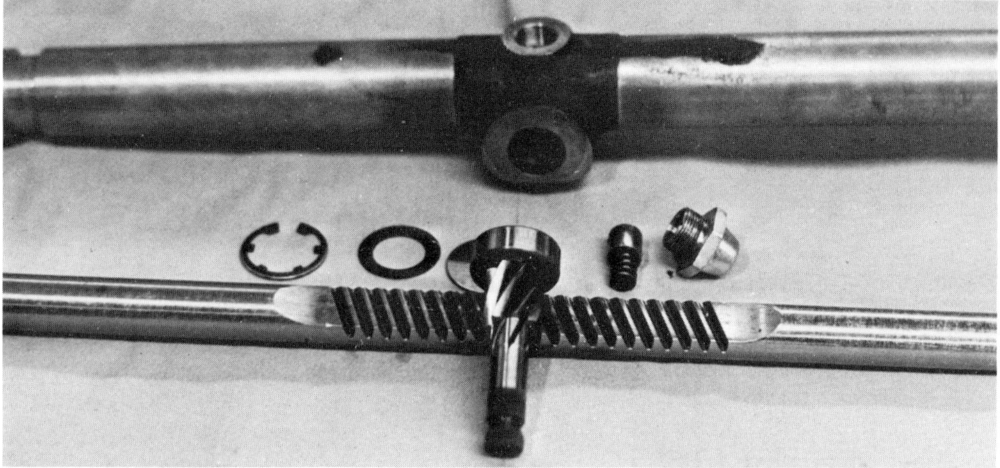

Steering rack and pinion arrangement.

describes a circle's circumference and it would be natural for the front wheels to go along this circumference tangentially. Because of the width of the car, the outside wheel is describing a larger circle than the inside wheel so ideally the outer wheel should be turned fewer degrees than the inner wheel. If the steering geometry does not give the right amount of compensation between the two front wheels, tyre scrub will occur. Ackermann steering geometry design can be used to provide an appropriate differential amount of turning of the front wheels.

Ackermann theory, dating from the good old days of 1819, says that to obtain the right differential of wheel turning angle, two lines should be drawn from the king pin point, passing through the outer track rod pivot points, and through the centreline of the rear axle. The (revised) theory is much applied, and works on road cars because of their relatively low cornering speed compared to that of a Formula One car, and because tyre wear characteristics remain an important design criteria. In high level car racing, the full Ackermann layout is not applied because, in cornering, weight transfer load concentrates on the outside wheel. The steering is mostly done by the same wheel and consequently a greater tyre slip angle is generated, creating a reducing tyre grip and requiring greater steering lock – therefore, with Ackermann compensation handling problems will occur.

On some Formula One cars, a theory called the Anti-Ackermann principle has been applied. This is done by putting the steering device's pick-up points straight with the upper ball joint, with equal length on both right and left hand side, and parallel to the car centreline. With this layout, in corners both wheels will be turned the same amount, forcing the inside wheel to toe-in, but generally a small amount of toe-out, previously set, would reduce the tendency of increasing toe-in, therefore putting the wheel on the proper radius according to the corner.

In practice, the steering ratio really depends on the length of the steering arm, which obviously is a lever, and also on the amount of steering wheel angle the driver can easily turn without having to take his hand off the wheel – in other words when he crosses his arms, the point where his wrists touch is the limit of the steering wheel movement. The effort to turn the steering wheel has greatly increased with ground effect cars, due to the fact that the tyres are a lot more loaded. Rack and pinion ratio along with the length of steering arms and castor angle has changed in order to lighten the whole steering input. Quick steering action is needed, in particular on twisty circuits, again like Monaco, where some corners are so tight that in going around them, the reverse action is almost

(A&B) Front and rear track; (C) Wheelbase; (D&E) Toe-in, toe-out; (F) Ackermann steering layout.

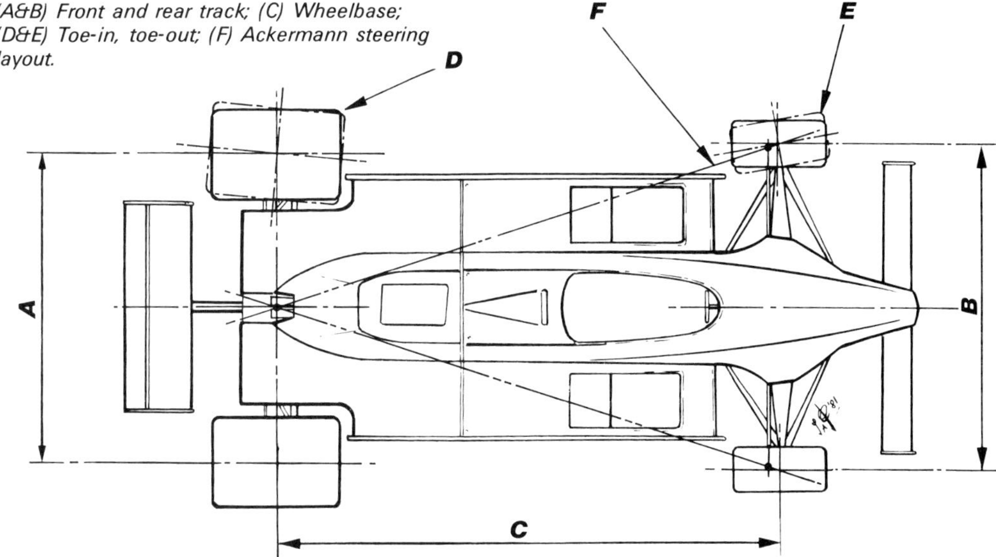

needed. Somehow drivers manage to go round them for three days without too many problems; of course sliding is quite "prohibited" and overtaking almost impossible.

Generally speaking a steering ratio of 8/1 (rack to pinion) is commonly used, being a good compromise for lightness and quick action. Lately big front tyre diameter has been introduced, mainly to cope with wear (front wheels turn a lot quicker than rear wheels because of differences in diameter) and handling problems and these offer at the same time an easier steering effort.

Toe-in – Toe-out

Toe-in and toe-out are terms applied to the directional wheels' leading edges, if pointing either toward or away from the centreline of the chassis. Any deviation of the wheels from a parallel relationship will generate slip angle. Both wheels attempt to track in accordance with slip angle, in opposing directions. In other words, the reason for toe-in or toe-out is that the forces which act on the tyres tend to cause toe-in – or toe-out and an initial setting is made to counteract this tendency.

At the front of the car, toe-in or toe-out is used to promote straight line stability and influence cornering, when the weight is transferred to the tyres. The amount of toe-in or toe-out varies from car to car depending on its handling characteristics and greatly influenced by the tyre specifications. Along with the camber angle, it keeps the tyres to a desired temperature for maximum grip and also helps the car's stability under heavy braking. To prevent tyre scrub and rolling resistance, toe-in or toe-out angle is set at around 1° for both wheels. At the rear toe-in and toe-out is also used to improve stability under acceleration loads and again, as for the front end, to keep an ideal tyre temperature for better grip in cornering. Also, the grip on rear wheel is very much influenced by the movement, and amount of power, transmitted by the engine, the amount of torque produced by the self-locking differential of the transmission, the tyre quality, and, of course, by the amount of downforce produced (see drawing, page 51).

Toe-in or toe-out is measured when the car is in a static position and measurement is given either in degrees, fractions of an inch, or millimetres. Both wheels are adjusted the same amount to achieve the desired figure of toe-in or toe-out and that becomes important since variables such as

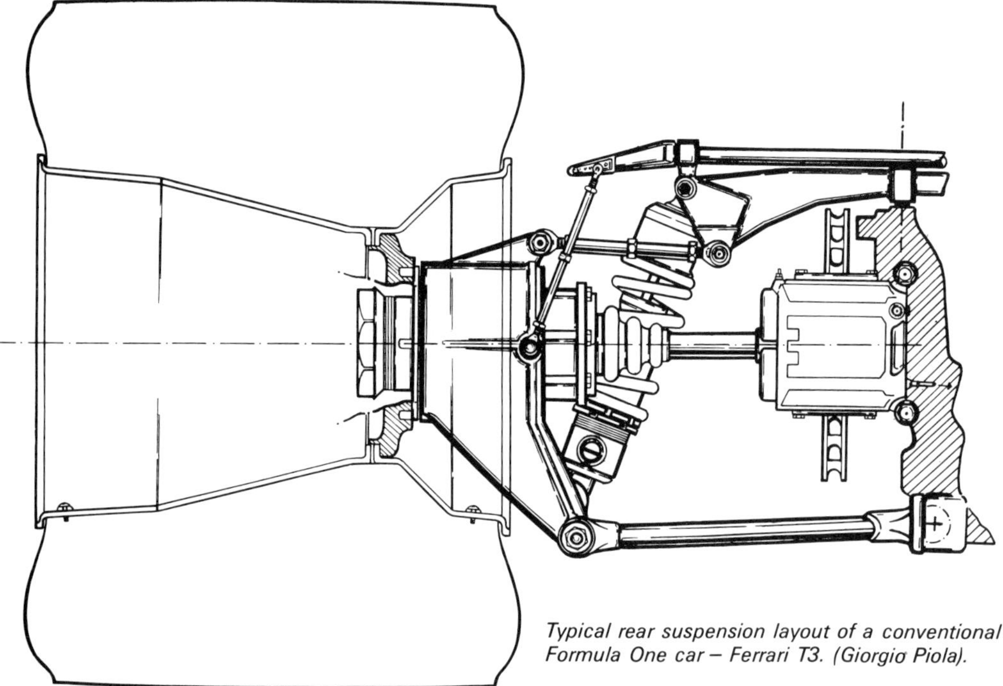

Typical rear suspension layout of a conventional Formula One car – Ferrari T3. (Giorgio Piola).

castor, camber angles and Ackermann effects have on the relationship of the wheels to each other when cornering. The most popular ways of statically setting a suspension geometry are the "Dunlop" optical mirror gauge and the "Muller" (electric) apparatus, the latter being the more accurate.

Alteration of toe-in or toe-out can be made at the front of the car by changing the length of the track rods. On most cars, altering the length of the link which joins the upright and cross beam of the rear suspension provides adjustment for the rear.

Linkage Geometry

The most obvious feature of a Formula One car is its independent suspension system. Suspension design starts with tyres, since the basic object is to get maximum tyre grip on any shape of corner. A fundamental of suspension geometry is the amount of camber change that takes place as the wheels move up and down in a limited travel from full bump to full droop. To obtain maximum cornering power the tyres must be kept vertical during cornering. Grip during acceleration and braking is also essential. The difficulty is to get all these requirements catered for perfectly, so suspension geometry is very much a compromise.

All ground effect Formula One cars today have a suspension layout which features the use of wishbones, rockers and outboard brakes. Suspension geometry covers the length and disposition of the four links attached to points on the chassis and connected with the uprights. The travel of the links, governed by wheel or chassis, lateral or vertical movement, is controlled by the spring-damper combination and anti roll bar. In the case of parallel wishbones and equal length chassis roll due to the centrifugal force in cornering, the wheel would lean outward (positive camber) at the same angle as the chassis roll. Obviously, the cornering power, or grip of the tyres, would be much reduced by this change of camber, because the tyres would run on their edges. At the front the steering system would also be affected. For this reason geometry linkage is based on unequal length, non-parallel wishbones or rockers, which are disposed so that the wheels remain as perpendicular as possible to the road throughout cornering and different movements of the suspension layout. The layout is also designed to give a certain amount of camber change when the wheel is deflected over bumps or hollows. An amount of camber change is specified initially on the drawing board, according to the designer's requirements and whether cross ply or radial tyres are to be used. With radial tyres more camber change is desired because of higher deflection compared to cross ply tyres.

Generally the surface of the majority of Formula One circuits is quite smooth, so the possibility of wheel deflection over bumps and hollows is limited; added to this is the fact that, as mentioned before, the downforce produced by ground effect cars necessitates very stiff springs and roll bars, consequently reducing the chassis movements, as well as the suspension travel. Overall, therefore, the amount of camber change that is liable to take place is limited.

Linkage geometry affects chassis roll under centrifugal force for the chassis tries to resist the roll, which is counteracted by heavy springs and roll bars, providing an amount of roll stiffness. The relationship between front and rear geometry determines how the weight is distributed on the outside wheels, between front and rear, in cornering. Also, the overall weight transfer is dictated by the front and rear tracks, position of the centre of gravity and the roll centres. During cornering, centrifugal force is counteracted by aerodynamic devices as well as roll stiffness. The attitude of the majority of cars as they are going around a corner shows little chassis roll, giving the impression of taking the corner without leaning over.

Designing a suspension geometry requires mathematical knowledge and practical experience. Simplicity in the layout generally ends up being most practical since all movements cannot be controlled as desired at the same time.

Springs

The use of springs on a Formula One racing car is not for comfort but to enhance the car's handling and grip.
Along with other suspension components, the job of springs is to keep the maximum tyre patch firmly in contact with the track throughout cornering and, of course, to keep the chassis at a pre-determined ride height. For roll stiffness, weight transfer and handling characteristics, springs are the first components having a bearing upon them, so their prime quality is ride. (Roll stiffness is also controlled with anti roll bars). In reality a car is riding on two components; the springs themselves and the tyres. The basic work of the springs is to isolate road shocks from the chassis, maintaining traction over rough circuits, so therefore bouncing frequency, bump, rebound travel and chassis ride height must be considered, taking into account, again, the roll stiffness, especially on wing cars producing a tremendous downforce, and thus putting a great load on the tyres through the springs. Basically the rate of a spring is calculated in pounds per inch or kilos per centimetre. This is determined by design and test.

With the MacPherson type suspension widely used on road cars, coil springs are mounted directly above the wheel and so deflect in a straight line; then the wheel rate is equal and constant to the spring rate. All Formula One cars have combinations of damper springs mounted inboard on the chassis, the suspension linkage being through different mediums, rockers or a progressive rate system, and the springs being operated by a leverage, the effect of which, of course, can be calculated. A progressive rate system can be obtained by all sorts of types of linkage, which cause the angle of attack on the springs to vary with wheel movement but as soon as the wheel moves further, the spring is attacked more directly, increasing the effective spring rate.

Typical Formula One rear suspension linkage seen on the Brabham BT49. Note the progressive spring rate arrangement and rising chassis hydraulics. 1981.

On conventional Formula One cars, progressive spring rate was once the fashion, but was abandoned later on for a more conventional system (rockers). Nevertheless, this sort of arrangement is back in fashion and can be seen on Gordon Murray's Brabham cars. Progressive has become the trend again for two reasons. 1) Because of the progressive spring rate advantages. 2) Because of the downforce and cornering speed achieved, combined with almost virtually no suspension, rockers might not be able to take the load applied.

The development of ground effects led to the use of high spring rates, ranging from 2,000lbs to 3,500lbs/in or more, which inevitably give a very stiff ride, much like that of a kart. This problem has been openly criticised by the majority of drivers.

Anti Squat – Anti Dive

Two interesting aspects of suspension geometry are what is known as "anti squat" and "anti dive". Anti squat is the aspect of the geometry design which minimises the effect of the back of the car squatting under acceleration while anti dive relates to the front suspension and minimises the effect of the front of the car diving under braking. Concerning anti squat, as a general rule if rockers and wishbones slope uphill ahead of the rear wheel centre line then the car has anti squat (on conventional cars by the radius rod). The amount of anti squat depends on the angle of the rockers and wishbones since the forces of an angled thrust can be resolved into two components, horizontal and vertical; the vertical component will counteract the weight transfer to the rear under acceleration.

Anti dive on the front suspension works in a similar manner; the suspension inboard mounting points are angled uphill to the rear of the front wheel centre line and in a similar manner the forces are resolved into horizontal and vertical components and the vertical component will counteract the weight transfer to the front wheels under braking since the braking forces at the front tend to be higher than the rear. This was quite important consideration on conventional Formula One cars, but it is not so on ground effect cars because the very stiff springs used tend to limit the dive anyway. With development of ground effects, theoretically anti dive and anti squat is undesirable for as the chassis moves up and down it also alters the height of the venturi section in relation to the ground. To overcome anti dive and anti squat an arrangement was tried on the 1979 Ferrari T4 using hydraulic devices (similar to slave cylinders), one attached to the chassis at the front, another to the gearbox at the rear, and both connected to its respective anti roll bar. Both cylinders communicated to each other and if any movement of the chassis under acceleration or braking acting on the anti roll bars, then to the cylinders would in turn offer a certain resistance to anti dive or anti squat, (see photo, page 176).

Bump Steer

The terms "bump steer" and "roll steer" are used to cover a number of steering effects when the chassis rolls in cornering, including weight transfer, and bump steer is associated with the steering geometry's relationship of rod linkage arms.

The front wheels, mounted on uprights, are connected by a track rod and steering arm to the steering rack clevis. When the suspension travels, bumps or droops, the steering arm and track rod pick-up point move inward or outward at a faster rate than the lateral suspension linkage, so a variation in the position of the wheel will occur.

Toe-in or toe-out will be induced if the track rod pick-up point does not travel in an arc equal to the arc described by the upright around its own attachment point. Ideally, the track rod should be the same length as the suspension linkage and parallel to it. Variations can also occur if the centreline of the chassis pick-up point is not in line with the track rod pivot. Toe-in or toe-out on bump or droop depends whether the steering system is mounted in front or behind the uprights.

At the rear end of the car bump steer also takes place. Variations are due to the fact that the top and bottom linkage are not parallel to each other in relation with their attachment point on the uprights. Here again, when the suspension is moving the linkages describe different arcs, therefore inducing bump steer.

Suspension and steering geometry must be accurately designed so that unwanted effects like bump steer are eliminated. Suspension and steering gear consists of many parts which are not always machined or constructed 100% according to the original drawing and this is why effects like bump steer do occur. Nevertheless, this is quite easy to correct when setting the suspension geometry statically.

Shock Absorbers

The function of the shock absorbers is to reduce the suspension spring oscillation. For Formula One use these dampers are all of the telescopic type, in which oil kept in reservoirs is displaced through fixed orifices and spring loaded valves by the movement of a piston inside a cylinder.

Shock absorbers do not affect roll stiffness but control spring reaction to roll and pitch. With a given load, spring frequency is highly related to road irregularity. When a spring is compressed and returns to its normal position, it will have stored some energy, and so it moves past its natural point, stretching in the other direction and again storing energy, and hence overshooting the starting point once again. These so called "amplitudes" depend on the spring rate. With hard springs a high natural frequency situation will occur. The impact of a bump is transmitted to the chassis which in turn will reach high frequency bouncing giving a feeling of hammering.

With soft springing the chassis will react less violently and therefore travel more smoothly. In racing both types of reaction are undesirable. Dampers are used to decrease the amplitudes by absorbing the springs' energy. For bumpy circuits such as Brands Hatch, softer springs are used, the chassis ride height is raised and the damper setting is softened in order to get the wheels to ride the bumps without losing grip. Obviously, this compensation can vary from car to car depending on handling characteristics. Dampers tend to be set to a driver's preference.

Because of tremendous reliability, effectiveness and compactness of their shock absorbers the Dutch company Koni have become world famous, particularly for their externally adjustable units. Almost without exception all Formula One cars are equipped with the Koni units. It has taken Koni a comparatively short time to grow from a local handicraft firm into an industry of one thousand employees with steadily increasing export trade all over the world. In spite of this spectacular growth Koni have stood by their first principles of skill and quality.

Shock absorbers take the "bump" and "rebound" motions generated by wheels moving in a vertical plane. "Bump" is the motion that compresses the shock absorber when wheels hit an obstacle such as a high spot on the road. "Rebound" is the motion that extends the shock absorber after bump has occurred.

The proper tuning of bump and rebound forces is of great importance for the modern suspension systems as an improper setting of the shock absorber either does not adequately absorb the shock (and the suspension hits the stops or "bottoms") or allows the spring to continue movement over a long period of time (wallowing). The Koni aluminium racing shock absorber works on the same principle as that for road cars, which is as follows:

Bump Stroke. At the bump stroke, the piston (3) travels down the cylinder (1), oil flows from below the piston (3) through the orifices, through the non-return valve (14) to the upper part of the cylinder, thus equalising pressure in the whole cylinder. The piston rod (2) entering the cylinder displaces a quantity of oil, which escapes through the valve assembly (4) to the reservoir (18). With every bump or rebound stroke a small quantity of oil escapes from the cylinder through a calibrated leak or bleed orifice via a nylon tube into the reservoir. The resistance encountered by the oil passing through the foot valve assembly produces the bump damping force of the shock absorber. The resistance can be altered simply by turning clockwise or anti-clockwise the knob assembly (5). By doing this, more or less, load is put on to the bump valve (4).

Rebound Stroke. When the piston (3) travels upwards, the oil above the piston is under pressure and escapes through the orifices (6) to the lower part of the cylinder. Bypass valve (7) opens against the pressure of spring (8). The resistance offered to the oil on flowing through the piston produces the rebound damping force. Via the foot valve assembly (9) oil flows from the reservoir to the lower part of the cylinder below the piston to compensate for the volume of oil displaced by the piston rod.

Like the bump setting, the rebound stroke can be altered by turning the ring (holes) (10) placed inside the head (11) and acting on the top (19) of the adjustment rod (brazed) going all the way down the main piston rod (2) turning the adjustment nut (20) thus putting more or less load on the bypass spring (8) acting on the bypass valve (7) controlling the oil blow off pressure.

When adjusting the rebound, the adjustment nut (20) is turned upwards. By doing this the tension on bypass spring (8) is increased. At the same time small leak orifices (18) in the piston rod (2) will be closed by the adjustment nut.

The damper is bolted to the chassis through the ball joint (12) and at the top to the suspension rocker, again through a ball joint (22) placed in the removable head (21). The suspension spring is located outside the damper and leaning on a platform (14) on the bottom and a platform (15) on the top. Depending on the mode of the damper attachment, some teams make their own platform to meet the rocker design, in this case room is allowed to set the rebound damping.

The chassis ride height can be altered

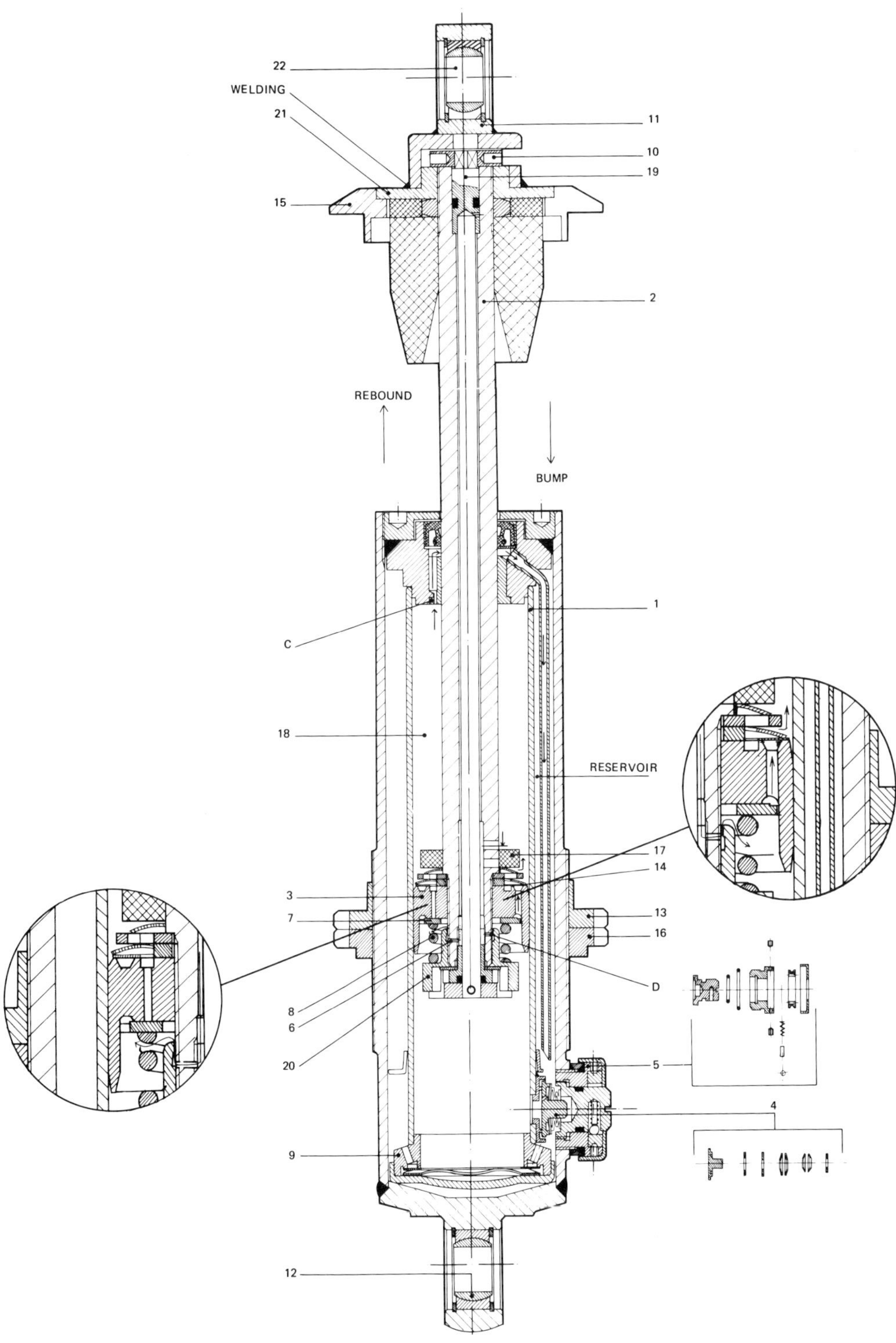

Internal view of the Koni shock absorber. (See text for key).

by adjusting, up or down, the platform (14), the setting being secured by a lock nut (16).

On conventional Formula One cars, because of the length of the spring, a light auxiliary helper spring is used to keep the spring against the top platform (15). This is when the suspension is on full droop – the platform stays located in the dampers head (21).

The interchangeable synthetic bump stop placed outside the piston rod allows a smooth bottoming of the suspension. In full bump the suspension travel can also be limited by adding another rubber washer packer so that in cornering the suspension leans on it, smoothing the chassis roll to give more load on the tyres for better grip. Obviously in this case the suspension linkages are under great stress and the packer's thickness must be carefully chosen for there can be a danger of suspension failure.

Anti Roll Bar

The anti roll bar is an essential part of a suspension layout. Its job is to control roll during cornering. As wing cars have a very low roll centre, (in order to make the car roll), so more load is put on the outside tyres and this is controlled by the anti roll bars and springs. The anti roll bar also controls weight transfer. Depending on the anti roll bar rate is the distribution of the roll and this has a great effect on cornering stability, or balance. In addition to that, the lateral movement of the chassis in corners governs, through the geometry linkages, the amount of camber change. As the tyres react to this camber change, the idea is to bring the tyre contact patch to an ideal temperature. Again, as roll stiffness and grip are controlled by the springs, the roll bars' torsional rate should be adequate for the spring rate. The amount of movement can be controlled by this torsioned rate and, of course, by the leverage. Usually the leverage is kept as per the original design and only the anti roll bar rate or size is changed. As the anti roll bar is an interconnection between the suspension linkage from the right side to the left side, and because the anti roll bar is resisting a great amount of toe-in under cornering, it is important that its mountings are rigid so loads cannot deflect or deform its support and thus stop it working freely.

Anti roll bars are generally mounted on the front bulkhead and linked directly to top suspension rockers. At the rear the layout is much the same. The rear anti roll bar is often adjustable from the cockpit. This little toy is composed of a notched tube fixed to the chassis and a push rod, manoeuvered by a little lever and attached to a rigid cable going to the rear. At the rear the leverage of either side of the roll bar, usually the left hand side, is connected rigidly to the rockers or wishbones. On the right hand side the leverage is simply a blade connected to the cable by a small lever. That makes the blade rotate by about 90° from full soft to full hard. Naturally the blade is designed to take the operational loads. The system allows the driver to change the anti roll bar "rate" as he wishes without stopping at the pits during practice. During the race, track conditions can change or tyre characteristics can change and then the little toy becomes very handy.

Wheels – Rims

The major forces carried by the wheels are those of cornering and braking and of acceleration on the driven wheels. During cornering, the side forces generated by ground effect cars are quite staggering and are trying to bend the wheels sideways. During braking and acceleration, forces are trying to rotate the rim off the rest of the wheel.

The critical high-stress area on a rim is the tyre bead seat, where bending and rotational torques are greatest. An important dimension of a rim is the offset, which is the distance between the centreline of the rim and the mounting face. Large offset is supposed to be best for minimum weight transfer but creates a stress on the suspension since it acts as a leverage.

However the offset is taken into account when designing a suspension geometry and cannot be altered with cast magnesium rims. Major offset can be seen on Ferrari and Lotus rear wheels.

A rim's internal diameter is limited by its suspension and brake components since large size discs and calipers are used, and little room is left for the balance weight which has to be fixed in the right place so that it cannot touch the suspension linkages and brake calipers when rotating or when in full bump or droop.

Rim width and overall diameter are limited by the regulations to match a specific tyre size. Therefore rims cannot be taken off the shelf but are designed according to the designer's requirements. Formula One rims are so wide now that a substantial saving in weight can be made in design and choice of material. These days, the choice of material lies between aluminium or magnesium in cast form. There are rims made from sheet aluminium, formed by spinning or stamping. These types of rims, made by Speedline of Italy are made basically of three pieces, two halves and a solid magnesium disc-shaped centre, assembled with 6mm bolts and the four faces sealed with two "O" rings located in a groove machined in the centre-part. This design is attractive since it allows replacement of either half, obviously a cheaper operation than changing the whole rim. It was introduced in the late '70's and is popular among the Ferrari, Alfa Romeo, Renault, Ligier and Lotus teams.

Die-cast magnesium alloy rims are still very much in use. The risk of corrosion failure is much higher. In the past complete wheels were covered with a varnish to

Cast magnesium wheel. Note the three safety bolts. (Courtesy Toleman Group Motorsport).

avoid any possibility of an air break but nowadays cast magnesium rims are black anodised which tends to overcome the problem of porosity and gives a good, clean finish. Rim spokes are crack tested from time to time for safety but apart from that, maintenance is simply a matter of cleaning.

In accordance with the regulations, all Formula One rims have safety bolts. These are screwed through the rim to prevent the tyre bead falling into the well in the event of a puncture. They are in numbers of three on the outside part of the rim and are sealed with a plastic washer.

For the same reason some rims also have a hump which is a circular portion raised just in the inboard area of the portion of rim that normally carries the tyre bead. The idea is that the tyre bead cannot move across the hump once it has been fitted, and thus it keeps a punctured tyre on its rim.

Chapter 4

Brakes

As on road cars, a Formula One braking system is based on hydraulics. However Formula One systems have some interesting peculiarities. They are under constant development and Formula One cars certainly have a tremendous stopping power.

The main considerations of the system are:

Constant braking power with no change in co-efficient of friction.
Resistance to fade under high temperatures.
Directional stability.
Pedal pressure.
Balance of proportioning.
Lightness.

Rigidity in the chassis, suspension linkage and pick-up points are vital to stability during intense braking since these elements receive tremendous loads thus attention to detail is a primary consideration of design.

Basic Hydraulics

In a closed braking system, the hydraulic pressure is the same in all parts of the circuit.

This pressure is measured in pounds per square inch (psi) or kilogrammes per square centimetre (K/cm^2) which expresses the force applied on the inner surface of the various components.

The pressure is caused by a force exerted from the brake pedal acting on a piston in the master cylinder which causes the fluid in the system to reach a high pressure. This pressure increases according to the effort transmitted to the pedal. The force on the pedal generated by the driver tends to be around 160–200 pounds.

Most Formula One cars have twin calipers with twin pistons. These pistons push the brake pads against the disc. The amount of mechanical force derived from the hydraulic pressure is determined by the area of each piston; if each piston is of one square inch in area and receives a force of 100 psi, it will produce a mechanical force of 100lbs. This mechanical force can be altered by changing the area of the piston. In reality, on Formula One cars, the area of the pistons is changed by replacing the whole caliper. Brake components are delivered as a package already set by the manufacturer so all one has to do is to bolt the calipers into the upright. As the brake pads wear out, the volume in each piston area increases.

Master Cylinders

The reason for mounting two parallel master cylinders is both to be able to modify the

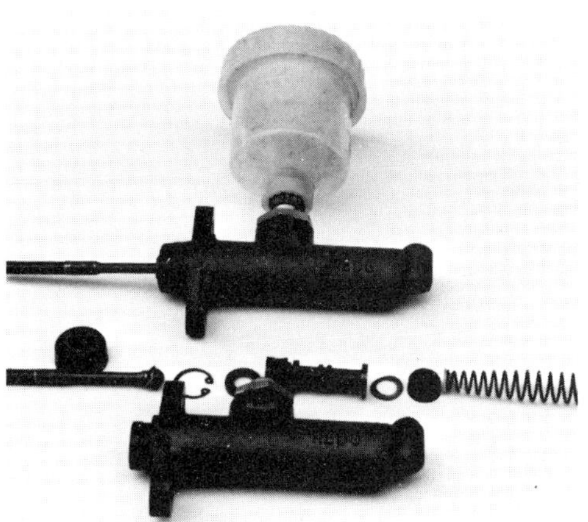

AP master cylinder with its reservoir (top) and internal components.

braking distribution from front to rear and for safety purposes. Although braking design and its components are known to be reliable, leaks and loose unions can occur, forcing the car to pit.

Master cylinders fitted to Formula One cars are similar to those fitted to road cars, except that they are designed to fit a diversity of bulkheads. Each master cylinder has residual pressure valve which maintains a small amount of pressure in the system to prevent air being drawn into the lines and to stop the piston calipers from being completely retracted from the brake pads. This avoids a dead moment while the caliper piston pushes the pads against the disc.

Brake fluid cannot be compressed so the hydraulic pressure develops a certain pedal force which will be inversely proportional to the bore of the master cylinder, and obviously the amount of fluid displacement will be proportional to the master cylinder bore.

Depending on the location of the brake pedal pivot joint, the travel of the pedal can vary considerably. Normally adjustment is down to replacement of the master cylinder bore size. In most cases braking is sufficient and this change in master cylinder is to accommodate the driver's preference, whether he likes a little softness at the beginning of the pedal travel or has the pedal hard like a brick wall. Some drivers prefer a hard pedal simply because it gives an impression of safety, others prefer it softer for a better feel.

The size of master cylinder bore is quite limited, ranging from ¾ inch, to ⅞ inch. Master cylinders are all made of light alloys with standard Imperial thread fittings and are compact and easy to fit. The rods come with them and are designed to cope with the force applied from the pedal to the master cylinder piston. Their length can be modified, either by shortening them or by adding an aluminium tube extension, depending on the layout and position of the pedal bracketry and quite often according to the length of the driver's legs.

Brake fluid reservoirs are generally mounted on top of the master cylinder by some kind of adaptor. On some cars the reservoirs are located elsewhere but still on the bulkhead and from there they feed the master cylinder through a pipe. The reservoirs, made of transparent plastic, provide enough capacity in order not to run dry when the pads are completely worn and the caliper piston is at full travel. A cap is screwed on the open top of the reservoir itself and is vented to the atmosphere to allow the fluid level to go down as the brake pads wear.

Brutal acceleration and deceleration and centrifugal force in cornering, makes the fluid move about in the reservoir, and each team has its own method of ventilation. Generally, reservoir caps (including that for the clutch master cylinder) are connected to three little plastic tubes, joined together at one point and the air is taken from one single point on a "T" junction where the three tubes are plugged. A non-abrasive sponge is inserted inside the reservoir to minimise the fluid movement.

Discs

Ventilated cast iron discs have been in service in Formula One for many years. Ventilated discs have a better heat dissipating capacity than a normal disc brake of the same diameter and thickness. The cooling of the disc is improved by introducing air into the centre of the upright

Rear brakes with extra air ducting required on hard braking circuits.

where it passes into a circular ring in the body of the disc and then centrifuges out through the radial channel cast in the disc.

Disc diameter is one of the factors of the brake pedal force multiplication. Before "ground effect" was introduced in Formula One, and for many years, a large variety of disc thickness, ranging from 1 inch to 10.2 inch, with appropriate single size calipers, were used. Many combinations of discs and calipers used for Can-Am cars were also used in Formula One at circuits where brake cooling is a major concern.

The theory was that because the disc was of a bigger diameter and thickness, it dissipated heat better. Added to this, enormous scoops were introduced to help cooling, and by the end of the first practice session many cars ended up having all sorts of ducting which gave an appearance of untidyness and certainly did not help aerodynamics.

All this is now largely unnecessary but nevertheless at some hard braking circuits extra heat problems still arise.

Discs come with tangential slots milled in the friction surface and on each face of the disc. The idea is to wipe the incandescent dust from the rotating disc as it comes into contact with the leading edge of the pad, since a boundary layer of dust between disc and pad would reduce friction. Slotted discs are normally left and right handed and they are mounted so that the slots become parallel to the leading edge of the pad as the disc rotates. More important, ventilated discs are also left and righthanded and are meant to be mounted in the same direction of travel as the curved vanes, functioning like an air pump.

Along with the pedal force multiplication, the disc diameters are designed to be fitted with calipers inside a front wheel of 13 inch diameter and when assembled to the car, little room is left between calipers and internal surface of the rim.

The disc fixing areas are designed to be rigidly bolted to a hub. In most cases, disc bells are inserted onto the hubs pegs and are clamped in position by the wheel itself.

Ventilated and drilled discs used to be

used in Formula One by Ligier the fashion having been introduced by Porsche on their sports cars. Drilled discs are supposed to decrease pad wear at the expense of disc wear but they do crack around the holes, though without danger of splitting apart. By drilling the four discs of the car, a considerable amount of weight is saved, although the drilling has to be done properly. Nowadays the idea has been dropped. The life of the racing brake disc varies between 400–600 miles, mainly because of changes in temperature.

Calipers

A law of physics says that "for every action there is an opposite and equal reaction".

Brakes calipers are subject to this law. What happens, in practice, is that when the brakes are applied, the caliper's pistons push the pads against the discs and as the discs become resistant, there is the opposite reaction. The disc does not move and instead the caliper flexes.

Brake manufacturers overcame this problem by producing compact and rigid calipers. The primary criteria of brake calipers is the piston area rate between front and rear calipers which is the braking distribution ratio. Piston area, size of master cylinder, disc diameter, and tyres specifications are part of the brake pedal force multiplication.

Formula One brake calipers are made from cast alloy. They are made of two halves, joined together by four high quality bolts. Each half contains a piston and a seal is made with a rubber ring retained in a groove. Pistons are made of light alloy and are hard anodised. Each piston is pushed slightly into the pads which helps, in some respects, the residual pressure system.

Fluid channels are drilled inside, so that when both halves are assembled a closed circuit is formed.

Because of the positioning of these channels, the calipers have their own respective position at the front or at the back of the disc.

Typical brake arrangement seen through a wheel rim. (Courtesy Toleman Group Motorsport).

Externally there is nothing special to be seen. The outer halves have pump and bleeding nipples. The inner halves have the inlets for brake fluid line unions. Finally, the whole caliper has little ears for inserting the pad safety pins.

Diversity of opinion among Formula One designers exists as to which brakes to use, each having his own ideas. But everybody is guided by the brake manufacturers who produce new, efficient products and eventually most end up with similar layouts: twin calipers, twin pistons, four brake pads, and it is likely to stay that way. Nowadays with ground effect cars, brakes are mounted outboard both front and rear, since the unsprung weight theory doesn't apply anymore.

Both calipers are bolted to the upright with two bolts, secured by lock wire. The hydraulics system is linked by a flexible pipe going from one caliper to another. The fluid comes from the master cylinder, goes through two flexible pipes running along the lower wishbones and these are connected to the front and rear caliper of each wheel.

With ground effect design the aim is to give the air the easiest flow path out through the back of the car and the biggest obstruction was the brake layout. Putting the brakes "outboard", or inside the rear

Brake caliper with its Ferodo DS11 pads and safety pins (left) and internal components (right).

wheel, allows a narrower gearbox lump and hence a better air flow.

The temperature of discs and calipers is frequently checked with an appropriate instrument. In addition temperature stickers are stuck to the calipers, giving accurate indications. An indication of good braking is that temperatures are equal, or close, between front and rear.

Pads

Developing a friction material is a black art that only brake specialists can deal with.

Racing friction material, or brake pads, is designed to have the following basic characteristics:

Excellent co-efficient of friction.
Because of the friction, ability to withstand extremely high temperature.
Resistance to wear.

The material pad rubs against the disc and its ability to maintain an almost constant co-efficient of friction gradually diminishes at temperatures exceeding 700°C.

Ferodo DS11 brake pads are widely used in Formula One. The DS11 pad is made of random fibre asbestos, evenly dispersed and including copper particles. Because of its characteristics the DS11 has a very poor grip when cold but extremely good grip once it has reached its proper working temperature.

Bedding-in of new pads is an important process, a fact that is very difficult to instill in some drivers. This bedding-in is done when a practice session starts by making a couple of slow laps and applying the brakes gently and frequently. The pads develop a glaze caused by the copper particles on the surface melting and forming a film over the faces of both the pads and discs. Bedded-in that way, the pads will provide a consistent co-efficient friction. Failing that, the pads get "cooked" immediately, cracking and losing their properties, causing what is called a "brake-fade" situation when the pedal, still fairly hard, does not give braking power.

Obviously the pads are designed to be fitted with free movement as they wear inside the caliper. On the latest type of Lockheed calipers, the pads are held by means of safety pins, or long split pins, for quick replacement.

Normally, depending on the circuit, new brake pads last 200–250 miles and new pads are fitted for the race and bedded-in in the warm-up session preceding the race or during a practice session.

Pedals and Bracketry

Details of the brake system include the essential rigidity of the brake pedal and its bracketry.

Bracketry may be called upon to withstand loads of 900lbs (400kgs) without flexing, to avoid spongy and therefore imprecise braking.

Usually a one piece bracket carries the throttle, brake and clutch pedals. It is generally fabricated in 18 gauge steel and is heat treated before being riveted to the front part of the chassis floor.

Some cars have a cast magnesium or machined aluminium bracket, also riveted to the chassis floor. Ferrari use cast magnesium, which has great rigidity and good finish. Before riveting, a special bond is applied to the surface facing the floor and the lower parts of the side panels. This bond is applied to the bracket mainly to prevent vibration, which can easily sheer off the heads of the rivets.

Brackets have different pivoting points in order to accommodate different drivers in the car. Bulkheads should be rigid to avoid flexing as well.

The brake pedal will be of much the same material and gauge, and fabricated as well. Its total height varies between 7 and 8 inches. At the base of the pivot bush is a small tube welded to the pedal and reinforced with a small welded gusset. Further up, the brake balance system barrel is also welded and reinforced with gussets.

Right at the top of the pedal, the foot area is also made of steel, boxed or flanged and welded. On some cars the foot area is adjustable, again to accommodate the driver's legs. On virtually all cars a thin mesh or an abrasive material is added in order to prevent the foot slipping. The complete pedal can be made in cast light alloy such as magnesium or machined from aluminium.

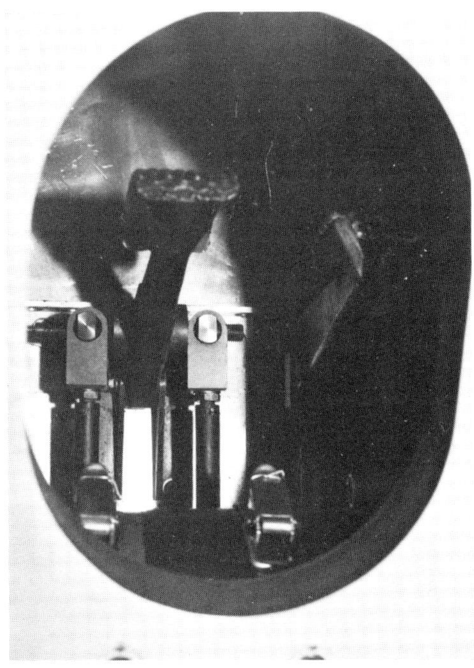

Brake pedal balance arrangement and bracketry. (Courtesy Toleman Group Motorsport).

The distances between the centre top pedal to the centre of the balance bush, and from the pivot point to the centre of the balance bush determines the pedal ratio. This ratio varies from car to car, depending on the size of the master cylinders and their design, to obtain a ratio varying from 5/1 to 7/1. This pedal ratio will determine the amount of pressure to apply to the pedal. Again the pressure exerted depends on the size of the master cylinder as standard brake calipers and discs are fitted most of the time.

Generally, lateral movement is neutralised by fitting the pedal in flanged mount. The pedal pivot point has a small greased, bronze tube slightly longer than the pivot bush going through it, holding the whole pedal in and mounted in double sheer with a hard material bolt.

Like in many other areas of the car, brake pedal and its bracketry are designed to take the heavy loads which designers are aware of, and pedal ratio and other details are taken from experience.

To reduce pedal effort, AP Lockheed produced a power assisted unit which was tried on a Renault in 1981. Although the system was efficient, the unit was removed simply because it was too heavy. Further development has reduced this unwanted weight, but it seems that no team is keen to try it, instead drivers are asked to press the pedal harder!

Brake Balance System

All Formula One cars have twin brake circuits, one for the front and one for the rear. Under braking, the weight transfer from rear to front makes the car dive and under hard braking this weight transfer becomes even more important. Depending on the amount of transfer, brake power distribution can make the rear or front wheels lock causing a difficult situation with a ground effect car, because of the load applied to the tyres.

The purpose of the brake balance system is simply to distribute the braking power between the front and rear wheels, to counteract weight transfer loading of the front and unloading of the rear wheels.

The inside surface of the balance barrel is round and perfectly machined. The barrel is crossed by a balance bar, threaded on either end. Right in the middle, a bearing, commonly called a "rose joint", is held by two circlips and this assembly should move freely inside the barrel.

The extremity of the bar receives a light alloy clevis fixed on a shaped pivot and locked, after adjustment, by a nut. From there a threaded rod is screwed into each clevis and this goes to its respective master cylinder.

Both clevis are screwed close to the side faces of the balance barrel with some play in respect of the forward movement of the master cylinder rods. As the balance bar is threaded on each end, the action of turning it displaces the "bearing" inside the balance barrel, going away from the centre of the pedal. When the pedal is depressed, more pressure will be applied whereas the position of the bearing is, to the right or to the left, putting more pressure to the front or rear brake master cylinder. In other words, if the bearing is displaced to the left and the left hand side is the front brakes, then more pressure will be applied on it in comparison to the right master cylinder, which obviously will work the rear brakes.

The system is very sensitive and can be felt by the driver down to a change of half a turn. Some years ago a gadget was introduced in the form of an adjustable balance bar, operated from the dashboard area by the driver. It consists simply of a cable running inside a sleeve and acting on the balance bar. This gadget is very useful and handy because it does not require a pit stop for brake balance adjustment, and it is especially useful when weather conditions change, for brake power can be distributed more to the rear in order to avoid the front wheels locking on a wet track. The knob controlling the cable is usually fixed next to the dashboard and clearly indicates the direction to turn the knob, in order to avoid confusion.

Initially, the brakes are set statically by two persons, one applying the brake pedal while the other turns one front and rear wheel alternately until friction is thereby equalised by changing the position of the balance bar. Then, during testing, the driver will determine the brake balance distribution that he requires.

Plumbing

Brake pipes also play their role in a braking system and should be of high quality so that they do not expand under pressure.

Aeroquip pipes are widely used in Formula One, in the brake system, and they are also used, in different sizes, in other areas like engine plumbing and gearbox oil circulation system, where pressure is also high.

Aeroquip lines are made of Teflon (a plastic) covered with braided stainless steel. The common size is dash 4 which has a ⅛ inch bore. The brake lines are flexible and

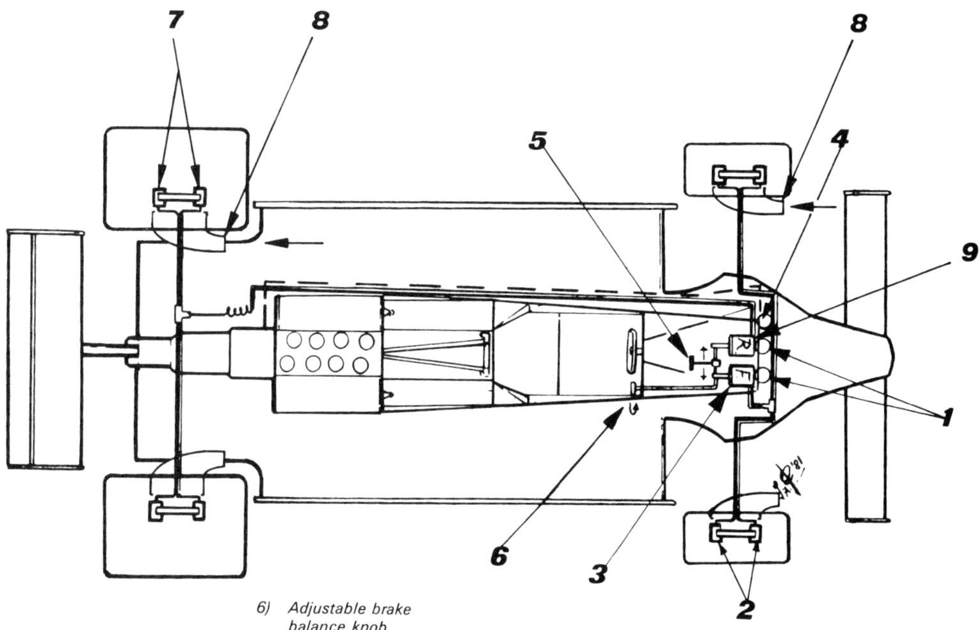

1) Brake fluid reservoirs
2) Front twin calipers
3) Front master cylinder
4) Clutch fluid reservoir
5) Brake pedal
6) Adjustable brake balance knob
7) Rear twin calipers
8) Front and rear brakes air ducts
9) Rear brake master cylinder

Brake and clutch pipe lines. (Giorgio Piola).

run from the master cylinders to the calipers along the chassis and suspension arms. The lines flex to follow suspension movement.

On some cars the Aeroquip lines run inside the bottom front suspension arms in order to reduce turbulence, so that the air goes under the side pods as smoothly as possible. For protection, they are covered with a thin plastic sleeve which prevents the braid deteriorating when rubbing against whatever it is fixed to.

Union lines are also made of high quality materials and are designed to be assembled to the Aeroquip lines. This type of product originated from the Aircraft industry.

Cooling

Brake temperature is reduced by the use of ventilated discs, but that is not enough.

Brake ducts are widely used in Formula One but there is a wide variation in design, the most popular type being a scoop protruding forward to collect cold air and feed it into an annular ring via the centre of the upright and then into the disc's channels.

Big scoops are sometimes needed at the front and they can produce a large amount of drag, but this problem is recognised and scoops and ducts have been slimmed down without loss of effectiveness.

Another method of cooling brakes is the system used on the front wheels of the Brabham BT49, on which the rims are designed to suck air from outside and send it onto the brake layout through the rim itself.

"Standard" scoops are made of fibre glass and are bolted directly to the upright, which is designed with this purpose in mind.

Manufacturers

Two manufacturers who supply the Formula One circus are, on a relatively small scale,

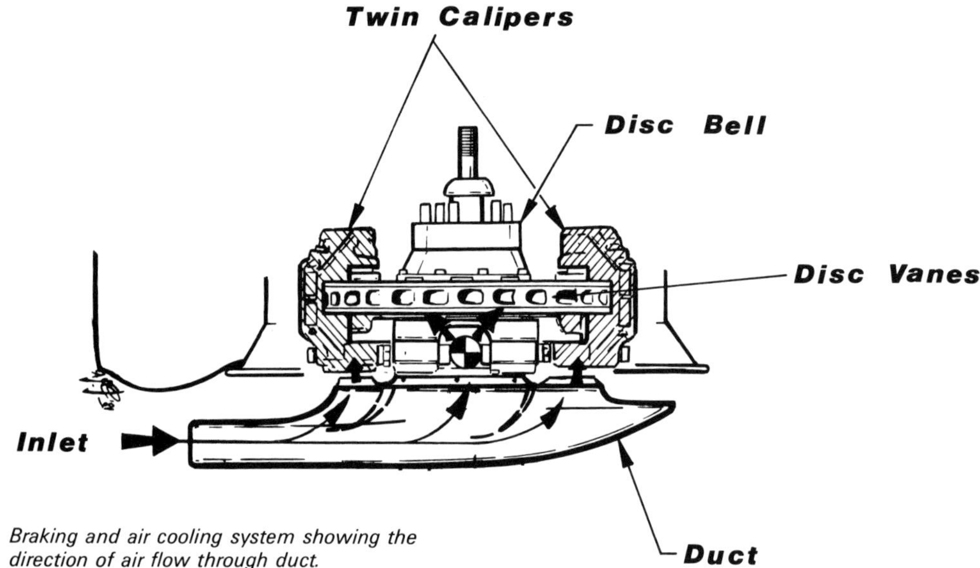

Braking and air cooling system showing the direction of air flow through duct.

Brembo of Italy (who, until the end of 1981, supplied only Ferrari) and, on a much larger scale, AP Lockheed and its associated company, Ferodo. Girling used to be a major brake supplier up until 1980 when AP Lockheed took over its market.

Automotive Product Lockheed was introduced to motor racing by McLaren in 1968 and has since expanded its interest considerably in various classes of racing.

Formula One certainly helps Lockheed to build an enormous amount of research information and experience, which would be almost impossible to obtain under only test bench and laboratory conditions.

Ferodo, Lockheed and Brembo, engineers assist Formula One teams at every circuit.

Chapter 5

Fluid Systems and Safety Measures

Water Cooling

One of the first priorities in the design of a Formula Car should be the provision of adequate engine cooling, having a capacity that is proportional to the horsepower output. The basic requirement is that the flow of coolant has to be sufficient to take the heat away from the engine. This does not mean that the engine must be kept cool, but it should be kept at a temperature close to 90°C, although it may be a good deal hotter during races held in South America or South Africa where ambient air temperature is much higher than in Europe. Good design and choice of radiator should keep the water within the 90°C figure.

A radiator consists of many fine narrow tubes held together by fringes and two separate tanks. As the water flows through the tubes when the car is in motion the passing air flow cools the water. The number of tubes, their length and the number of rows of tubes also influence the radiator's performance. Optimum tube length generally leads the shape to be rectangular.

Since the ground effect cars have been introduced, the trend has been to use all aluminium radiators. Most Formula One cars, with the exception of manufacturers of road cars such as Renault Sport, Alfa Romeo, Ferrari and Lotus, use French made Sofica water radiators, originally designed for Volkswagen and Citroen road car models. French and Italian Formula One cars have the radiators custom built to suit their specific requirements. Radiators by Sofica are light, well made, inexpensive and easy to obtain. Serck radiators also equip some British cars and were the first to introduce aluminium radiators into Formula One.

Copper has excellent ability to transfer the heat to air and was once popular in Formula One. However, copper radiators are heavy and expensive, since they are made in very small quantity. Aluminium radiators are strong enough to absorb any vibrations and their efficiency is as good as the copper ones, the only drawback is that they are not as easily repairable as copper radiators.

Over the years, radiators have been mounted in various locations. Originally it was popular to mount the radiator(s) in the nose. The lateral side mounting started with Lotus on its 72 model and the idea was widely copied. Although some constructors, like Tyrrell and Brabham, remained faithful to nose installation.

Now, on ground effect Formula One cars, the universal solution to radiator location is to lean them forward alongside the chassis (within the area of the dashboard) covered by the side pods which open at the front for air intake. Air escapes through the top surface by means of a ramp

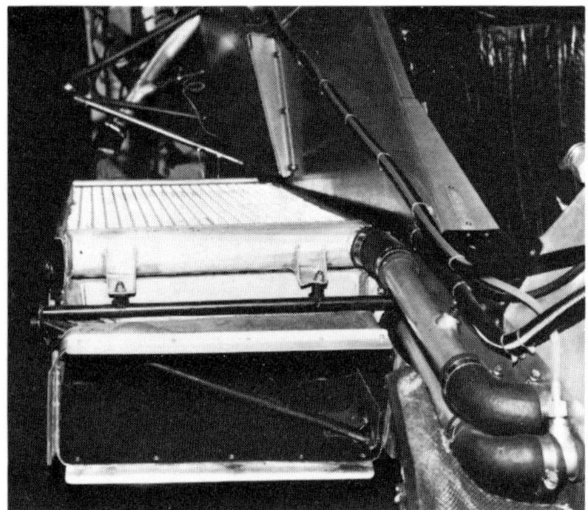

Water radiators arrangement of the Toleman TG181. The top one being of the main system as the lower one is part of the secondary system assisting the cooling of the turbo's intercooler layout underneath the air duct.

and ducts. Wherever the radiators are placed, they create considerable air resistance. Air intake is regarded less critical than the exit, but the shape and size of intakes is generally designed to get sufficient air flow into the radiator without restricting the amount of air passing over and under the side pods, which can affect the overall ground effect performance.

For the same reason, top and bottom front suspension arms are made of aerodynamic section steel tube to reduce drag for a better air flow around the side wings as well as into the radiator air inlet and ducting. However, this is still disturbed by the overall wheel when in motion, for it creates a great amount of turbulence. Obviously designers are aware of this but nothing can be done because aerodynamics devices around the wheels are not permitted by the rules. Radiators are very vulnerable components, they are protected with a wire mesh, positioned away from the surface. The size of the core is carefully chosen in order to stop any sharp object yet not to restrict air flow hitting the radiator.

Radiator air exit ramps are part of a good cooling system. The total exit surface is larger than the inlet. It is important in order to let the air through the radiators without restriction.

The ramps are either incorporated in the whole side wing or are added on afterwards, or are part of the top body work section. From the bottom of the radiator to the top exit the ramp resembles a large arc so the warm air can pass freely at high speed over the top surface of the side pod.

A good example of the importance of adequate radiator exit ramps was provided in 1979 by the Ensign N179. The idea was to obtain a truer wing section by placing the oil cooler and a massive water radiator in front of the driver, sloping forwards from the dashboard area. At the time the layout looked good; unfortunately the exit ducts could not cope with the amount of air hitting the radiators and because of their restricted area caused over-heating.

Some cars have flaps called "louvres", inclined slightly upward and fixed at the front of the ramp surface. The idea is that the difference of air speed passing over them and the air speed coming out of the radiators, activates air exit. They are positioned so that they do not affect the air flow passing on top or alongside the side pods (Ligier JS17, Renault RE30, RE31 etc. and Ferrari 126C). However there is a difference of opinion among designers about the effectiveness of louvres.

All current Formula One engines are provided with at least one or two pumps to circulate water. The water goes around the cylinder barrel and to the hottest zones of the cylinder heads, the combustion chambers, spark plugs, boxes and exhaust parts. This requirement applies to any engine, but cooling is more important with a racing engine because of the higher power output and normally one water pump is provided for each bank of cylinders in order to get uniform water flow. The plumbing is important insofar as it is designed to avoid an air trap forming in the system, since formation of air pocket traps will cause overheating.

From engine to radiators, water circulates in aluminium pipes of 1" – 1¼" diameter running uphill toward a little header tank from which air can escape. After an engine installation the water system is bled. Before attempting to start

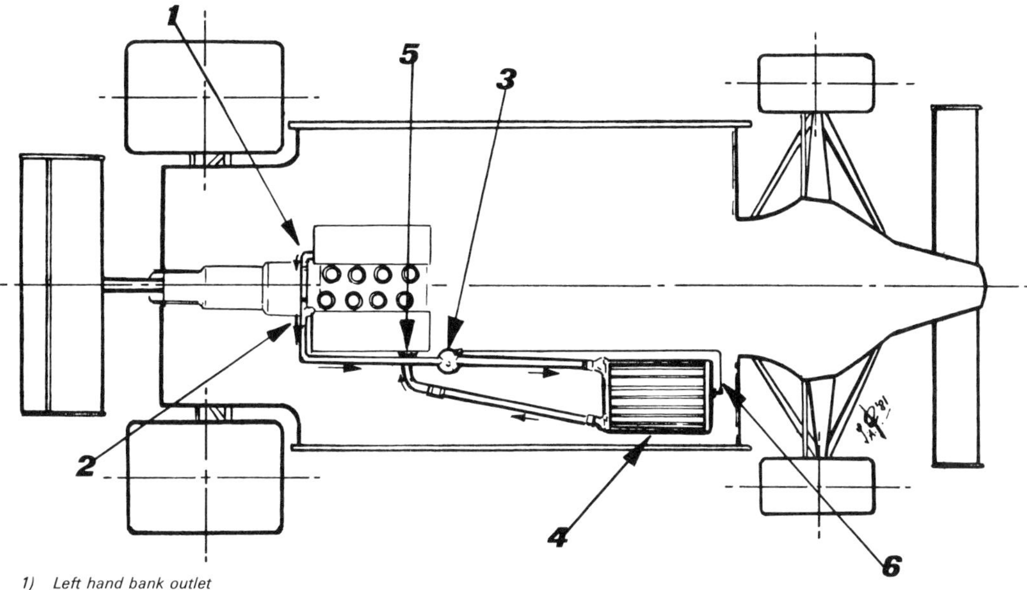

1) Left hand bank outlet
2) Right hand bank engine outlet
3) Header tank
4) Radiator
5) Water pump
6) Bleeding line

Simplified drawing of the cooling system.

the engine it is customary to pressurise the system by means of an appropriate tool, by doing so any leak can be spotted, otherwise difficulties occur in locating them after the whole bodywork has been fitted.

An appropriate water cap is fitted on the header tank to close the system after it has been properly bled.

The coolant is a mixture of water and other liquids as used in small aircraft, which is supposed to have a lower boiling point. At running temperature the pressure rises up to about 13psi.

All these components and their positions vary from car to car according to the design concept and its general evolution.

Oil System and Cooling

In addition to the water cooling system, it is vital for the well being of a Formula One engine that the oil should be adequately cooled. Oil cooling systems are in two parts – the engine's own oil lubrication system and the car oil cooling system layout, designed to work with it.

All Formula One engines have a dry sump oil system. The dry sump system consists of a remote oil tank, one or two pressure pumps and one or two scavenge pumps which collect the oil from the crank case and return it to the car's oil tank.

Basically, the pressure pumps fed from the car oil tank, send oil to all internal moving parts and then the oil is returned to the tank by means of one or two scavenge pumps, depending on the engine make. The reason for using scavenge pumps is to get the engine's centre of gravity as low as possible, preventing a large quantity of oil being whipped around by the crankshaft. Thus, oil is better controlled which improves lubrication and cooling.

The sump is merely an oil collection point and it is deep enough to clear the path of the travel of the con rods and crankshaft bob-weights. In the case of the Cosworth DFV, the bottom half incorporates the main bearing cap which is integral with the sump, also helping make a compatible structure for chassis loads to pass through the sump, the sump being part of the engine attachment to lower part of the chassis. (See relevant illustration).

Oil reservoir incorporated into the bellhousing – McLaren MP4.

The function of the oil tank is obviously to contain oil, and to separate trapped air from the oil. Its design is relatively simple: baffles with flanged holes are incorporated to reduce deceleration and acceleration movement and to keep the oil from going to the side of the tank under centrifugal force. At the top of the tank the scavenge oil lines are positioned tangentially in order to calm the returned oil, avoiding any formation of air bubbles.

Malfunctioning of an oil tank starves the oil pressure pump which results in an instant destruction of the engine internals. Design and location of the oil tanks have varied over the years from car to car. On some cars they are within the chassis, just behind the fuel tank area, a location first used on some American racing cars. Separate oil tank units are still in use, located between the chassis and the engine or alongside the chassis. A long time Ferrari technique, the trend is towards having the oil tank built into the bell housing. This idea requires an unusual length bell housing to hold 2–2½ gallons of oil, the usual contents of an oil system. It also calls for a longer input shaft and in most cases an internal channel sealed from the engine/gearbox units. An additional header tank is screwed on top of the housing, including all fittings as well as the ventilation piping. The oil pump is fed from the bottom of the main tank.

The majority of British Formula One cars are equipped with Serck coolers. They are made of aluminium and therefore are light, they offer better heat rejection per unit weight and volume, less oil pressure drop and cause less aerodynamic drag than any other type of oil cooler known. They come in several sizes with different male or female parts which make a neat and secure plumbing. They are also used for cooling gearbox oil.

Because the amount of heat to be extracted is similar to that from the water radiators, on conventional Formula One cars oil cooler installation has gone full circle from nose mounting, to under rear wing position, to alongside the chassis. Now with ground effect oil cooler(s) installations are pretty well defined. The already crowded engine area of wing car has led to the mounting of large coolers on top of the water radiators, although this is not the best area because of the extra drag produced.

An alternative is the so called "intercooler". This gadget is placed away from the external air flow and so is generally located inside the bottom of the side wing. The system is quite simple; the entire cooler is encased in an aluminium container and connected to the engine and to one of the water radiators. The cooled water coming out of the radiator goes through the container, cooling at the same time the oil circulating in the oil cooler. The container is shaped for easy water circulation and is supported by rubber mounts to avoid cracks from vibrations. The best quality of piping is always used in order to cope with the temperature and high pressure lines are rubber reinforced all around with braided wire and are flexible. Different bore sizes are chosen according to the oil flow recommended by the engine department. Finally the fittings are designed to be assembled with the piping and oil cooler parts supplied from the same source and made of aluminium in a variety of configurations to meet the requirements.

On turbo-charged engines the oil system is further complicated by the addition of an

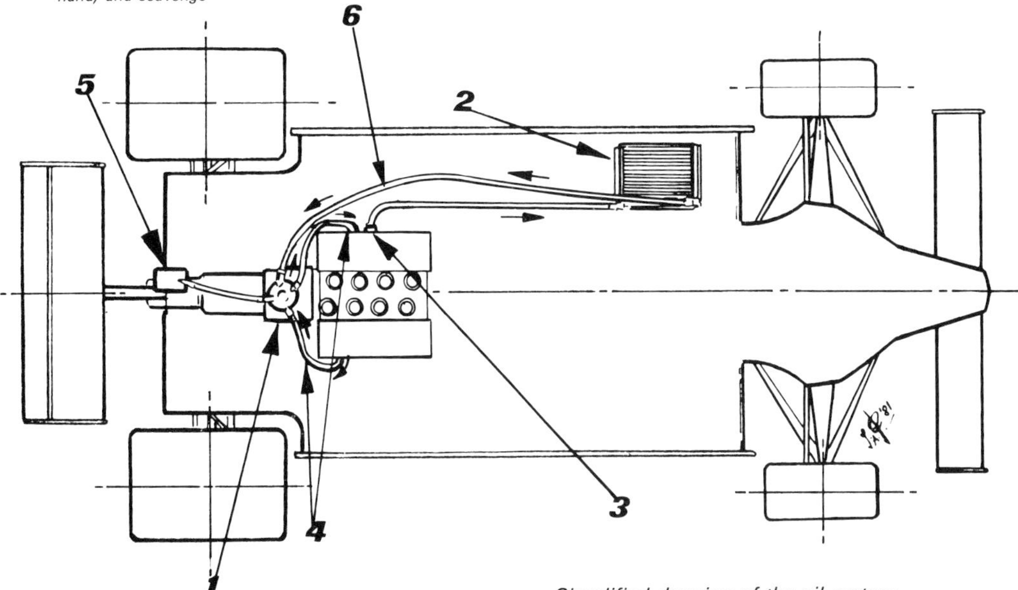

Simplified drawing of the oil system.

extra scavenge and pressure pump, solely circulating the oil around the turbine(s) shaft.

Fuel System

A Formula One fuel system is not quite as simple as running a hose from the tank to the engine. The whole idea is to feed the engine continuously during any attitude of the car under braking, acceleration and cornering without failure. The fuel load is calculated to last a full length race without surplus and the system must be capable of picking up the last pint of fuel remaining in the fuel cell. All Cosworth engined cars use some sort of "surge tank" fuel pick-up system. It is difficult to know what the continental cars are up to. However, they must have a similar system for without exception ground effect cars have a single fuel cell within the main structure, right at the back of the chassis. According to the rules, the cell capacity may not exceed 250 litres and must be made by a manufacturer recognised by the F.I.A. (1982),to specifications complying with the rules for safety reasons. The cell is put in through a large oval trap and expands against the housing walls which are designed to accept its shape.

After installation of the cell and the collector plumbing, the housing is closed by an aluminium trap bolted over the oval hole. The trap carries the different fuel return unions, all breather valves and the fuel filler.

Before the fuel goes to the engine it passes through a collector pot or tank located inside the main fuel cell. Its purpose is to pick up and to keep the fuel which will then be called by the engines mechanical fuel pump.

The collector pot is made of aluminium, usually with four inlet pipes going to the four corners of the main fuel tank. The extremity of each inlet pipe has some sort of scoop resting in a housing especially designed for it.

Right at the bottom of the collector tank are four one-way valves corresponding with the appropriate tube. Under braking,

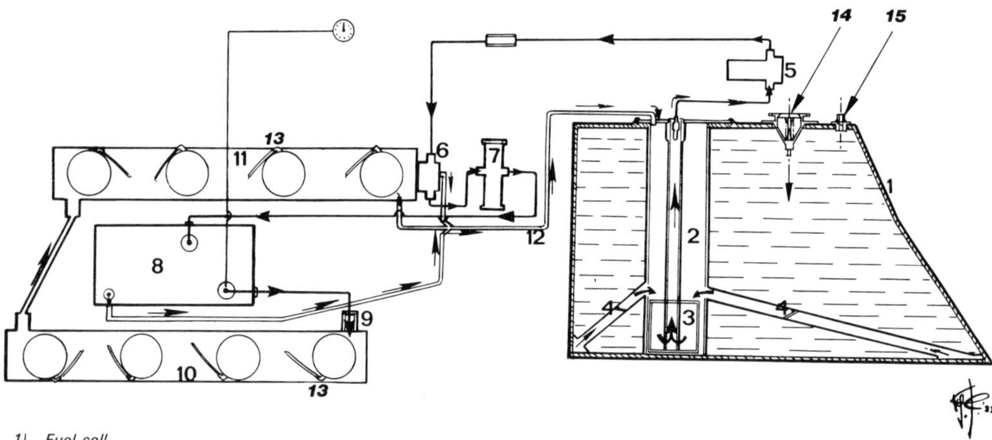

1) *Fuel cell*
2) *Collector pot*
3) *Filter*
4) *One way valves*
5) *Electric high pressure fuel pump*
6) *Engine fuel pump*
7) *Engine fuel filter*
8) *Metering unit*
9) *Pressure relief valve*
10) *Right hand bank manifold*
11) *Left hand bank manifold*
12) *Return fuel line into collector pot*
13) *Injectors*
14) *Quick release fuel filler*
15) *Tank breather*

Simplified drawing of the fuel system. (Giorgio Piola).

acceleration and cornering, the fuel contained in the main cell runs around the scoop and is forced through one or more valves, which let the fuel go into the collector tank and prevent it from escaping, so always keeping the collector full. The collector is fed by intertia surge, thus ensuring that all the fuel within the main cell is picked up, and, assuming that all the valves work properly, the collector provides a sufficient amount of fuel for the engine fuel pump to prevent any momentary fuel starvation during any attitude of the car, especially when the fuel level is low.

The collector tank usually incorporates a filter, unless this is placed externally, different engine returns and by-passes and is ventilated to the atmosphere through a one way valve located on top of a trap to the main tank. The ventilation valve is also required by the safety rules.

Tank filling is through a quick release sealed with a spring loaded valve opened only when the fuel funnel is put in position. the funnel pushes down the valve, letting the fuel run into the tank.

The procedure for starting the engine is relatively simple. The engine builder will recommend an external warm-up of the engine with the aid of some kind of heater, or at least a warming-up of the metering unit itself. This warm-up should be observed before attempting to crank the engine, especially in cold weather. The injection pump mixture datum adjusting pin is then set to full rich, the electric fuel pump is switched on, raising the pressure, and the engine is run at 2,000 rpm. When the oil and water temperature has risen to about 30°C the rpm's are increased then the mixture setting is weakened by turning back the adjustment pin to a given notch, usually the middle one. The car will not be allowed to leave the pits before the temperature has reached at least 70°C.

The fuel system on turbocharged engines uses similar principles as the normal atmospheric engine but more complicated because of the general layout in conjunction with the turbines and inlet manifold.

On turbocharged cars electronic fuel-injection is becoming a necessity in order to tailor fuel flow to boost at varying rpm and temperature.

Starters

Cranking the engine is usually done with a starter motor. Current British and French Formula One cars do not have electrical starter motors, unlike Ferrari. Air starters have replaced the electric ones because they are lighter, more compact and crank the engine a lot quicker. The only disadvantage is that a bottle containing compressed air is necessary to feed the starter itself. The air device was introduced by McLaren in the days of the M23 and was soon copied by other teams. The air starter principle has been taken and developed from an air drill design. It is composed of an aluminium housing of relatively small diameter, bolted to the bell housing. A complex gearing system incorporates an ellipse running on a shaft, sending the "bendix" forward and engaging into the engine flywheel crown, so rotating the engine when the pressurised air is activated. The air starter can be activated from the cockpit by means of a mechanical lever or an electric switch, both acting on a one-way valve which lets the air through from the small inboard air bottle, which allows 5 or 6 starts before running out of air. Air can also be supplied from outside when a pipe is plugged to a quick release union mounted at the back of the gearbox for easy reach and operated by a mechanic.

Electrics

Because of air starters, the heavy battery has become unnecessary – instead tiny motorbike batteries are popular and are of sufficient capacity to feed electric pumps, electronic ignition and injection systems.

Wiring diagrams are simple, and the wiring is the most reliable component when laid out properly. In England the wiring is done by Lucas, although a few teams do it themselves, as do Renault and Ligier. The wiring on all the Cosworth engined Formula One cars does not have fuses because there are few low tension electrical accessories and the current output of the DFV engine is relatively low. The current is controlled by a rectifier incorporated within the "spark box".

A cheap looking but efficient spark box is also made by Lucas and is designed to be fitted to the Cosworth engine. The Lucas spark box is usually located in the middle of the "V" between the manifolds and is quickly replaceable. Magnetti Marelli is taking over the Lucas system. The Formula One circus is usually asisted by Lucas and Magnetti Marelli personnel.

The Ferrari/Alfa Romeo wirings are quite complicated but nicely arranged. Fuses always come as standard. Their engines drive a fair sized alternator which has to provide sufficient amount of current for the Varley battery which in turn activates the electric starter motor.

On any Formula One car, all the dashboard switches come from the aeronautic industry; they are very well made and reliable.

Safety

Safety considerations are always very much in mind when a designer lays down a new car. The aim is to ensure maximum structural strength and stiffness of the chassis, which is an asset to a competitive Formula One car in terms of road holding. Suspension, steering and braking system components should all be up to their job so the driver has the maximum degree of control in difficult conditions. However, the problem of complete safety is not easy to resolve satisfactorily due to the high cornering and straight line speeds reached by ground effect Formula One cars.

Safety rules have steadily developed over the years for the benefit of driver protection. General circuit layout, protection such as catch fences, guard rails, fire and medical assistance etc., have all greatly improved thanks to Jackie Stewart, Formula One safety pioneer. Crushable chassis structures which are part of the integral chassis and covers the entire fuel tank area of the car in direct contact with open air are mandatory. The thickness of the structure is variable from 1 cm – 10cm, according to the

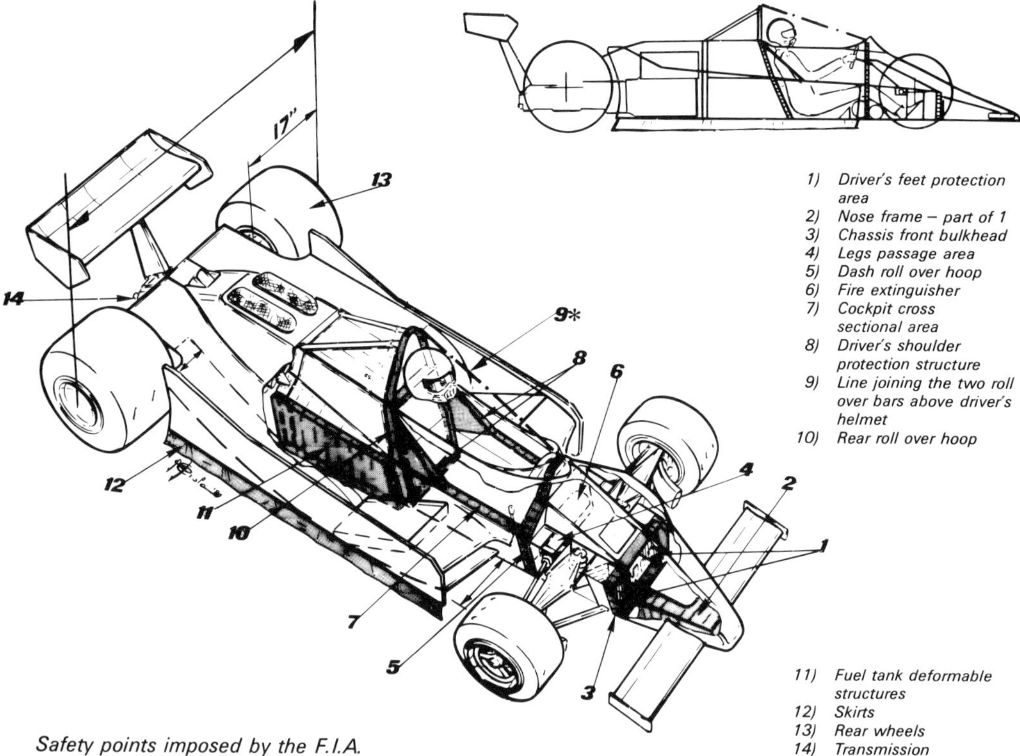

Safety points imposed by the F.I.A.

most vulnerable point of the fuel tank.

The conventional Formula One car had a deformable structure area which was filled with expandable foam around the fuel tank area. Now, with the narrow chassis of "wing cars" the large removable side pods are considered as deformable structures capable of absorbing a fair amount of side shock impact. There is also a rule which states that a protective structure at the back of the driver's shoulders, and in front of his feet, should be part of the chassis and capable of withstanding a given load.

All Formula One cars have a roll bar bolted or riveted a minimum of 25cm forward of the steering wheel and at least as high as the top of the steering wheel rim. In most cases the loop is part of the main dashboard structure. A second roll over bar (also bolted or riveted) is situated on top of the fuel tank and is high enough for a line extended from the top of it to the top of the dashboard loop to pass over the driver's helmet when he is seated in the car. The seat belts, fastened to these structures, are designed to withstand specific loads, which simply means that the roll over bar should be strong enough to resist an impact if the car goes upside down.

Fuel cells are made of rubber, therefore deformable. Although all bladders are crushproof, they are not always leak-free; they can still be cut or punctured. They are located inside a fuel cell department, built within the chassis and protection is by the deformable external structure mentioned above. Fuel cells are made according to the F.I.A. specifications and are proven by manufacturers. Piping, air vents, tank collectors and other fittings are fire proof and are positioned within the internal areas of the car, obviously away from hot areas such as the engine's exhaust. "Break away" self sealing valves are compulsory, their purpose being to stop the petrol running out in case of an accident where the engine might separate from the chassis or the car could turn upside down, but fortunately in Formula One this sort of shunt is very rare.

Fire is much feared by the drivers. Fire extinguishers are fitted within the chassis, the general system having two bottles, one of 2.5kg the other of 5kg, containing a chemical made according to the F.I.A. ruling.

The lines of the biggest extinguisher are routed within the driving compartment, and the line of the smaller extinguisher is run towards the engine, mainly around the fuel injection metering unit or injector pipes.

Fire extinguishers can be activated manually by means of some sort of lever, or electrically, by pressing a button.

All Formula One cars carry a life support system composed of a medical air bottle mounted somewhere in the car and connected to the driver's helmet by a flame resistant flexible pipe. The system is designed to feed the driver with air for around 30 seconds, in the hope that the rescue party arrives before that time expires.

Electrics have to be fire proof and all electrical circuits can be cut-off by means of a spark proof circuit breaker which is simply a master switch. These safety devices are set at the same time, either by the driver or externally by a marshal. The location of the external handle or switch is normally within the rear roll over bar area. The activating systems are clearly indicated, so rescue personnel can operate at a distance by means of a hook on a pole or similar.

Seat belts or safety harnesses are mandatory and a "must", otherwise the "G" forces at the first corner would send the driver into the crowd!

British made Willans seat belts are popular in Formula One and other forms of racing. The belt comprises two abdominal straps, two so-called crotch straps and two shoulder straps, all initially set when fitting the driver in the car. All straps are adjustable. The different anchorages are securely fixed to the chassis. The design of this type of seat belt allows a quick and easy release. A detachable steering wheel is an extra safety item; it allows the driver to get in or out of the car easily.

Crash helmets are also part of the safety requirements, of course, and must be approved by the F.I.A. They are fire proof and quite a few drivers wear an additional chamois leather stuck to the lower part of the helmet to prevent flames reaching the neck. The helmet has a mandatory life bottle connecting to a tube on the left hand side and an intercom device in order to communicate with the engineer during practice sessions.

The driving suit is equally fire proof, and compulsory, as well as fireproof underwear and balaclava. Shoes are of the same material, except for the sole which is leather.

The gloves complete the uniform and are also made of the fireproof material. The inner face is also of leather for better grip of the steering wheel.

Other rules minimise dimensions for both the cockpit area and its opening to ensure that the driver can get in or out without undue difficulty. The use of magnesium sheet less than 3mm thick is forbidden, as is chromium plating of steel suspension members so most cars' suspension components are not painted at all, but black. A little red light, of 15 watts, hanging around the lower part of the rear wing is used during wet weather conditions and can be switched on by the driver.

More details of rules and regulations can be found in the annual F.I.A. Yearbook.

Chapter 6

Transmission

The transmission is the unit which transmits the movement of the engine, through the clutch, to the wheels. In a Formula One car it is a beautiful piece of engineering, extremely accurate in design and machining. Modern Formula One cars have very good grip and power of around 500 bhp; the torque attained during violent accelerations and decelerations puts tremendous stress on the transmission.

For many years the name of Hewland has been closely associated with motor racing. Hewland produce gearboxes and final drive units for many forms of racing such as Formula Ford, Formula Three, Formula Two, Formula One and sports cars. In Formula One the majority of the cars on the starting grid are equipped with Hewland gearboxes. The units are widely used because of their compact construction, versatility and reliability. In general conception, they accept many parts of the suspension as well as the inboard brakes (now brakes are generally outboard thanks to ground effect requirements), starter motor and other big accessories such as the rear wing. Due to its great popularity in racing, we shall explain how the Hewland gearbox and final drive work. The differences between the Hewland FG400, FGA and FGB are minor. The FGB is the latest design which has replaced the long serving FG400 and FGA.

Hewland units have gradually been improved, according to the going trend. For a long time the FG400 with inboard brakes was used. Its recent replacement by the FGB was due to the fact that higher engine outputs plus the extra loads produced by "wing cars" required a stronger case where most suspension components are attached to it and that brakes were mounted outboard and a narrower overall box was called for.

Internally, the crown wheel and pinion (CWP) and its bearing received a better way of being lubricated; an oil channel cast within the main case, on the FGB.

Hewland FG400, FGA, FGB

On the FG400, starting inside of the gearbox, we find the differential, working also as a limited self-locking device, and composed simply of the outer cam track, inner cam track and eight plungers, all enclosed between the plunger carrier and the outer housing, all in case hardened steel all the way through, (also known as spyraldo graphite iron), which is extremely tough. The advantage is that the outer cam track runs in the outer case, giving good lubricating properties with cast iron. The design and working order of the unit is simple as well as being efficient and reliable. The complete unit is bolted on to the crown wheel with ten 7/16 inch UNF

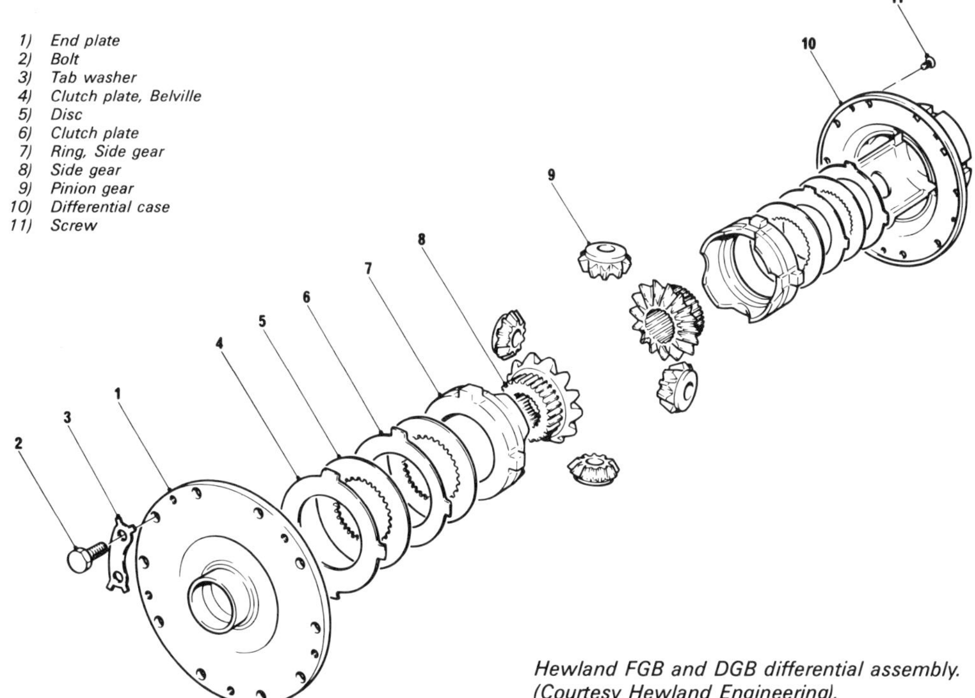

Hewland FGB and DGB differential assembly. (Courtesy Hewland Engineering).

bolts secured by tab washers. The outer housing and inner cam tracks are splined to receive the drive shafts. The system works as described below.

The power comes through the crown wheel into the outer case, which in turn is bolted to the plunger carrier. The plunger carrier then transmits the power into the plungers and the torque is then split onto the inner cam track and the outer cam track. These in turn are connected straight to the drive shafts coming out either side of the side plate. Any break-away of one wheel will cause the wheel to spin freely for a period until such time as the speed limit of the differential is reached. Because of the centrifugal force, the plungers then split, equalising the differential and then the wheel stops spinning, locking both wheels and giving a better traction.

The latest FGB is delivered with a standard Hewland self locking device which functions in a similar manner to the Salisbury system, which is described later in this chapter. The differential unit is supported by two roller bearings, the bearing cages being located in the side plates. The pre-load can be set by altering the thickness of the shims. Outside the plate one ball bearing (double track) supports the drive shafts retained inside the side plate by a circlip. A retaining plate complete with an oil seal holds the whole thing together.

Cast magnesium side plates take the very high load from the crown wheel and pinion, in fact the movement tends to push the side plates outside; this is reduced by a series of studs, with four long studs going through the main cage and side plates.

The movement is transmitted from the pinion to the crown wheel, both hardened steel and always paired. Another very high load comes from the pinion being forced back into the box, and this is why there is a large pinion head bearing. The rear of the bearing is threaded so that when the pinion and bearing are positioned in their

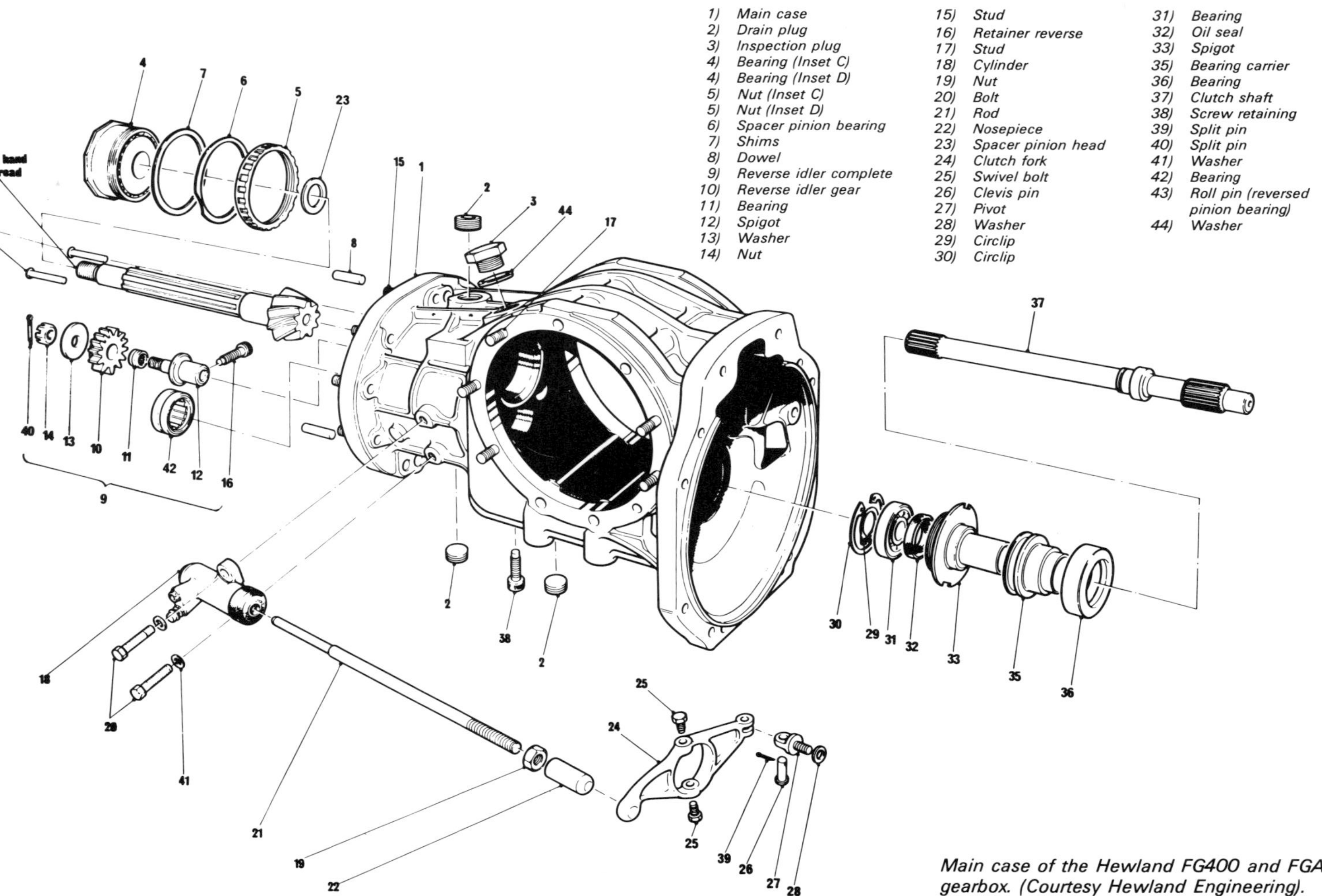

Main case of the Hewland FG400 and FGA gearbox. (Courtesy Hewland Engineering).

respective bore, a big nut tightens them together with a certain load obtained, again with shims. The rest of the pinion body is splined to receive three hubs, the rear of the pinion is located into a bearing at the back of the bearing carrier and tightened with a left hand thread nut for safety. On the FGB, the pinion bearing is located in a steel housing, bolted to the cage with a series of six bolts.

The life of the crown wheel and pinion is around 800 miles. Because the gearbox is mounted in unit with the final drive, it is quite difficult to change the crown wheel and pinion rapidly for the complete gearbox has got to be dismantled. In any case, the setting of the crown wheel and pinion must be very precise for reliability. Nowadays, it is normal to change the ratio of the crown wheel and pinion as well as the gear ratios to suit the different circuits. The FG400 and FGA accept several crown wheels and pinion ratios.

Moving to the main cage, or box, in cast magnesium, nicely designed and also very strong and light, we notice the several external nerves for maxiumum rigidity. The sides of the crown wheel housing are accurately machined to receive the side plates. The front section is designed to accept the bell housing and also the clutch fork, the spigot and the thrust bearing assembly. This small unit is crossed by the clutch shaft, more commonly known as the input shaft, which turn in a bearing, located in the spigot and secured with a circlip. Between them, an oil seal completes the assembly.

On the FGB, now widely used in Formula One, an oil channel is incorporated at the top section within the cage; the oil sent by the oil pump goes to a dowel screwed at the rear section of the cage and distributed by an oil feed or by-pass at the same time. Externally, the FGB carcass has been reinforced because of the loads produced by ground effect cars.

Looking from the rear of the main cage (see illustration) we see the idler reverse unit with the spigot located in the cage and retained with a bolt from the side. The gear is held by a washer and nut, also secured by a split pin. The lay-shaft part of the first gear and reverse takes place in a roller bearing, again secured by a retainer bolt. On the top of it, the pinion bearing can clearly be seen, (see page 80).

Outside the box on the right hand side, we find the clutch slave cylinder and its rod. On the left hand side, the electric starter motors, brackets and supports also have their own location, if they are to be used. Still outside, on top of the box one plug is situated right on top of the bearing bore for oil filling. A second plug is situated on top of the differential and is used mainly to check the state of the crown wheel and pinion. On the bottom there are two plugs to drain the oil. The threaded bosses have been designed for a possible anchorage of lower suspension links or wishbones.

Gear Ratios

Driving one's own saloon car around a twisty circuit, such as Las Vegas, one can be certain to find that one has the wrong ratios for some corners. The Hewland gearbox allows the fitting of the right ratio at the right time, so that the maximum amount of power can be transmitted when needed. A Hewland offers a wide range of gear ratios, plus, as mentioned above, different ratios of crown wheel and pinion to suit any corner on any circuit.

Construction: 5-Speed Unit

The following description is in the same order as when put together as shown in the drawings. Bear in mind that the gears are paired, one from the layshaft and one from the pinion shaft, and that each ratio is etched with two sets of numbers.

Starting from the pinion shaft we have on the bottom of the bearing carrier:

1 thrust washer – inner track for 5th gear – rear hub – 4th and 5th clutch ring – needle bearing and 4th gear – needle bearing and 3rd gear – centre hub and 2nd gear – needle bearing and

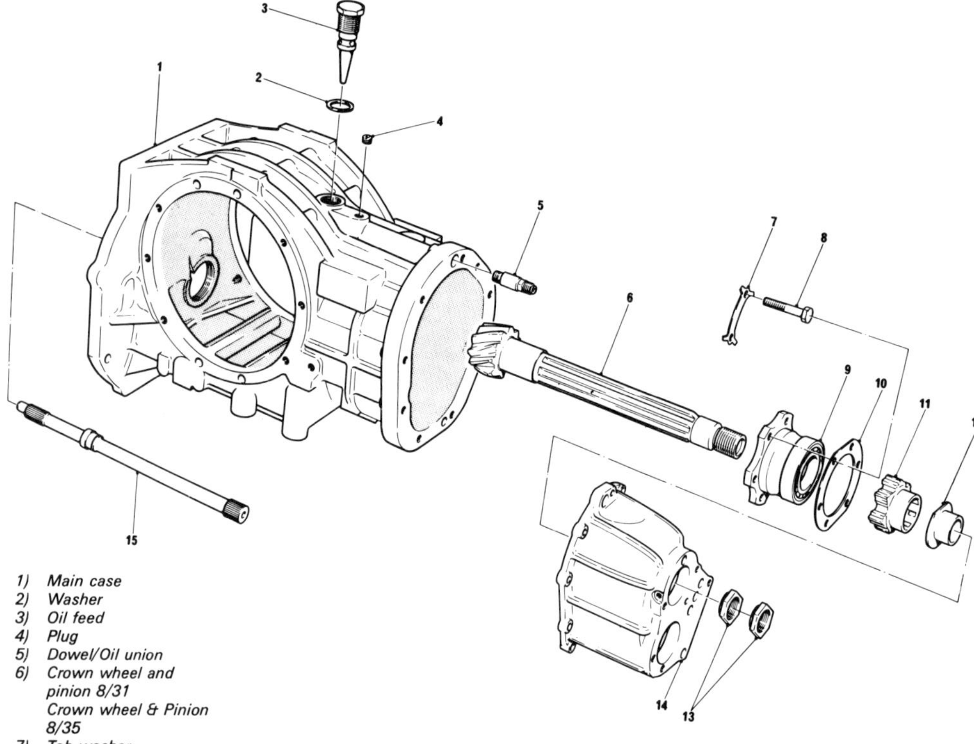

1) *Main case*
2) *Washer*
3) *Oil feed*
4) *Plug*
5) *Dowel/Oil union*
6) *Crown wheel and pinion 8/31*
   Crown wheel & Pinion 8/35
7) *Tab washer*
8) *Bolt*
9) *Pinion bearing*
10) *Shim (various sizes)*
11) *Hub, Rear*
12) *Inner track*
13) *Nut, Pinion LH*
14) *Bearing carrier*
15) *Clutch shaft*

Hewland FGB gearbox components. (Courtesy Hewland Engineering).

> *1st gear – needle bearing – front hub and finally the 1st and reverse sliding gear.*

On the layshaft there is from right to left:

> *1 thrust washer – 5th gear – 1 spacer (fork passage) 4th gear – 1 pinion – 3rd gear – 1 pinion – 2nd gear and the layshaft itself making the 1st gear and reverse.*

The gears on the layshaft are all splined as the layshaft itself connects to the clutch shaft or input shaft, coming from the engine through the clutch.

The bearing carrier contains one roller bearing and double ball bearing to support the two assemblies. The pinion shaft and layshaft are both tightened with two big nuts and are secured by split pins at the rear. The three selector rods in hardened steel are in the interlocking mechanism. At their threaded end the forks are locked with nuts and tab washers, and three forks are cast aluminium bronze. Obviously the forks have got to be set correctly and individually in the dog ring and at the same time they have to be perfectly centralised in the hub. Failing that, overheating of gears, excessive wear and possible seizing up of the forks can occur. The three selector rods are slotted to take the plungers pushed with little springs, and their bead is machined in a sort of "U" shape to allow the selector finger to travel from right to left to select the gears. All this takes part on the interlocking mechanism. As we can see

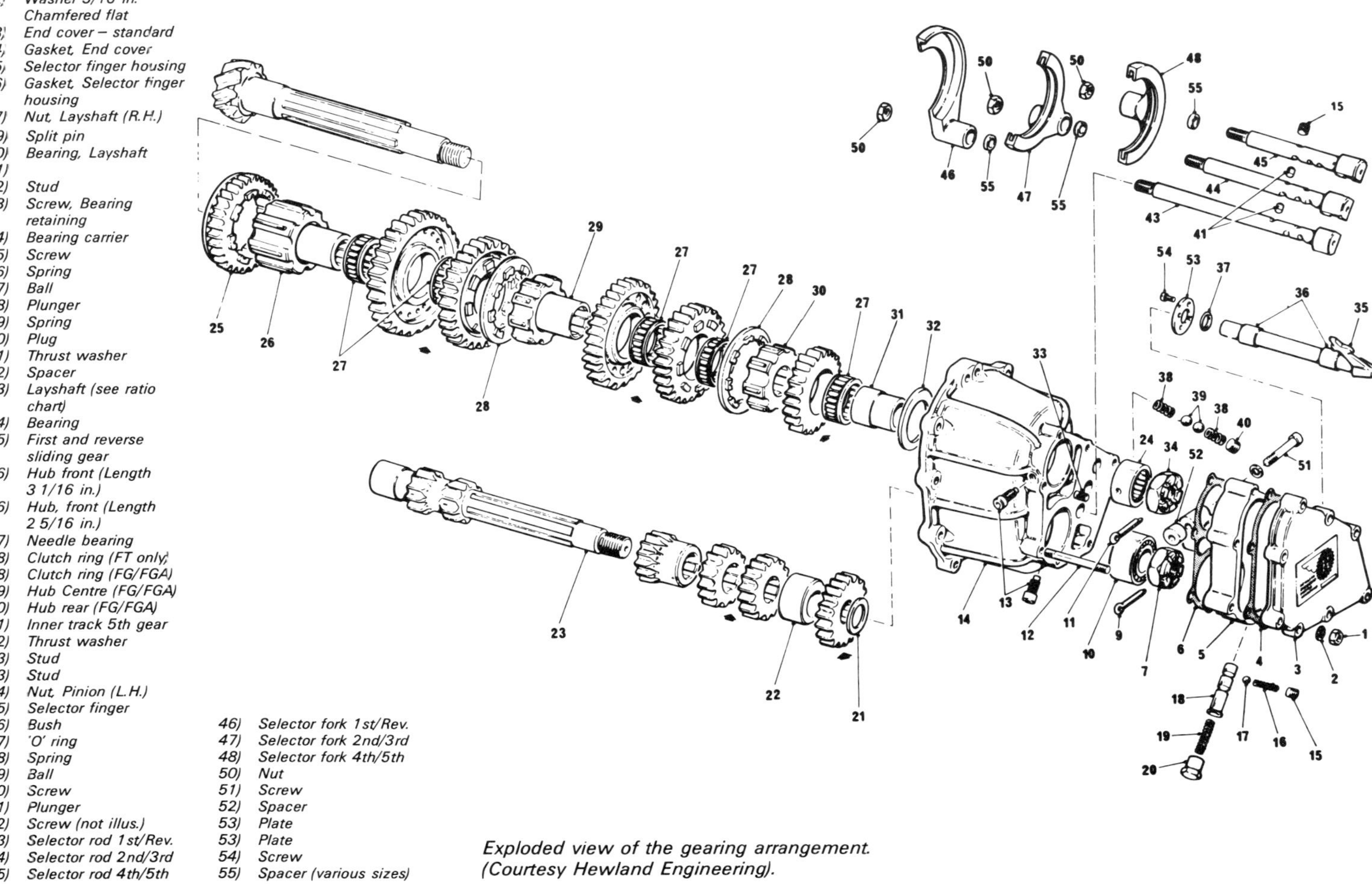

Exploded view of the gearing arrangement. (Courtesy Hewland Engineering).

1) Nut 5/16 in. UNF Nyloc
2) Washer 5/16 in. Chamfered flat
3) End cover – standard
4) Gasket, End cover
5) Selector finger housing
6) Gasket, Selector finger housing
7) Nut, Layshaft (R.H.)
9) Split pin
10) Bearing, Layshaft
11)
12) Stud
13) Screw, Bearing retaining
14) Bearing carrier
15) Screw
16) Spring
17) Ball
18) Plunger
19) Spring
20) Plug
21) Thrust washer
22) Spacer
23) Layshaft (see ratio chart)
24) Bearing
25) First and reverse sliding gear
26) Hub front (Length 3 1/16 in.)
26) Hub, front (Length 2 5/16 in.)
27) Needle bearing
28) Clutch ring (FT only)
28) Clutch ring (FG/FGA)
29) Hub Centre (FG/FGA)
30) Hub rear (FG/FGA)
31) Inner track 5th gear
32) Thrust washer
33) Stud
33) Stud
34) Nut, Pinion (L.H.)
35) Selector finger
36) Bush
37) 'O' ring
38) Spring
39) Ball
40) Screw
41) Plunger
42) Screw (not illus.)
43) Selector rod 1st/Rev.
44) Selector rod 2nd/3rd
45) Selector rod 4th/5th
46) Selector fork 1st/Rev.
47) Selector fork 2nd/3rd
48) Selector fork 4th/5th
50) Nut
51) Screw
52) Spacer
53) Plate
53) Plate
54) Screw
55) Spacer (various sizes)

from the drawing, the three selector rods with their individual fork, each select two different gears. On the back of the bearing carrier comes the selector finger housing, sealed by a gasket. On the lower part of the housing a slotted plunger is pushed up by a loaded spring. Another little spring pushes a ball bearing in the slot of the plunger; like that the plunger maintains the selector finger opposite 2nd and 3rd gear (neutral). To put in first gear or reverse the gear lever is leaned more to the left; by doing this the plunger is pushed also towards its bottom and comes back in its normal position when going from reverse or 1st or 2nd gear, pushed by its spring. In fact the little ball and spring keep the plunger in its slots which gives a "feeling" to the driver.

The interlocking mechanism is designed so that the selection of two gears at the same time is impossible, and it gives the assurance that the selector finger will come out of 1st gear and go across the gate, and not slip back into 1st gear which can be disastrous for the engine. Again, it's a driver preference to have a very heavy plunger spring to really come against the "stop" so that when they go from the 1st to the 2nd part of the gate they've got to slam it over. The rear unit is closed by a cover and sealed with a gasket. An oil breather is located on the top of the selector finger housing.

Selecting the Gears

The system consists of very straightforward constant mesh gears, with the exception of the reverse gear. All gears are treated with gas carbonise which provides a very tough core and very hard "skin". All the gears themselves are in constant mesh with the input shaft, itself obviously connected direct to the engine via the clutch, so that when the clutch is depressed the whole mechanism starts turning. All the gears on the pinion shafts are slotted and assembled in only one face with a simple roller bearing and all are free except the gear which is in use. The hubs carry the clutch ring, slotted in its two faces sliding from one gear to another, the gears guided by the forks when required by the driver.

How the clutch ring engages the gear is a simple matter. When the fork drives the clutch ring towards the gear the slots (straight machined) slow down the free gear; instantly the clutch ring engages into the slot. When the driver releases the clutch the power comes from the input shaft into the pinion gear shaft then it goes through the dog clutch ring onto the hub which in turn is connected to the pinion shaft. That then drives the pinion and crown wheel through to the drive shaft and wheel, putting the car in motion. For the rest of the gears, including reverse, the working order is the same. Note that the amazing thing is that the power is going through one of the smallest parts, which is the clutch ring.

As the gears are to be used for any circuit, the teams base their choice of ratios from previous year or else compromise on first gear, which illustrates the advantage of changing the gear ratio rather than the crown wheel and pinion to suit the particular circuit. Once the top and bottom gears have been chosen, the other gears can be easily set to meet the demands of the circuit.

The bigger the step you get in the gears, the bigger the problem you are going to have with the gear change. The closer the ratios, with the five speed gearbox, the easier the change will be, because there is obviously a speed difference between those gears. Ratio matching is a little more difficult with turbocharged cars because of the small power range at top engine speed. Even with a set of close ratios the driver may find that coming out of one particular corner he could do with a few more or less engine r.p.m.'s, in that case the ratio or ratios in question can be changed rapidly.

The FG400, FGA and the FGB accept no less than about 30 different sets of ratios; that gives an idea how small the gaps between the gears can be. It is possible to replace the gear ratios in about 20 minutes, when the accessibility is good. Accessibility has become difficult on some cars because of the design of the rear bodywork which covers the gearbox on

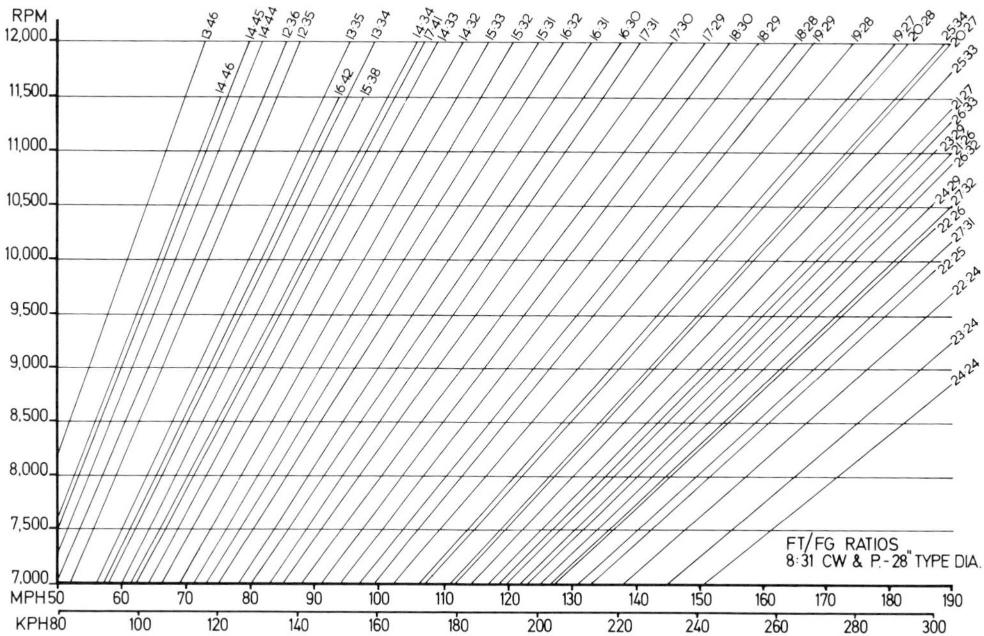

Ratio chart. (Courtesy Hewland Engineering).

some wing cars to gain a clean air flow from underneath the side pods. The synchromesh system of road cars is not used because it would add weight, and this alone would tend to make gear shifting slower.

6-Speed Gearbox

In spite of large selection of gears, the problem of wasting maximum engine torque and r.p.m. in difficult corners led McLaren to become the first team to modify the FG400 to make it a six speed gearbox. Without changing the outside look of the unit, the sixth speed was incorporated. The clever idea was to make the reverse gear on the layshaft a first gear. Reverse was then placed on the back of the bearing carrier and the existing oil pump, inside the main cage next to the crown wheel, was driven by a redesigned input shaft. In fact the original Hewland oil pump could not fit, so McLaren produced its own pump to cope with the room left in the main cage. For reverse, another very small fork had to be made, still manoeuvred by the same selector finger, and the whole unit was closed at the rear with a cast magnesium cover supporting the oil filter, also redesigned by McLaren. Later on Hewland produced a six speed gearbox based on the McLaren design, with the exception that the oil pump and reverse were kept in a thick housing placed on the back of the bearing carrier. On both gearboxes the grid of gear change is the same, except for the reverse. The gears are either straight cut or in helix angle, all machined within very close tolerances. Reliability is mainly down to preparation and assembly.

Oil Pump

The pump is of a very simple design. An amount of oil flows between the gear teeth, is then sent around the outside cones and is transmitted from one side around both gears and squirted out the other side. The lubrication system starts through the pinion shaft and centrifugal force throws it out

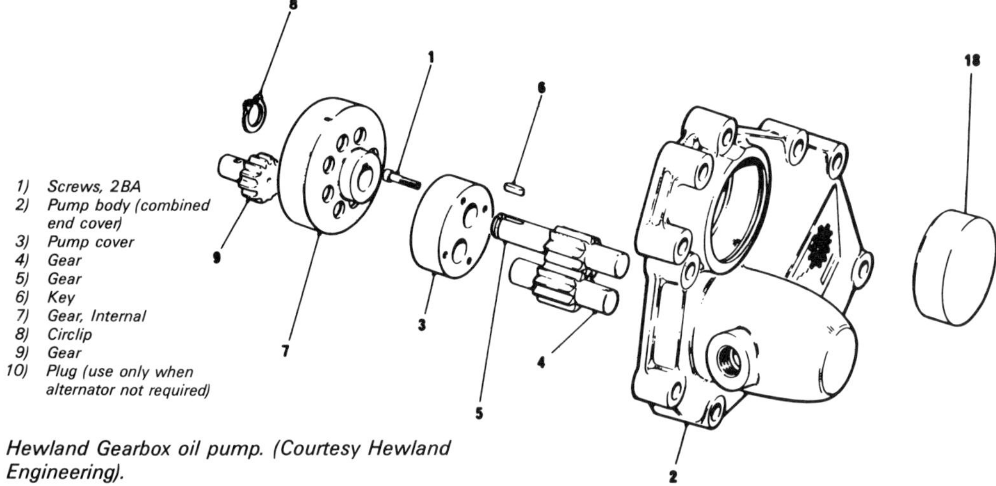

Hewland Gearbox oil pump. (Courtesy Hewland Engineering).

around the unit. Starting from the pump, it's usually put up through the back of the hollow pinion shaft, drilled with little holes along it, up to the crown wheel and this allows the oil to pass out through the inner tracks of the needle rollers, passing over these rollers and in turn to the gears. The whole lot is being flung out against the edges of the gearbox and it's atomised straight away and that really lubricates the whole gearing. At the same time oil is squeezed into the crown wheel and pinion. In addition to that, a good idea is to squirt it on the trailing edge, as the pinion comes out of mesh. In effect what happens is that the layshaft is cooled at the same time because the heat is mostly generated from that point. Over-heating can cause premature failure and in the gearbox the lower set of gears dip in the oil, splashing the gear. However, as the gears churn the oil around, a lot of resistance and heat are generated. In order to prevent or reduce this temperature problem, most of the cars are equipped with an oil cooler placed in the air stream. To keep the oil as clean as possible a filter is added to the back of the gearbox, but this late feature wasn't originally designed as part of the unit. Although nearly all teams, except Ferrari have used the Hewland unit, their individual modifications are very interesting. Tyrrell has its own ideas, mainly about the oil system, using a dry sump. Brabham have designed a different cage, oil system and many other details to fit the Alfa Romeo engine. The latest trend is for quite a few teams to redesign the main cage in order to slim the whole transmission to comply with ground effect requirements. The McLaren MP4 has a typical and nice example of the sort of reduction that can be made in the width of the gearbox.

Self Locking Differentials

Team Lotus have designed their own gearbox altogether, in collaboration with the German manufacturer Getrag. Little is known about it except that it uses a different gearing. Its concept has been kept secret, as it is still used on the Lotus 88, 87 and now 91.

Nowadays, it is rare to see a car retiring with gearbox problems. Formula One cars have gone faster and faster every year, until a lack of traction coming out of slow corners was discovered. The problem was down to the percentage of locking of the differential, as the Hewland locking device was not high enough. To solve the problem Team Lotus was one of the first to use a self locking differential. The system was available from Salisbury, and consequently was called the Salisbury self locking differential, but a ZF unit is also available. Rapidly the majority of teams appeared with this system. Later on, Hewland produced a similar unit which now comes as standard on FGB's. The Salisbury or ZF arrangement can give better traction, according to the geometry of suspension, and design of tyres, and suits some cars better than others.

During recent years the demand for self locking differentials has increased steadily. This confirms that the installation of a self locking differential is of great advantage, if not an absolute necessity for ground effect Formula One cars. Below, we look at two examples.

In a conventional differential gearing, just called the differential, the initial torque is transmitted via the differential cage to the differential bevel gears, and these then transmit the torque in equal proportions to the left and the right drive shaft. If road conditions are such that on one side the torque transmitted to the driving wheels cannot be taken up by the wheel, this wheel will begin to turn faster; it "spins". Due to this, the engine torque is used up mainly for speeding up the gears and shafts of the gearbox, the drive shaft, the differential, one wheel axle and the spinning wheel.

If the accelerated wheel now reaches firm ground again, it will be slowed down with a jerk and a shock torque will be transmitted via the differential gears to the other driving wheel. The car is likely to skid. This condition can occur when a powerful Formula One car is travelling on a wet track, at high speed, because, due to a wedge-like water build-up, the drive is distributed unevenly to the two driving wheels. Starting on uneven ground can also be a great disadvantage when the vehicle is equipped only with a conventional differential.

In order to overcome such situations, differentials were developed which have a braking effect on the drive axles when one driving wheel is turning faster than the other. They are the so-called self locking differentials.

High quality engineered self locking differentials equip the majority of cars, supplied by Salisbury Transmission Ltd., and ZF (Great Britain) Ltd. The two companies also produce self locking differentials for road and sports cars, machinery and other commercial industrial vehicles.

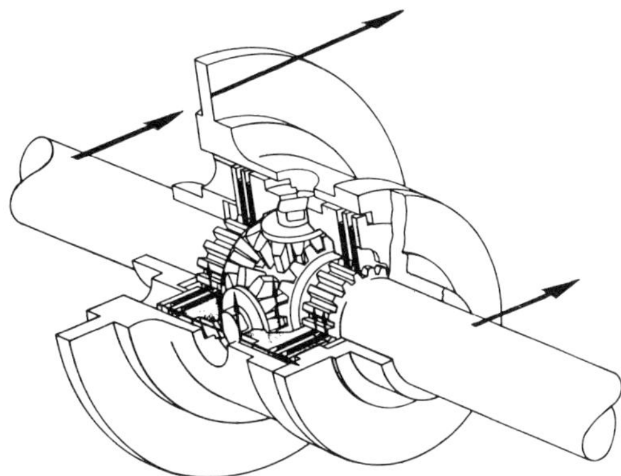

Schematic drawing of power transmission in the differential. Assuming that each axle is taking equal torque. For better observation the power flow is shown as being transmitted to the axles from one differential axle only and one differential bevel gear. (Courtesy ZF Gear (GB) Ltd).

ZF Construction

The crown wheel is bolted to the cage of the self locking differential. The inside diameter of the differential cage has four axial grooves for receiving the two pressure rings and the outer discs. The components have lugs on their outer diameters, which engage in the grooves of the differential cage and thus only permit axial movement. The inner rings, which are arranged alternately between the outer discs, are coupled to the axle bevel gears by the engagement teeth. The inner faces of the pressure rings are wedge-shaped for receiving the differential axles, which have similarly shaped surfaces at the ends. The two differential bevel gears, carried on each differential axle, are in mesh with the axle bevel gears.

Function

The locking effect is due to the internal friction of the differential. It is produced by two multiple disc brakes arranged symmetrically in the differential cage. In the case of a conventional differential, one wheel can be braked or held in position with hardly any resistance when the vehicle is jacked up, the engine is running and the gear is engaged. The other wheel will then turn correspondingly faster. However with a self locking differential, the above procedure will be rendered considerably more difficult, due to the multiple disc brakes, in fact it will become more difficult with increasing input torque.

This behaviour is caused because the torque action on the differential cage is transmitted to the differential axles via two pressure rings, which are unable to turn radially but can move axially, whereas with a conventional differential the torque is transmitted direct to the differential axles. The contact surfaces between the differential axles and the pressure rings are wedge-shaped. Outward axial forces are caused by the reaction of those surfaces when torque is transmitted. Therefore an increased pressure will be produced on the pre-loaded discs. Since the outer discs engage with the differential cage, and the inner discs with the axle bevel gears, relative motion between axle shafts and differential cage is rendered more difficult. The ZF multiple disc self locking differentials have the following two advantages:

Firstly, a constant locking torque is obtained due to the axial preload of the discs, so that a locking effect is available immediately, even under most unfavourable travelling conditions.

Secondly, due to the outward forces occurring on the wedge-shaped surfaces, a load dependent locking torque is produced in the multiple disc clutches, which is always directly proportional to the input torque. The locking effect, therefore, adapts itself to the variable engine torque and also the torque increase in the different gear speeds. This is especially useful for operations when large torques are transmitted.

The locking effect is influenced by:

1) *The number of discs.*
2) *The angle of the wedge-shaped surfaces.*
3) *The disc preload, which increases the locking effect in cases of very bad road conditions or small input torque.*

Installation

The ZF multiple disc self locking differentials have been dimensioned so that they can be installed without any difficulty in place of conventional differentials. The crown wheel, the differential housing and the axles remain unaltered, only the differential has to be changed, so that a subsequent installation can be carried out without any difficulty.

Self locking differentials alter the load conditions of the axle shafts. Although, actually there is no shock loading and it also has no influence on the driving performance.

Salisbury Powr-Lock Mk1 and Mk11

The Salisbury Powr-Lock assembly is basically a conventional bevel gear differential with free action inhibited by multiplate clutches, loaded in proportion to the torque transmitted. In order to minimise, as far as is practicable, the lubricant sensitivity of the device, the clutch plates have a low coefficient of friction. The necessary frictional torque restraint is achieved with a small number of plates, as a consequence of the loading obtained through the normal separating forces of the differential gears being supplemented by axial forces imposed by cam action.

Additional clutch loading may be provided by forming one or more of the clutch plates as "belleville" springs. The resultant pre-load of the clutch assemblies ensures a degree of constraint under extreme conditions when one driving wheel is off the ground.

The initial torque, to turn a free

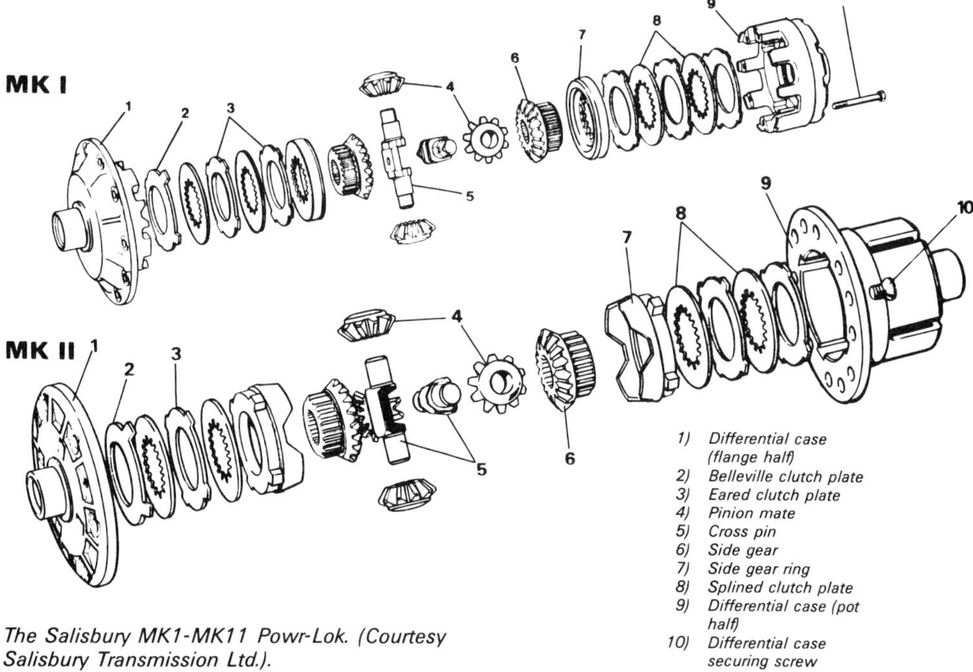

The Salisbury MK1-MK11 Powr-Lok. (Courtesy Salisbury Transmission Ltd.).

assembly, is dependent not only on the frictional torque capacity of the clutch packs, but more significantly, the degree of belleville spring loading. It should not be assumed that a low free torque figure necessarily implies a lack of adequate torque bias through the functional range of the assembly.

The Powr-Lock system performance may be varied by re-arranging the stacking order of the clutch plates and the addition or deletion of belleville plates. The above principles apply to both Mk 1 and Mk 11 designs which do however differ in construction as follows:

Mk 1 Design

The differential spider is made in two parts which move relative to each other. These cross pins are flatted to provide cam surfaces engaging in "V" slots, machined and hardened in the differential case, one pin being located in the flange half of the case, the other being similarly positioned in the bottom half of the case. The differential case is cut away to permit movement of the cross pins. When torque is applied to the assembly, the separating forces which result at the cam surfaces are transmitted through the cross pins to the differential side gear rings, via the abutment shoulders on the differential pinions, thereby loading the clutch packs. The side gear rings are attached to the side gear hubs by means of splines and rotate with them.

The clutch plates are restrained by means of lugs engaging slots cast in the differential case and interposed between the clutch discs located on the splined hubs of the side gears. When the clutches are loaded, by a combination of the cam forces on the cross pin and the separating forces of the differential gears under load, free differential action is inhibited by the frictional resistance of the clutch plates.

Typical driveshaft with Glenzer-Spicer crosses seen on Ligier JS15 and Renault RE series.

Mk II Design

This configuration incorporates the same basic principles but differs in construction as described below:

The two piece differential case is split at the drive gear flange and incorporates a cylindrical internal form with four rectangular cast grooves, designed to accommodate the lugs of the clutch plates, and also similar lugs on the side gear rings which are further modified to incorporate "V" cam grooves in which the shoulders on the differential pinions are located.

The bore of the side gear rings are plain and do not engage the splined hubs of the side gears, on which are located the clutch discs. As compared with the Mk 1 parts, the two cross pins have been shortened since the cam action is exerted between the cam surfaces of the side gear rings and the mating abutment shoulders of the pinion mates. Drive is, therefore, transmitted from the differential casing to the side gear rings thence through the pinion mates to the differential gear assembly.

Drive Shafts

From the final drive unit, power is transmitted to the wheels by means of drive shafts. Shafts and joints are designed to take torque with continual stress and are, therefore, because of this "abuse" subject to constant checking for safety, since any excess torsional motion may result in failure which is usually sudden and total, and can destroy the suspension.

McLaren, up to the M28, used their own design of final drive which was composed of large diameter titanium drive shafts, steer Glenzer-Spicer forks and crosses on either end. The telescopic movement of the suspension was obtained through the stub axles sliding sideways and rotating on two roller bearing units located in the uprights. The assembly was a bit bulky, as was the McLaren tradition before the MP4, but very reliable and safe. The team replaced the arrangement with "standard" lobro constant velocity joints and steel drive shafts on the MP4.

Another type of drive shaft was used by Renault and Ligier some while ago. These were drive shafts with Glenzer-Spicer joints at each end, with a male and female shaft to provide the necessary plunge when the suspension or chassis rises or falls. The two half-shafts slide into each other on steel balls, making the assembly "frictionless". Grease is kept inside the inner half-shaft by a plastic washer held with a threaded steel cage. This type of splined drive shaft takes tremendous torques from tyres (grip) and engine. As with the old McLaren system, they are a bit bulky and don't quite conform with today's ground effect concept.

Nowadays the most common drive shafts are plain or hollow steel shafts and lobro joints are mounted on either end of the shaft. The shafts themselves are

Popular driveshaft with Lobro joint assembly. (Brabham BT 49)

machined from a block of purified steel called "maraging steel" and receive special heat treatment which gives them the necessary high tensile characteristics. The lobro joints are also made of high tensile steel and form an outer balls track which is also the housing bolted to the gearbox output shafts and stub axle. The inner balls track is splined in its centre and comes to be assembled to either end of the shaft leaning on one face and secured to it simply by a circlip. Both tracks are machined in spiral (semi-circular) to receive the six steel balls, each one having its own track lubricated with high quality grease.

Although movement is quite limited, it is sufficient to take the chassis and suspension movement and therefore these shafts can be called "telescopic".

The Lobro constant velocity joint components.

Tracks are protected with a conical rubber cover and when assembled to the car, it represents a neat and up-to-date arrangement. Although the transmission is not the most attractive part of a Formula One car, it certainly is a very accurate piece of engineering.

Ferrari Gearbox

The Ferrari transmission is a unique arrangement originally designed to bring the weight distribution closer to the centre of gravity. That is why the gearbox is very short. However, it is fairly large in the transversal axis, which with the Boxer engine is not the most convenient design for maximising the potential of ground effect. Where the nomination of the car was "T4" or "T5", the letter T stands for transversal (gearbox). However, the box is also used on later cars, such as the Ferrari 126C turbocharged.

Compared to the Hewland FGA, the Ferrari unit is heavier and a lot more complicated. Nevertheless, its design and casting are most attractive, as befits the Ferrari tradition.

The general appearance of the gearbox is of a "square" casing, which certainly gives great rigidity. The bell housing is part of the box itself, and takes the different accessories such as clutch cylinder, oil cooler, starter motor and, of course, all the

Ferrari transmission seen on the 126C turbo.

suspension pick-up points and aerofoil mounts. The general layout of the gears and shaft can be compared to a front wheel drive road car layout, except that, instead of receiving the movement directly from the crankshafts, on the Ferrari the movement from the engine via the clutch is transmitted by an input shaft having a 90° spiral bevel inside the box, so that the transmission revolves at only 70% of the engine speed. The layshaft and output shafts are enclosed by a central housing with bearings and are supported again by bearings on their ends, on each side of the box. The gearbox is five speed with reverse. Most of the pinions are straight cut and revolve on needle bearings. As on the Hewland unit, a clutch ring is used to engage two different gear ratios. The first gear ratio is fixed to the shafts and cannot be changed. The oil pump is incorporated within the main casing and is driven by the output shaft. The final drive is composed of straight cut teeth, crown wheel and pinion (the latter being part of the output shaft) and a self locking differential. Everything is designed and made at Ferrari.

At the race track, ratio change requires the dismantling of the gearbox which is usually carried out "in discretion".

Clutch

The clutch generally used is a multi disc arrangement, designed to transmit in excess of 500 bhp. It is lightweight, has a relatively low inertia and is capable of reliability even when transmitting high power outputs at engine speeds of up to 12,000 rpm.

The most common clutch used is the AP Borg and Beck 7¼ inch twin plates version. This unit has a lightweight toothed outer ring to drive the two pressure plates, which are also toothed on their outer diameter. The main pressure plate is made of high strength carbon steel and the intermediate plate is spring steel.

The two discs slide on central splines on the input shaft of the gearbox and are made of steel with copper plated surfaces. Sintered bronze linings are built up by an

the AP Borg & Beck clutch. (Courtesy AP Lockheed).

application of powered metal to copper plating at extremely high pressure and temperature. Before being fitted to the engine flywheel, the clutch is accurately balanced to provide a balanced engine assembly.

The clutch is mechanically or hydraulically activated, the latter being more popular. The thrust or release bearing itself is fitted onto a bobbin sliding on a spigot and guided by a fork, the whole lot being located inside the bell housing. The hydraulic arrangement is relatively simple and comprises a master cylinder and its reservoir located on the front bulkhead of the car and a slave cylinder which works the fork, bolted underneath or on top of the gearbox. Naturally a high pressure resistance line connects both cyclinders.

In the case of a bell housing forming an oil tank, the slave cylinder and fork are replaced by an annulus cylinder arrangement, all located inside the bell housing.

The clutch pedal pressure can be controlled first by the pedal ratio and secondly by the size of the master and slave cylinders which displace the fluid. The fluid used is the same as that for brakes.

Chapter 7

Turbocharging

In the course of the last few years, required limitations of exhaust emission have resulted in a considerable reduction of the potential power output per litre of passenger cars. In the past power increase was obtained mainly by displacement increases. Now exhaust turbocharging offers the possibility of returning to engines with small displacements and high power output. The turbocharged engine does not present any more problems than the induction engine. This has been confirmed by its successful application to US vehicles. As far as the fuel economy is concerned, the turbocharged engine has turned out to be especially favourable in comparison to an induction engine with an identical power output.

The exhaust gas turbocharging, in connection with a boost pressure control by means of a by-pass valve at the exhaust side, is a real alternative to an increase in engine displacement. By comparing both possibilities of increasing power output, one will find that the turbocharging system offers a distinct advantage.

Fuel Economy

In the case of the turbocharged engine during idling and under partial load, the reduced consumption due to the lower displacement balances and increased consumption due to the lower geometric compression ratio. Under full load, the turbocharged engine, thanks to its high overall compression ratio, fully matches the consumption values realised by the normally aspirated engine. However, the above claims become debatable when applied to motor racing. Motor racing requires speed and power. A Formula One turbo engine runs at around 11,000rpm and can obtain a maximum power output approaching 600bhp (and probably more in the near future). But as the turbo engine develops more power than a normally aspirated engine, for the equivalent capacity, more petrol is required in order to complete a race distance.

In this case the cost of the amount of fuel consumed is totally disregarded. The major concern of competitors is the fact that the car has to be as light as possible on the starting grid.

A typical example of normally aspirated 3 litre car is the DFV Cosworth engined Williams FW08, carrying 39 gallons (177 litres). In comparison the BMW turbo engined Brabham BT50 carries 46 gallons (209 litres). The difference of seven gallons represents a drawback in terms of weight, but this should be compensated for by the extra power output of the turbocharged engine. However, this figure may well be greatly reduced with development along with fuel consumption control. Presently,

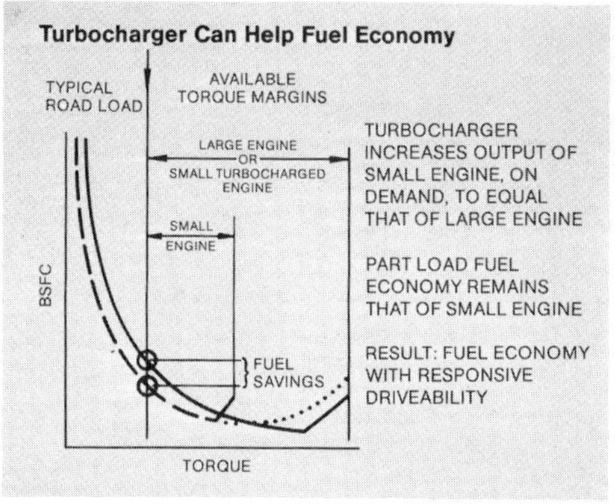

Chart of fuel economy with turbocharging. (Courtesy Garrett AiResearch).

almost without exception, all major passenger car manufacturers are experimenting intensively with turbocharging. Although the principle of increasing power and torque of piston engines by housing the Kinetic energy of the hot exhaust gases has been known for some seventy years, it is only now that this logical method is being widely used to increase the thermal efficiency of engines (thus improving their fuel consumption).

Originally turbochargers were destinated for commercial vehicle power units. In this field the turbocharger has become a "natural" part of any newly designed unit. Quite obviously, therefore, there are also very good chances for application to passenger car mass production in the near future. Several manufacturers have already marketed models with turbocharged engines fitted as standard. Furthermore, turbocharger tuning kits are available, for various categories of road cars, and their number is likely to rapidly increase. One may ask: if turbochargers are so good, why are they only just becoming popular in racing? Three major problems delayed the adoption of Turbos:

1) The first problem is bound up with the sporting regulations. These regulations do not always authorise the use of the turbo-compressor (Formula Two, for example). In addition, the actual cubic capacity of the supercharged engine is affected by an "equivalence factor", sometimes ill-adapted to the Formula in question. The present equivalence factor, ruled by the C.S.I. (now F.I.A.) is: 3 litre capacity for normally aspirated engine, 1.5 litre capacity for supercharged or turbocharged engines.

2) The second problem is of a technical nature, in direct relationship with the very nature of the functioning of the engine equipped with a turbo-compressor. Because the speed of the turbocharger depends upon the exhaust gas pressure, a delay between the opening of the throttle, by the drivers and the building up of the necessary boost, (called lag), is a handicap typical of the turbocharged racing engine. Although today the turbocharger(s) response (lag) is still there to some extent, a major improvement has been achieved.

3) The third problem is of a metallurgical nature. Today, the speed of turbo-compressor rotation may go as high as 140,000rpm. It has been necessary, therefore, to find very sophisticated steels for making the turbine wheels. This is done in a precision foundry. The turbine must stand up at the same time to the effects of centrifugal force and to the temperature of the exhaust gases of over 1,000°C. Progress of the same nature has had to be made for the steels of the valves and for the aluminium alloys of the pistons and the distribution system.

To these three main problems have been added others concerning the adaptation of the supercharging.

As opposed to the manufacturers of diesel engine who design their engines from the outset to be supercharged, which is certainly the best way of exploiting the advantages of supercharging, the manufacturers of racing engines are still adapting a turbo-compressor to an existing atmospheric engine. If to increase the inlet pressure appears, at first sight, to be a simple operation, it nevertheless cannot be carried out without precautions being taken. To limit the increase of mechanical loads, the automobile engineer does his utmost to control, as best he can, the maximum pressure of combustion, which may, if it is too strong, be the cause of damage. Generally speaking, it can only be avoided, for a given engine, by increasing the octane index of the fuel. In addition, progressively increasing the inlet pressure will increase the thermal loads. In this way engine builders are confronted with these two practicalities: to find, on the engine to be supercharged, the limits of the thermal and mechanical loads and to remain on the right side of these in order to provide the engine with adequate reliability.

The limit on the thermal loads (apart from the resistance of the turbine wheel, which is not generally the weak link in the chain) will be provided by the "resistance when hot" of the exhaust valves and pistons. It is generally necessary to review the circulation of the water or air at the level of the cylinder head, in order to evacuate the excess heat. The thermal aspect is certainly the most difficult to resolve, because the engine builder lacks reference data. Precise measurements of the temperature are difficult to take where they might be necessary.

The limit of the mechanical loads is given by the dimensions of the shaft line, block, connecting rods and the bearings of the connecting rods. In order to control the maximum load which the engine will take, the volumetric ratio is juggled with. This latter will be lower the greater the supercharging pressure. Thus, an engine supercharged to 1 bar above the atmospheric pressure will have a compression ratio of 7 – 7.5 to 1 if it runs on petrol (much higher if it runs on alcohol, as do the U.S.A.C. (Indy) racing engines).

Two of the main manufacturers of turbocharger units used in Formula One are: KUHNLE, KOPP KAUSCH AG, known as "KKK", and US Garrett AiResearch. Both also produce turbochargers diesel engine for light and heavy commercial vehicles as well as for other industrial purposes.

BBC Comprex is a third supercharger manufacturer, recently introduced through Ferrari. As the Comprex pressure-wave supercharger system works on different principles than those of the turbocharger, its characteristics are reviewed in a separate section.

KKK

KKK has been developing and manufacturing turbochargers since 1952. In 1959, the interest in its products intensified. In 1960, KKK therefore established a plant at Kirchheimbolanden, especially designed for the manufacture of turbochargers in series. The steadily increasing demand for turbochargers led to a large extension of the plant.

The first turbocharger manufactured by KKK was equipped with an axial turbine. During the following years, this design was extended and improved, step by step, by using radial turbines and was primarily employed for stationary, marine and rail application. The interest of the engine manufacturers in turbocharging truck engines then started to develop.

Utilisation of exhaust gas turbochargers for commercial vehicles called for smaller and more favourably priced units. This know-how was acquired by KKK in 1961/62 by taking over a licence from Schwitzer, of Indianapolis USA. By consistent further development, KKK steadily adapted its range of turbocharger models to meet market demands. After intensive development and research work, based upon a 25 year experience, and making use of the knowledge gained in turbomachinery, KKK developed and brought to the stage of serial production the K turbocharger range. The current KKK turbocharger programme stretches from chargers for 55 to 740bhp per turbocharger unit.

Garrett AiResearch

AiResearch has an extensive technology base, which has been acquired from 24 years of turbocharger development and manufacture and from an even greater number of years as a major manufacturer of gas turbines. The gas turbines are manufactured by another division of Garrett for auxiliary power units, turboprop engines and turbofan engines for aircraft.

AiResearch Industrial Division (AID)

KKK turbocharged version of the Ferrari 126C Formula One car.

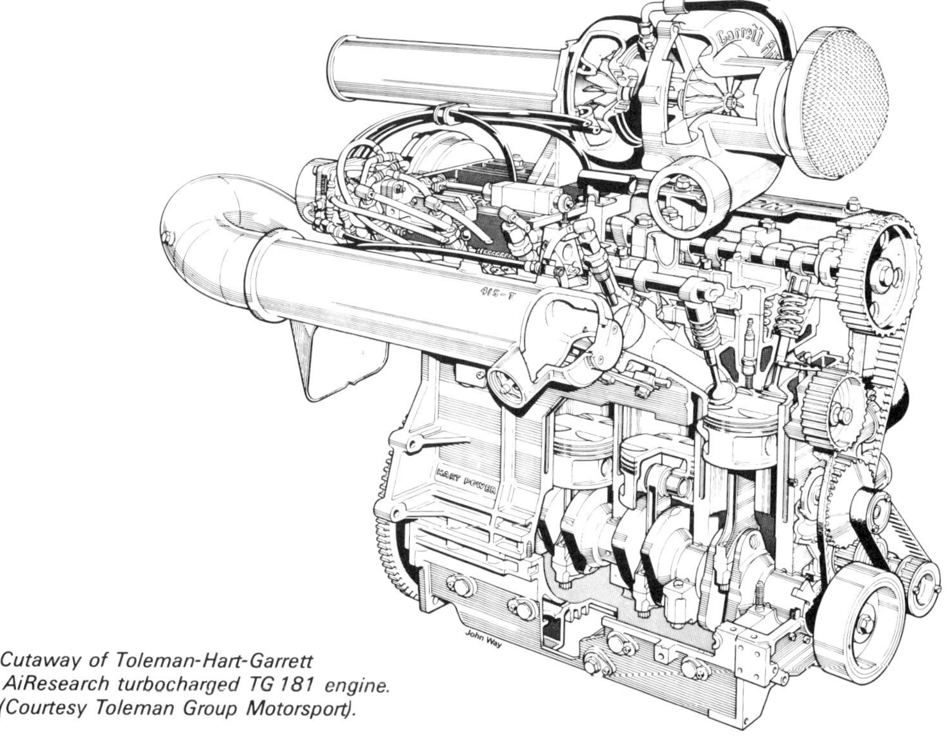

Cutaway of Toleman-Hart-Garrett AiResearch turbocharged TG 181 engine. (Courtesy Toleman Group Motorsport).

produce turbocharger controls and heat exchangers for engines in the 50 to 1,000bhp range. In addition to its own specialist skills in turbomachinery/heat exchanger design technology and precision production techniques, AID can call on other major Garrett manufacturing plants for expert advice and specific technical knowledge.

AiResearch Industrial Divisions is based in Torrance, California.

Turbocharging

The power of an internal combustion engine depends on the weight of the air on the respective fuel quantity that is available to the engine for combustion. If it is intended to increase engine power, more air for combustion and more fuel have to be delivered. In case of a naturally aspirated engine, this power increase is obtained by increasing the swept volume or by raising the speed. Increasing the swept volume, however, as a general principle leads to heavier engines, having larger dimensions. Especially with larger engines, a speed increase involves considerable technical problems and disadvantages.

A power increase with unchanged swept volume and the same engine speed can be obtained by turbocharging the engine by means of exhaust gas turbochargers. This principle was first proposed in 1905 by the Swiss, Buchi.

The heart of an exhaust gas turbocharger consists of the rotor assembly, comprising a turbine wheel, a compressor wheel, and a shaft. The turbine wheel is driven by the hot exhaust gases of the engine that normally exhaust to the atmosphere. The compressor wheel being firmly connected to the turbine wheel by the shaft, it always has the same speed as the turbine wheel. The compressor wheel draws in fresh air and delivers the pre-compressed air to the cylinders. In accordance with the larger weight of the air, more fuel can be converted and consequently a higher power can be obtained.

The exhaust gas turbocharger is connected with the engine merely by the air and exhaust gas flows; it is self-controlled via a waste gate. As soon as more fuel is injected, the exhaust gas energy of the engine rises, the speed of the rotor assembly increases, and the boost pressure rises too. Consequently, an air quantity sufficient for the combustion of the increased fuel quantity is delivered to the engine.

There are different methods of turbocharging, the kinetic energy of the exhaust gas is partly used. Individual exhaust gas lines are necessary for this purpose.

In the case of constant pressure turbocharging, the exhaust gas of all cylinders is led into a manifold from where it is admitted to the turbine wheel with nearly constant pressure (controlled by the waste gate). This latter method is generally used in motor racing. The method to be chosen depends on the number of cylinders, on the engine design and on various other criteria.

Apart from the power increase described above, an engine with a turbocharger has further technical and economical advantages as compared to a naturally aspirated engine. As more power is obtained with the same engine dimensions and the same speed, a turbocharged engine has a more favourable power to dimension ratio than a naturally aspirated engine of the same power.

Thanks to exhaust gas turbocharging, the torque characteristics of an engine can be improved. With passenger cars it is thus possible to obtain the so-called "high-rise torque". Gradients can thereby be taken more rapidly with a relatively few number of gear changes, thus realising higher average speeds. Moreover, the possibility of reducing the number of ratios, as a rule, permits utilisation of smaller gears. As it is possible to modify the torque characteristic, the fields of application of the engine series can be extended.

Despite increased power, a turbocharged engine develops less noise. This is especially true on the exhaust gas side, for

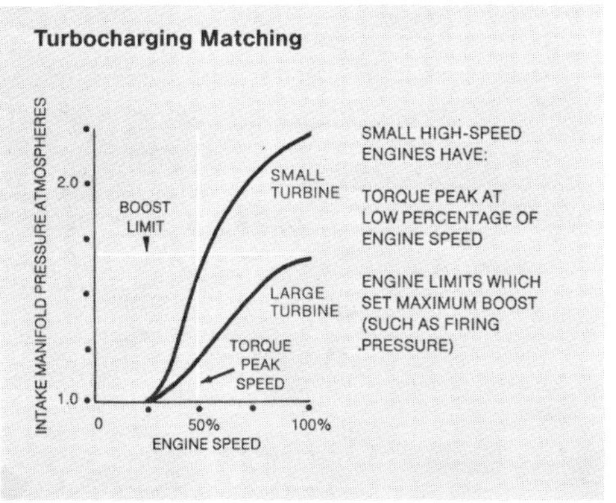

Chart of turbocharging matching. (Courtesy Garrett AiResearch).

the exhaust gas turbochargers act as an additional silencer.

The exhaust gas turbocharger is more closely connected with the engine than is generally presumed. Although mounting to the engine is relatively simple, matching is always necessary. What is more, the engine must fulfil a number of conditions with regard to the design. As a general principle, an engine is suited well for turbocharging if, under thermal and mechanical aspects, it was designed from the very beginning for an optimum turbocharged power and efficiency.

It is, however, possible to successfully turbocharge well-designed naturally aspirated engines so as to economically enlarge an existing engine series. It must be checked to what extent design changes of the engine have to be made, given the desired power increase. The object of matching an exhaust gas turbocharger to an engine therefore is to find the right combination of the different component variants of the turbocharger by a close cooperation between engine and turbocharger manufacture.

In motor racing, KKK and Garrett AiResearch turbochargers have been utilised for a number of years with extraordinary success on spark ignition engines. Owing to its many advantages, the turbocharger is increasingly being fitted to production car spark ignition engines.

Different compressor sizes, twin-flow turbine housings and single-inlet turbine housings are, as a rule, available. This offers the possibility of achieving an optimum matching to the different operating conditions of the engines by selecting the appropriate compressor sizes and turbine housings. Like all exhaust gas turbochargers, the turbochargers of the K range consist of four main parts: rotor assembly, bearing housing, turbine housing and compressor housing.

Rotor Assembly

The rotor assembly comprises the single-stage centripetal turbine wheel with shaft, the single-stage radial compressor wheel, and some small parts. The turbine wheel is made of a high-temperature austenitic alloy. It is precision-cast and is attached by friction welding to the shaft made of quenched and tempered steel.

The compressor wheel is precision-cast and made of an aluminium alloy. With the finger sleeve, the thrust rings, and the spacer sleeve it is fastened to the shaft by a nut.

Shaft and turbine wheel assembly and compressor wheel are each balanced dynamically. It is not necessary to rebalance the rotor assembly after mounting, the components being inter-changeable due to their individual balancing. On the turbine and compressor side, piston rings are fitted sealing off the oil chamber of the bearing housing against the gas chambers.

Bearing Housing

The rotor assembly is supported by floating lead bronze sleeve bearings in the bearing housing. The turbocharger is lubricated with finest-filtered oil from the oil system of the engine. There is a heat shield arranged between the gas chamber of the turbine and the bearing housing. A special step bore in the bearing housing avoids wear of the piston rings with exhaust brake operation of commercial vehicles. On the compressor side, the bearing housing is

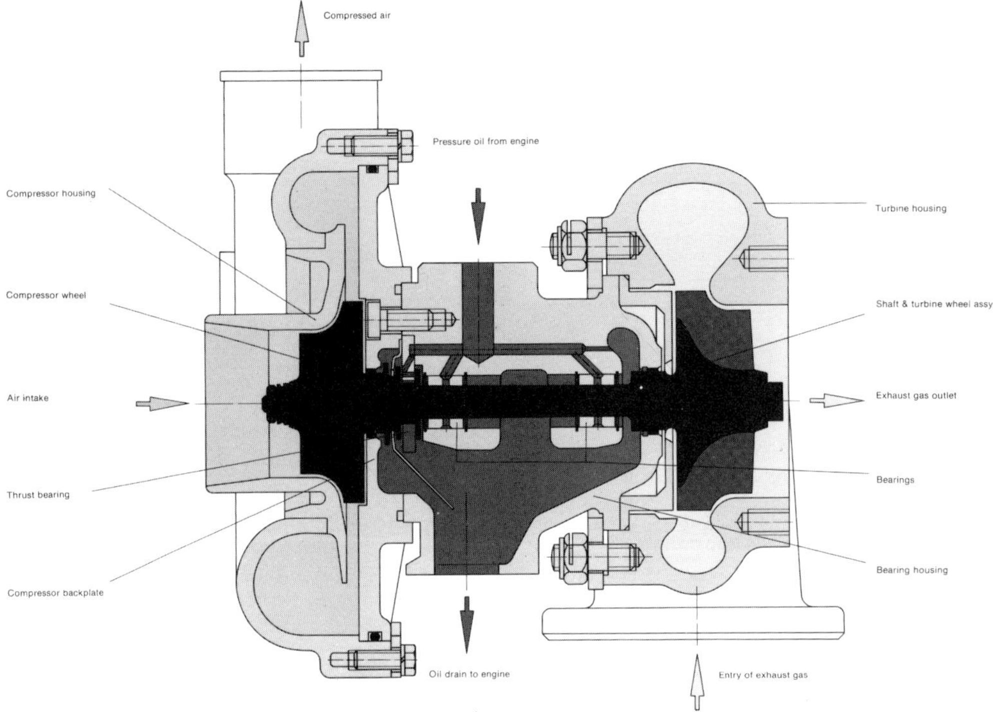

A cutaway view of KKK turbocharger (K type). (Courtesy KKK).

closed by the compressor backplate. Bearing housing, rotor assembly and bearing form the core assembly.

Turbine and Compressor Housing

By means of screwed clampings, the housings of turbine and compressor are fastened to the core assembly; they permit infinitely variable angle adjustments between the branches of the turbine and compressor housings. The turbine housings are made of spheroidal graphite cast iron. For higher temperatures, austenitic nodular cast iron or silicon molybdenum cast iron are employed. The turbine housing is designed in such a way that even in the case of extreme damage occurring, the parts of a bursting turbine wheel are retained.

The simple design of the exhaust gas turbocharger and selected, proven materials make it a robust element of the engine. For passenger cars experience shows that the turbocharger reaches the service life of the engine. Apart from engine inspections at regular intervals, no additional or particular maintenance services are required for the road turbocharger. However, this does not apply to racing because the turbocharger was designed originally for road cars where engine speed is relatively slow. On a racing engine the turbines run at about 100,000rpm and frequent maintenance is required.

Intercooling

Intercooling is to cool the air/fuel mixture somewhere between the compressor(s) discharge and the engine intake. The units for this purpose are called either heat exchangers or intercoolers. Basically, the idea is to reduce the air intake temperature (thermic loads) which automatically decrease the exhausts temperature, making it easier for the exhaust valves and to cut

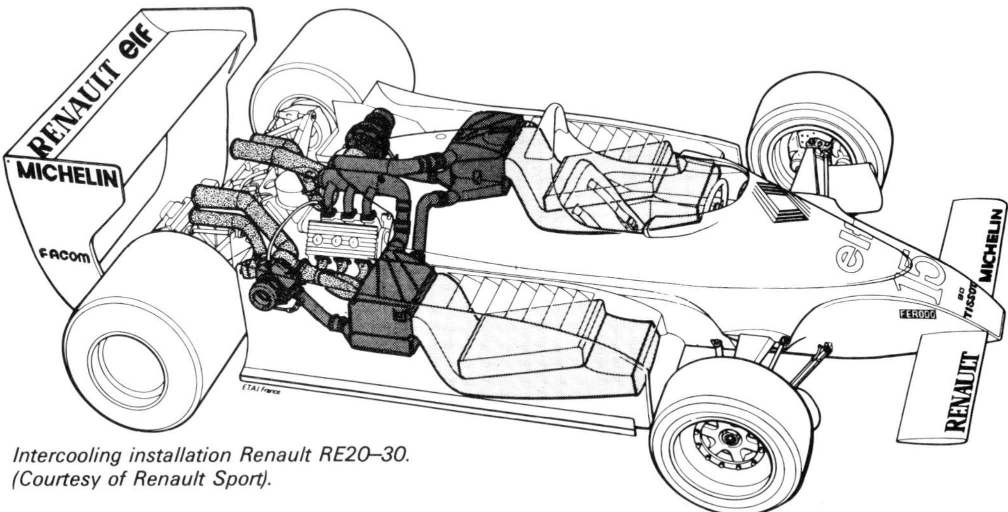

Intercooling installation Renault RE20–30. (Courtesy of Renault Sport).

down the overall heat rejection of the engine. This leads to higher charge density which will allow more of a given mass of air to flow into the engine at any intake manifold pressure. In turn more fuel can be burned to produce more engine horse power without exceeding thermal load limits or mechanical stress limits.

The drawback of an intercooler is that it causes a slight drop in pressure charge, and that it is a weight and space penalty which is difficult to avoid. The two basic methods of intercooling used in racing are air to air and air to water, both being raced initially by Porsche in their prototype sports cars. In Formula One originally Renault and Hart used an air to air intercooler, the cooling depending on a ram effect. The ram effect was created by the car's speed and was also subject to ambient air temperature variation during the race. These temperature variations caused important variations in the density of the charge, reducing the engine power output as the temperature rose. This in turn provoked an inconsistency in the air-fuel mixture, since the Kugelfischer fuel injection system is known to be insensitive to the density of charge. As a result, as the temperature rose, the mixture became over-rich causing dilution of the oil film in the cylinders which destroyed the pistons and consequently the whole engine.

The situation improved for Renault, the pioneer of turbocharging in Formula One when an air-water intercooler was tried at the 1978 Monaco Grand Prix. The layout was assisted by the car's left hand radiator which sent cooled water into the compound water-air intercooler and thence to the engine. This seemed to contribute to a steadier level of temperature, a more reliable engine, and more reliable performance with a better throttle response.

Because turbochargers normally produce more pressure than the engine can stand, controls are designed to limit compressor outlet pressure. These controls sense pressure overloads and through pneumatic or hydraulic activators modulate the position of an exhaust by-pass valve commonly called waste-gate.

Waste-Gate

In motor racing the most common and simple waste-gate control is a differential pressure sensing waste-gate where the difference between two pressures (compressed air and exhaust gas pressure) acting directly on two sides of a diaphragm, against a loaded spring, moves a poppet valve. It will open when the compressed air pressure has reached a determined level, thus by-passing the exhaust gases not required for maintaining the boost around the turbine(s).

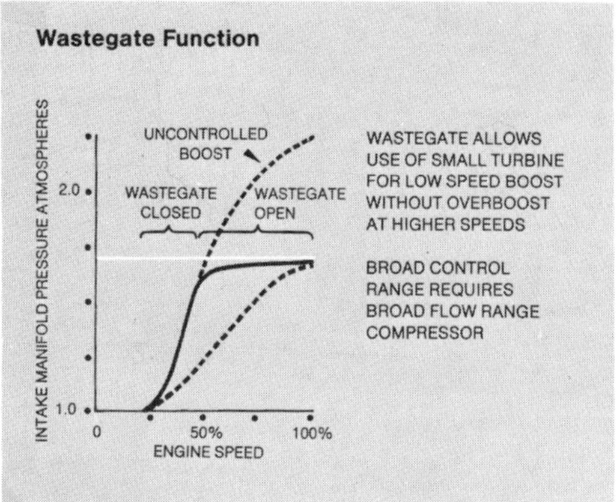

Waste gate function. (Courtesy of Garrett AiResearch).

Exhaust turbo and waste gate arrangement on Renault RE30 – right hand side.

Lag

Improving throttle response and widening the useful torque range has been and still is, one of the major preoccupations in the development of the Formula One turbocharged engine. With the high boost pressure needed on a Formula One turbocharged engine, the main problem is the delay between the time the driver opens the throttle and the required pressure build up. On the same lines, turbine size (flow density) and waste-gate working characteristics (spring loading) have to be carefully matched in order to achieve a useful speed range. Because of the speed of the turbocharger(s) depends on the pressure in the exhaust gases, on the overrun the turbo(s) are not running quickly enough to obtain an instant boost, and it is not until the engine reaches a certain speed that there is sufficient gas energy to accelerate the turbine(s), thus providing the needed boost pressure.

Lag can be a particular draw-back of the turbocharged racing engine on slow circuits such as Monaco or Long Beach, where instant availability of engine power is needed to come out of the corners quickly. At the other extreme, on fast circuits such as Monza the turbocharged engine is superior to the normally aspirated engine, running at an almost constant high speed.

Having said that, with development lag is being considerably reduced.

Boost control can be operated by the driver from the cockpit, as is standard on USAC cars. But in Formula One the boost control "screw" should be kept away from the driver's reach.

Excessively raising the boost raises the charged air temperature and consequently causes lag. Just as there is a limit to the compression ratio of a normally aspirated engine, where detonation will result in a blow-up, so there is a limit to a boost pressure.

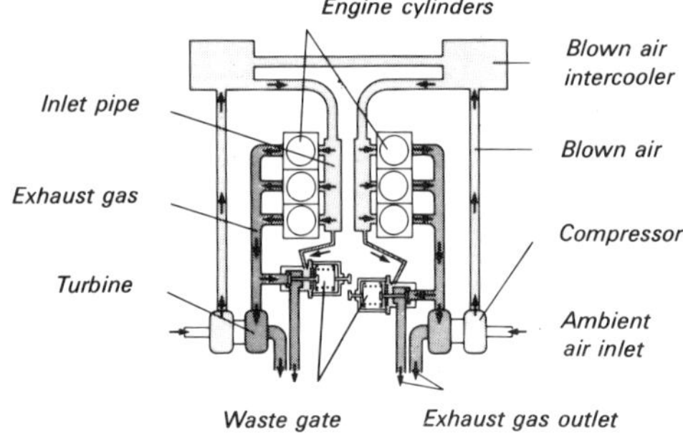

Example of turbocharged installation. (Courtesy Renault Sport).

Ferrari engine Comprex version (supercharged).

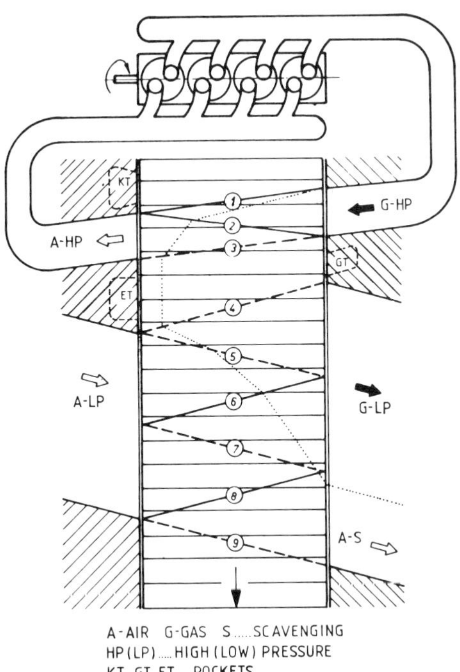

Unrolled view of comprex pressure wave process. (Courtesy BBC Brown Boveri).

BBC – Comprex Supercharged System

A totally new system of supercharging Formula One racing engines was introduced by Scuderia Ferrari early in 1981. Like the turbocharger the "Comprex" system was originally developed to suit heavy commercial vehicles. Although the name "Comprex" is not familiar to motor racing enthusiasts, the firm's association with Ferrari dates back to 1978 when the Scuderia started carrying out engine bench tests with a view to an application to future Formula One projects. The development programme accelerated as Renault showed competitiveness, and more and more reliability, with their 1.5 litre turbocharged engine. By the end of the 1980 season the normally aspirated 312 Ferrari 3-litre boxer engine seemed to have arrived at its limit in terms of power output. This was the main reason for which the decision to change engine technology was made.

Originally the "KKK" turbocharger was tried out by Ferrari and later it was replaced by the Comprex system in order to get

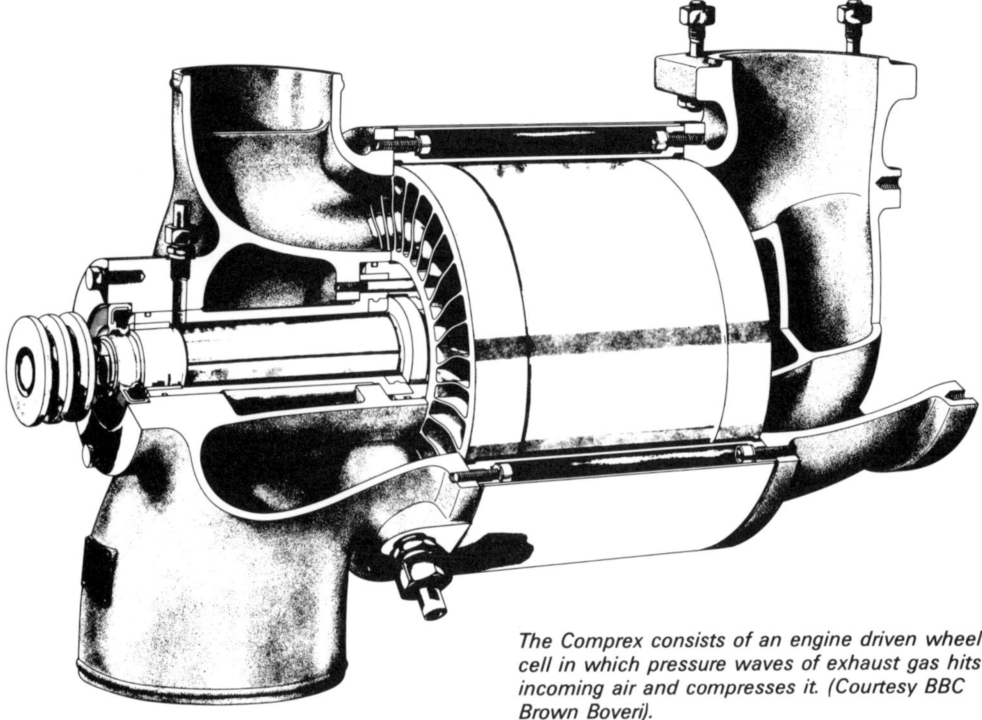

The Comprex consists of an engine driven wheel cell in which pressure waves of exhaust gas hits incoming air and compresses it. (Courtesy BBC Brown Boveri).

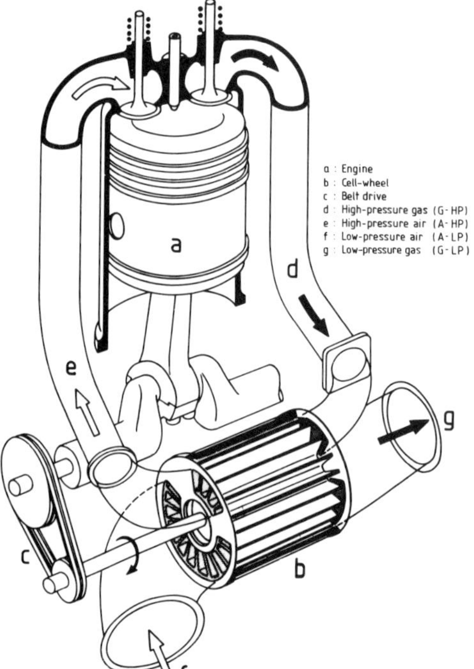

Engine and Comprex supercharger schematic arrangement. (Courtesy BBC Brown Boveri).

comparative tests in several areas such as, power, reliability, response and so forth. The conclusion was that the "Comprex" offered considerably improved throttle response. The other advantages were that the Comprex's rotor ran at a relatively low speed of 30,000rpm compared to the turbocharger equivalent of 140,000rpm. As for power output, torque and fuel consumption, the two systems offered similar results.

The only public outing of the Comprex supercharged Ferrari was at the 1981 Long Beach Grand Prix where constant breakages of the rotor shaft under severe acceleration and deceleration saw the car withdrawn from official practice. Thereafter, Ferrari concentrated on a conventional KKK turbocharging set up, although development of the Comprex system is continuing with a view to being used in 1983.

Chapter 8

Aerodynamics

Since the creation of the Lotus 77, the beginning of the era of the wing car, aerodynamics has had a greater effect on the design of a Formula One car than ever before.

Aerodynamics may be considered an art. It was after the convincing domination of the Lotus 79 in 1978, that Formula One designers started to reflect on the complexities of ground effects, through which rapid development was soon to change the face of Grand Prix cars.

No matter how much has been learned about ground effects in some cases it still seems that aerodynamic design is based more on trial and error than on a systematic analytical approach. To understand the phenomenon of aerodynamics as applicable to Formula One, we must begin with theoretical definitions.

Boundary Layer

Airflow behaviour depends on the shape of the car bodywork and on the shape of any foil surfaces. The thin layer of air adjacent to a solid surface is called the "Boundary Layer". The movement(s) of the boundary layer may be laminar or turbulent. In a turbulent flow, the layer undergoes transition; it becomes thicker and is characterised by turbulence of air. In laminar flow, the speed distribution in the layer indicates a steady increase from zero at the surface to a maximum corresponding to the speed of the main airflow. In this case, the airflow is relatively smooth and moves in a layer parallel to the surface in question, hence the term Laminar.

The airflow around aerofoils starts at the leading edge, which is the front point of the wing, and is laminar up to the transition point, where turbulence takes place. Normally, the boundary layers separate themselves from the trailing edge of the wings, where turbulence develops.

If the separation of boundary layers occurs too far forward towards the leading edge, it will result in a loss of down force and a major increase in drag. This is called stalling angle and is liable to happen if the angle of attack of the wing exceeds its critical angle value. But this is unlikely to happen on Formula One cars since front and rear wings are set to a small degree of angle of attack.

Even though the surfaces of the bodywork and wings are smooth and unbroken by rivet heads or other irregularities such as a gear lever hand bulge, it is not possible to prolong the laminar flow all the way from the leading edge to the trailing edge, except at low speeds. Inevitably, molecules of air from each layer collide, creating an interchange of energy between layers, which causes a large increase of drag. Naturally designers

Scale model of the 1981 Talbot-Ligier JS17 made for wind tunnel testing. (Courtesy Talbot Gitanes).

try to avoid drag. The line of the general bodywork, especially the frontal area, is pretty much determined when the car is designed, therefore the scope for aerodynamic modifications in this region is quite limited.

Aerofoils

Aerofoil profile and ground effect systems are based on the oldest principles of aviation. A couple of hundred years ago an Italian scientist, Bernoulli, found out that for a given shape (in our case a wing) the pressure and speed of a gas (or liquid) flowing around it are interchangeable forms of equal energy. In other words, when the pressure increases, the velocity falls, and vice versa.

A racing car wing works just as an aircraft one does, with the difference that on the car the wing is mounted upside down so it produces downforce instead of lift. The wing is subject to turbulence provoked by the air passing around the car, and by its closeness to the ground.

Basically a wing is defined by:

Aspect Ratio

The size of a wing determines the amount of downforce it produces. The width is called span, and the length is called chord. Dividing span by chord gives "the aspect ratio", which can be seen as the efficiency of the wing. As a high aspect ratio will give most efficient wing; a typical example is the design of a glider. Span multiplied by chord is the area of the wing and this area determines the total downforce. Naturally the larger the area, the larger the downforce will be.

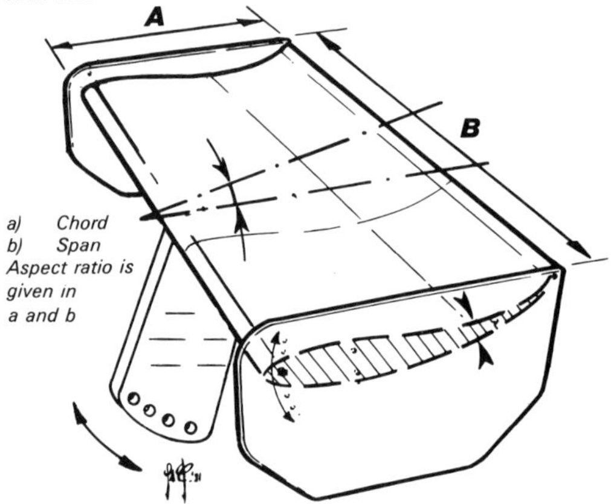

Aerofoil section mounted on its pylon with the various positioning points.

Angle of Attack

The efficiency of a wing is the ratio of its downforce to drag. The amount of downforce produced depends on the angle of attack, or tilt of the wing. Drag also increases with the angle of attack and each wing has a certain angle of attack where the downforce to drag ratio is maximum. It can be noticed from photographs that top ground effect Formula One cars have very little angle of attack of the wings. Because the main downforce is produced by the large side pods alongside the monocoque, the front and rear wings become "trim tails" to balance out the car, especially on fast circuits where very small angle of attack becomes a bonus for straight line speed.

Downforce : Drag Ratio

Downforce : drag ratio is the ratio of the downforce that a given wing provokes at a given speed and angle of attack, to the total drag produced by the wing under the same conditions. The performance of a wing depends upon the aspect ratio and the airflow conditions with which it is surrounded.

The Centre of "Lift" (Pressure)

The centre of "lift" is the point on the chord of the wing through which the downforce acts. The centre of lift is usually located about 2/5ths of the distance across from the leading edge, but varies in design depending on whether the wing operates by itself or if it has a flap added to it.

Downforce

The wings of an aircraft generate lift due to the pressure differential between the bottom and top area of the wings.

When the wing of an aircraft moves forward through the air, the flow of air along the lower surfaces arrives at the trailing edge before the flow along the upper surface, due to the different profiles of the two surfaces.

The lower surface airflow attempts to expand around the trailing edge, and as a result of this a vortex is formed. The rotation of the vortex accelerates the upper surface airflow, so that the length of time required for a molecule of air to move from the leading edge to the trailing edge becomes the same for the upper and the lower surface airflow. The increased speed of the upper surface flow eliminates the formation of vortex by the lower surface air at the trailing edge, and produces a lower pressure at each point on the upper surface than exists at the corresponding points on the lower surface. It is this difference in pressure that produces an aerodynamic lift.

This dynamic lift force depends on the composite airflow, is proportional to the speed of air circulation, to the power of air circulation, and is a function of the difference between the curvature of the lower and upper surfaces.

The magnitude of the aerodynamic lift force changes with the angle of attack. The force acts at the centre of pressure which varies with the angle of attack. The stability of an aircraft is significantly affected by the displacement of the centre of pressure. By increasing the angle of attack this point moves forward. But if the angle is increased beyond the angle that produces maximum lift, what is called a "stall" will occur, resulting in loss of flying speed and lift, and consequently loss of control. The air detaches itself from the upper surface.

By mounting a wing of a given shape upside down, the same force will be created but the opposite effect will take place. Dynamic lift force becomes a dynamic downforce and can be made to act on a chassis through the suspension springs to the tyres, thus improving adhesion, or grip.

Drag

Unfortunately, a wing produces drag as well as downforce, which hinders straight line

speed. The drag is produced by the air creating certain frictional resistance.

Formula One wings are designed to give a calculated amount of downforce for a minimum of drag resistance.

Drag also increases with angle of attack and each wing has a certain angle of attack where the downforce to drag ratio is at its best. This is the most efficient angle of attack for that wing. The downforce created acts at a right angle to the direction of the air flow and drag acts in the opposite direction to the air flow. Drag is also created by various components of the overall car. The uncovered wheels of a Formula One car bring about extraordinary turbulence, which is additional drag and in fact the four wheels are the cause of about 60% of the aerodynamic inefficiency, of the car, the distribution of which is approximately 35% attributable to the front wheels and 25% attributable to the rear wheels. The aim for a Formula One design should therefore be first of all to eliminate as much of the turbulence as possible from around the wheels. Unfortunately, the present regulations do not permit covering wheels. However, some years ago the problem of the turbulence created by the front wheels was reduced by mounting a full "sports car" type nose as seen on "conventional" cars such as the Tyrrell P34 six wheeler. Now, on ground effect cars a full sports car nose cannot be used simply because maximum airflow to the side pods is required.

Drag is produced at all speeds. In motion, a car's body displaces each particle of air perpendicularly to the frontal surface and the absence of friction of the particles results in the air returning to its original position. When deciding on the form of a Formula One car, the whole of the frontal surface hitting the air including the various accessories like cockpit surround, windscreen, mirrors, brakes, scoops, etc., creates turbulence which becomes drag. Nevertheless, since the application of ground effects, aerodynamic discoveries have changed the thinking on this subject, which has led the majority of designers producing effective Formula One cars as regards a very good downforce : drag ratio compromise.

Wings

The principal objective of racing car aerofoils is to provide a downforce on the tyres to increase cornering speed. The aerodynamic form of a wing depends on the individual designer; that is why numerous sections and shapes have been seen in Formula One. At the front, the two aerofoils mounted on the nose are used not only to produce the needed downforce but are also used as "trim-tails" to balance the fore and aft load on the car for a better overall stability since they affect the air flow going around the side pods of ground effect cars.

The different shapes and sizes of the end plates bolted on the outer section of a wing reflect different opinions among designers. End plates vary from almost nothing to a huge size, depending on what is asked of them; to spill air off the end of the wing, to guide air around the side pods, to improve air flow into the brake duct by reducing turbulence around the front wheels, or as is most often the case, to improve handling.

The pair of nose wings commonly fitted is joined transversally by a tube section going through the nose and resting on the nose frame, or support. The inner part touching the nose has a slotted piece of riveted aluminium to allow adjustments to be made. Usually a graduation on the nose allows a quick and accurate change of the wing incidence.

Ferrari have their own idea of front wing in the forms of a single piece aerofoil with small end plates, located ahead of the nose cone. It is mounted, and is adjustable, on a central frame, which is replaceable as a single unit. The design has been used on all "T" series Ferrari Formula One cars, and is featured on the current 126C, Mk 1.

On some circuits the removal of front wings is quite normal, firstly because the downforce produced by the side pods gives sufficient loading to the tyres and secondly because of general weight distribution and

Front wing seen on the Ferrari 126C.

the location of the centre of pressure "lift" can be improved when seen in the context of tyre characteristics. The absence of front wings gives an extra bonus in presenting less drag and allowing a much cleaner entry for the air going into the water/oil radiator ducts, and that passing over and under the side pods. The absence or otherwise of front wings depends on the overall behaviour of the car, even at fast circuits such as Monza.

Rear Wings

Rear wings have their own history of shape, size, position and improvisation. The introduction of rear wings began around the mid sixties. It started slowly with small aluminium sheets across the rear end of the car between the engine and gearbox which later developed into automatically controlled wings, and wings which eventually rose high on pillars above the rear wheels of the car. Dangerous heights of both front and rear pillar mounted wings and the fragile way they were secured brought quite a bit of concern about safety. Soon new F.I.A. rules put an end to them finding a compromise on height above the ground, and distance behind the rear wheel centre line for rear wings. Rear wings are designed to produce downforce which is combined with the load produced by the side pods. The rear wing is larger than the front wings because of the down force required for the size of the rear wheels. It is simply a question of aerodynamic balance between the front and rear ends of the car.

Rear wing support can vary from car to car, but most common is a single fabricated pillar, as on the Ferrari 126C and Toleman TG181 for example. Teams that believe that the air flow should run clear across the top of the car to the wing prefer the wing to be mounted between twin vertical plates, in order to avoid an obstruction occurring in the form of the pylon.

On some conventional Formula One cars the wing was supported by large twin end plates bolted to a 4 or 5 inch diameter tube, this tube attached at the back of the gearbox. The tube was also used as an oil catch-tank, having the different breather pipes connected to it.

The majority of front and rear wings are made of aluminium. The surface is glued and riveted onto a series of frames which form the wing's shape.

An additional small wing added further aft, on top of the main wing and called the Gurney Flap is commonly used. It is adjustable since the end plates have slotted holes to allow changes of incidence. On the central pylon layout only this flap can be adjusted, as desired. The main wing incidence has to be altered by changing the complete wing pylon, which is mounted on small aluminium plates bolted on the gearbox (McLaren MP4 Toleman TG181).

According to its profile, the effectiveness of an aerofoil starts at 50mph and can reach maximum value at about 200mph.

Rear wing with Gurney flap and lip seen on Renault RE series.

Gurney Flap

This type of flap is used in aviation in connection with the take off and landing of high speed aircraft. It is bolted upside down and is adjustable on racing cars, and the main wing and its flap work together. A plain wing flap aft of the main wing, the Gurney Flap increases the curvature (camber) of the wing, with the result that the downforce is improved and the angle of attack at which separation occurs is increased, so the air speed can be reduced without "stalling". The flow of air through the important gap between the trailing edge of the main wing and the flap gives a further increase in downforce without separation of the boundary layer. The Gurney Flap was first introduced on Indy cars where the flap was liable to work better with high speed.

Lip

The lip is simply an aluminium sheet bent at 90° with a high variant front ¼″ bolted to the trailing edge of the Gurney Flap. The lip creates a low pressure behind itself which accelerates the air flow from under the surface of the flap and therefore delays the separation. Hence there is an increase of downthrust, without a significant increase of drag.

Ground Effect

The term "Ground Effect" is used to explain the difference in the aerodynamic behaviour between bodies operating in close proximity to the ground and, in some respect, those operating in clean air as aerofoils. Although there is a difference in concept, the principle is similar.

The general shape of a pre-Ground Effect Formula One car created lift and the more the body was streamlined, the greater the lift, which meant that pressure on the ground diminished.

In the late '60s, to get over this problem, the Formula One brigade mounted curved pieces of aluminium around the gearbox in the form of an aircraft aerofoil, but upside down.

Later on, two more little wings appeared on the nose. Attempts at different shapes, widths and positioning of these wings reduced a good part of the problem of lift since the aerofoils created a negative lift (downforce) of about 250lbs at the front and of about 400lbs at the rear, at about 80mph. Thus better grip was obtained, which was demonstrated by a distinct increase in cornering speeds.

The Lotus 78 was the first ground effect car and was followed a year later by the Lotus 79 which dominated the 1978 season with impertinent ease. It is from there that the face of the Grand Prix car technology changed dramatically not only in the field of aerodynamics, but also in suspension and tyre development.

The application of Mr Bernoulli's law shows that when air is accelerating into a narrowing passage (the venturi-shaped gap under a Formula One car) it is subject to a fall in pressure. This reduced pressure beneath the car acts equally on car and ground, but as the ground can't move

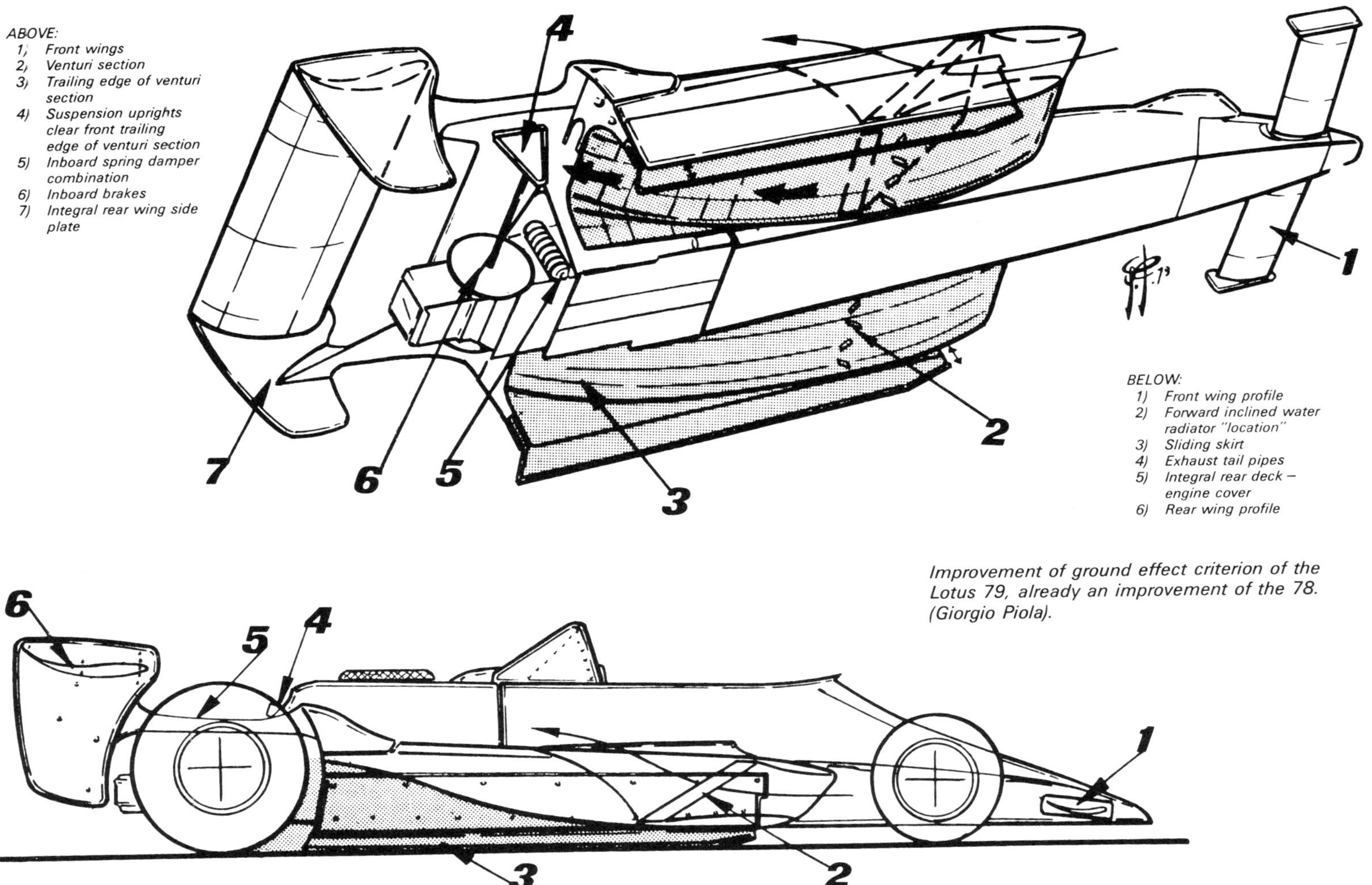

ABOVE:
1) *Front wings*
2) *Venturi section*
3) *Trailing edge of venturi section*
4) *Suspension uprights clear front trailing edge of venturi section*
5) *Inboard spring damper combination*
6) *Inboard brakes*
7) *Integral rear wing side plate*

BELOW:
1) *Front wing profile*
2) *Forward inclined water radiator "location"*
3) *Sliding skirt*
4) *Exhaust tail pipes*
5) *Integral rear deck – engine cover*
6) *Rear wing profile*

Improvement of ground effect criterion of the Lotus 79, already an improvement of the 78. (Giorgio Piola).

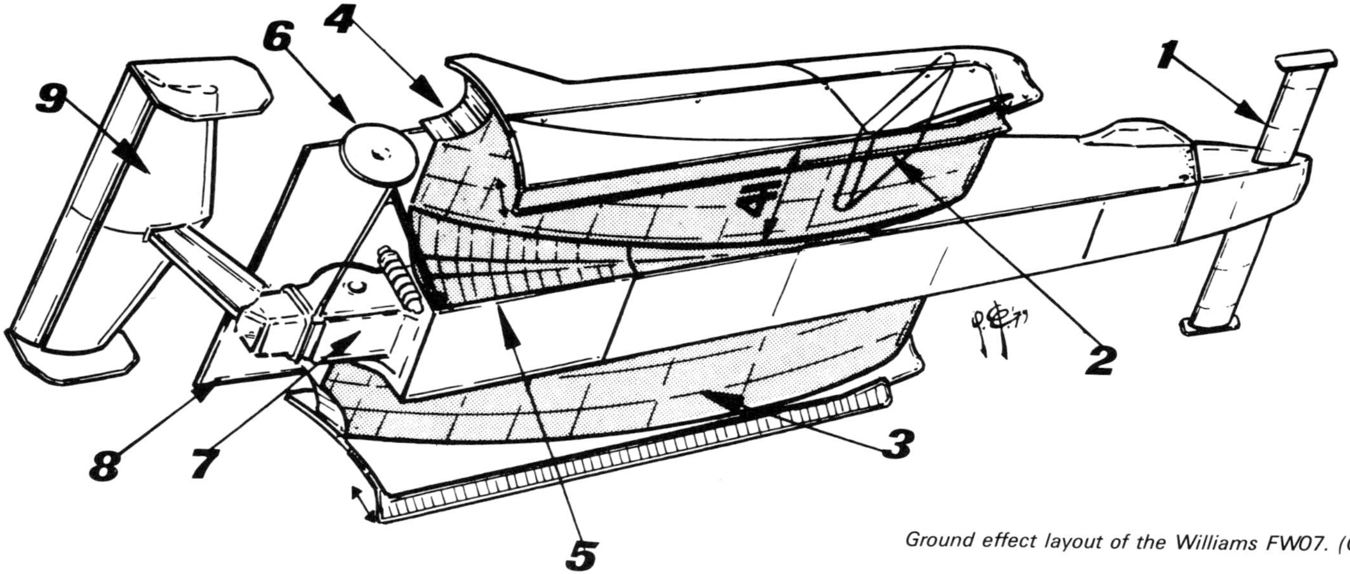

Ground effect layout of the Williams FW07. (Giorgio Piola).

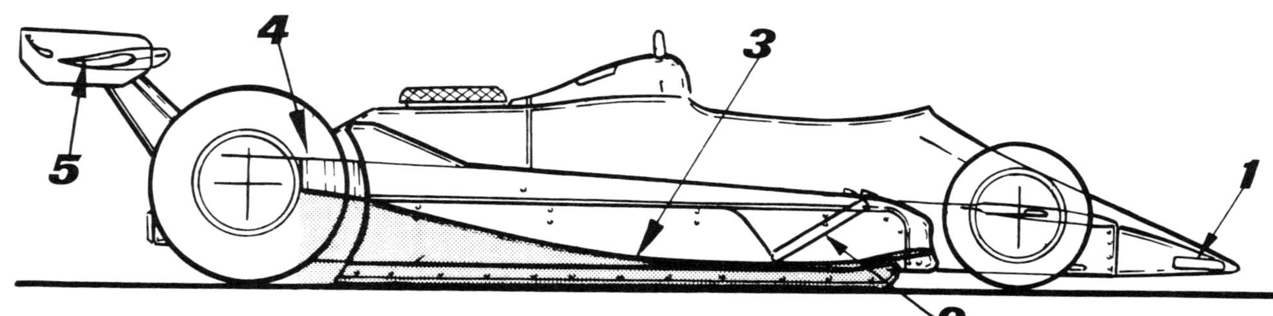

ABOVE:
1) Front wings
2) Skirt
3) Under wing
4) Honeycombe area of wheel passage
5) Engine undertray
6) Outboard brakes
7) Gearbox
8) Rear deck

BELOW:
1) Front wings
2) Water radiator
3) Venturi section
4) Honeycombe rear deck
5) Rear wing profile

upwards the car is "sucked" downwards. This phenomenon is called "Venturi effect" (note that the venturi principle is applied on carburettors). On a ground effect Formula One car, the venturi is created by mounting a large aerofoil section upside down, close to the ground alongside the chassis.

The venturi principle depends a great deal on the front and rear aerofoils since these influence the inlet and exit of airflow passing along the upper and the under sections of the side wings.

The form given to a side wing is able to reduce the incidence, or angle of attack, of the front and rear wings whilst retaining the same overall downforce for a reduced drag, because the side wings themselves are capable of producing a downforce nowadays of more than 4000lbs, but this is only achieved with a good approach to an overall design.

A ground effect car is basically characterised by:

1) Narrow chassis, in order to achieve maximum side pod, air passage areas (upper and under surfaces), which means that the fuel cell has to be located in a single unit just behind the driver, which in turn means that he has to sit further forward. (Rethinking of the weight distribution). Water and oil cooling radiators are located within the "leading edge" of the wing, the air coming in through an opening at the front and finding its way out just behind the radiator, channelled through smooth ducts.

2) At the back end, to allow the air flow under the wing to escape freely and smoothly, "bodywork" envelopes the entire engine, and extends back around the gearbox to finish under the rear. The upper surface of the body is equally smooth so that the air circulating at high pressure creates a minimum of turbulence. The bodywork extending up to the back of the gearbox, the two exhaust tail pipes (DFV engine) emerge through an opening in the middle of the rear cover, just after the engine cylinder heads.

3) At the front, the chisel-nose is quite slim. Its general shape is designed to produce downforce and also to let the air run freely around the upper and lower surface of the entire body. The suspension units, that is to say spring dampers, are placed inside the driver's foot well and are covered by aluminium bulges and operated by fabricated top rocker arms. Still at the front, the bottom wishbones are of aerodynamic shaped tube and the braided pipes run inside them, emerging at the outer end to feed the twin brake calipers buried inside the wheel rim, out of the air stream.

The rear suspension arms and general layout is quite similar to that at the front, except, of course, for the drive shafts. Bodywork envelopes the damper as well as the entire gearbox, leaving a small opening for the drive shafts. On some cars, this air channelling is pushed to the extent that the inner part of the uprights, brakes and bodywork layout surrounding the rear wheels and outer drive shaft joints are also covered to allow the airflow to exit freely behind the car.

Only a few years ago another way to activate the airflow after exiting the venturi (low pressure area) was by means of a device called an "extractor". The idea was to curve up abruptly a portion of underside area of bodywork, in front and within the inner part of the rear wheel, the curvature of this extractor ending after about 2/3rds of the wheel diameter. The effect starts as the rear wheels in motion create high pressure turbulence which is projected backwards around the top section of the tyres. At the same time this high pressure activates the exit of the low pressure airflow from the venturi. The design of the extractors was very much in accordance with the results obtained by wind tunnel tests, and led to the outward appearance of the famous "jaws" on the Ligier-Ford JS11 and JS15.

Lotus 88

The aerodynamic downforce principles of the controversial Lotus 88 are, in a way, a reversion to a much earlier arrangement seen on the Lotus 69, of 1968–69. The idea was to apply dynamic downforce directly to

Extractor and "jaws" of the Ligier JS15.

the rear wheel uprights, thus by-passing the car's suspension springs. At the time the downforce was produced by a single rear wing mounted on two high pylons which were bolted directly to the wheel hubs. This was later banned by the CSI on safety grounds.

The 88's featured integral rear wing, side pods and undertray, and bodywork, the underbody area closed with soft plastic skirted side panels held by an arrangement of cross beams and the whole forming an independent rigid structure. This downforce generating primary chassis was supported on four small, visible spring damper combinations, two at the front end of the side panels and two at the rear axle centre line, each combination resting directly to the external part of the bottom wishbones and assisted by a thrust rod directly bolted to the top part of the uprights.

The other "part" of the car is described as a "secondary chassis" which is simply the complete rolling chassis without bodywork and aerodynamic aids. With such a design the primary layout is independent of the secondary, because of the use of suspension springs. The arrangement then allows the wheels freedom to move independently, while the secondary chassis is insulated against track irregularities thus offering a comfortable ride.

From around 50mph onwards, a significant downforce is generated, literally squashing the "primary chassis" on its small spring damper combinations. This action of squatting closes up the venturi section and at the same time the spring-damper units become fully compressed, thus transmitting the downforce loads directly to the tyres through the hubs. If the car slows down again, the primary chassis comes up again to leave the 6cm side pod to track gap imposed by the 1981 F.I.S.A. rules.

The 88 was banned from racing. The opposition insisted that the car had a movable aerodynamic device, which Lotus refuted by referring to it as a "primary chassis".

The question is if the 88 is "illegal", why then is the jacking suspension system that others employed classed as legal?

Skirts

A very important component of the ground effect system are the lateral skirts, which were able to slide vertically, taking up any deformation of the track, keeping the tracks sidepod gap sealed at all times. In effect, they boxed off the venturi area, and also prevented the external high pressure air spilling into the venturi area.

Generally, sliding skirts were of honeycomb construction, or carbon fibre, a very light and strong material and slid freely over small rollers against the external and lateral surfaces of the wings, in order to avoid the danger of jamming towards the top of their passage which would cause instant loss of downforce. The bottom of the skirts were constantly in contact with the ground, and in order to avoid premature wear, ceramic tube sections held in small plastic or aluminium tubes were placed at the bottom of the skirts, resisting relatively well to the constant friction on the track. The way of keeping the skirts on the ground was the subject of a lot of research, from a couple of tension wire springs pushing them down, to leaving it to gravity, the latter course being the most commonly employed.

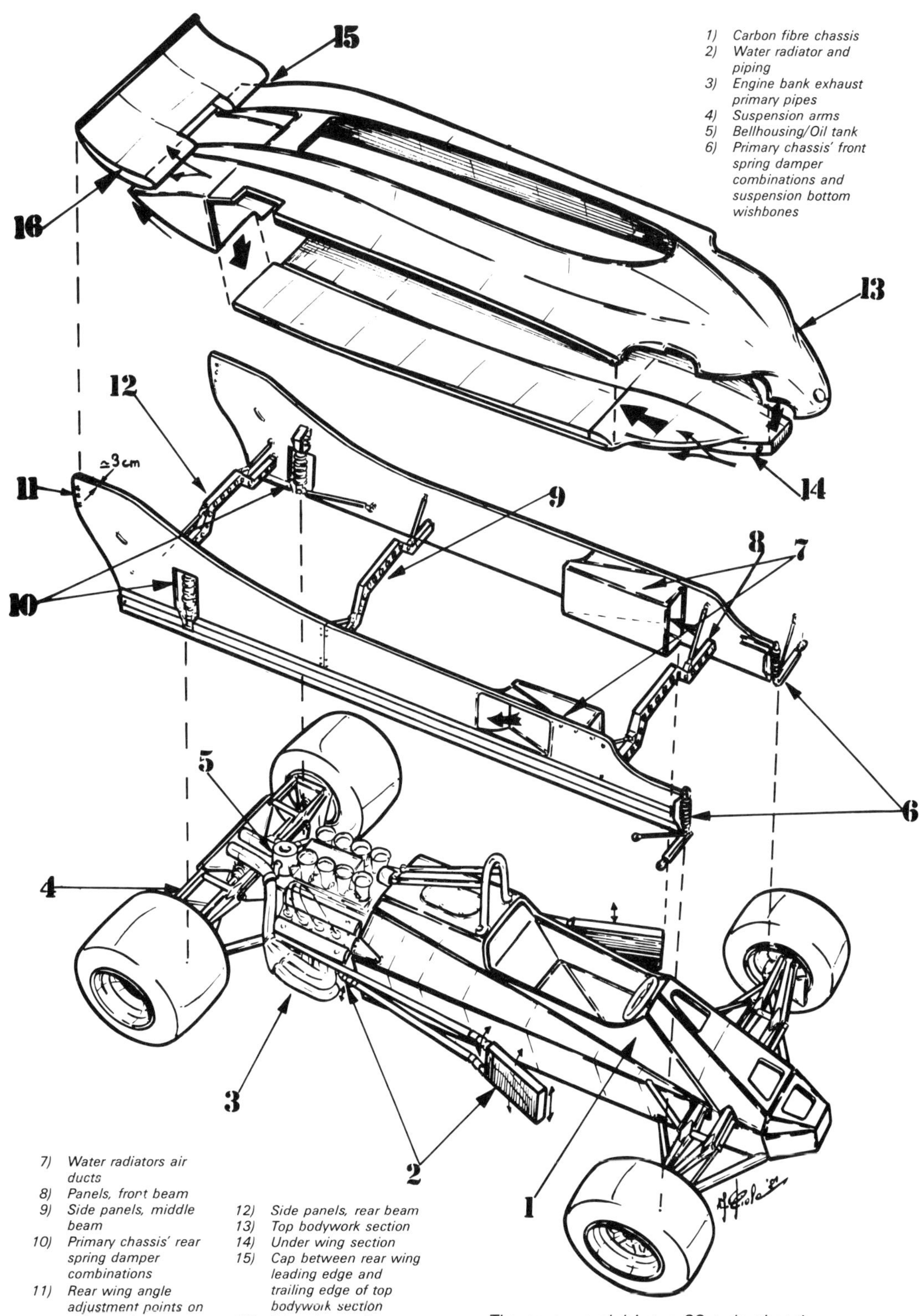

1) Carbon fibre chassis
2) Water radiator and piping
3) Engine bank exhaust primary pipes
4) Suspension arms
5) Bellhousing/Oil tank
6) Primary chassis' front spring damper combinations and suspension bottom wishbones
7) Water radiators air ducts
8) Panels, front beam
9) Side panels, middle beam
10) Primary chassis' rear spring damper combinations
11) Rear wing angle adjustment points on side panels
12) Side panels, rear beam
13) Top bodywork section
14) Under wing section
15) Cap between rear wing leading edge and trailing edge of top bodywork section
16) Integral rear wing

The controversial Lotus 88 twin chassis.

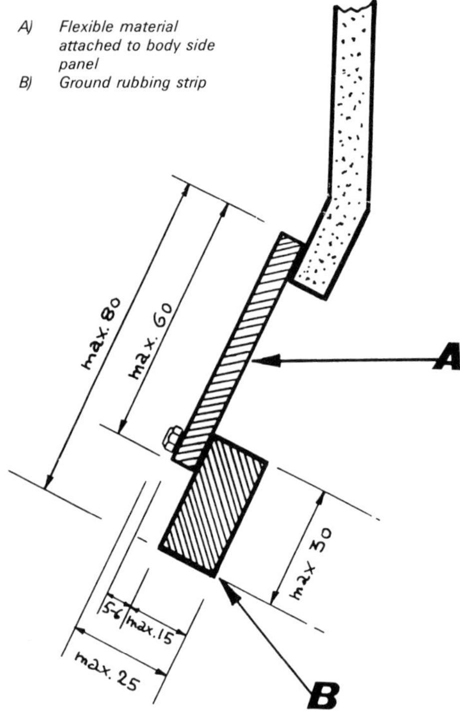

Sectional drawing of 1982 skirt assembly R/H side (F.I.S.A rules).

After the 1981 skirt ban, with suspension jacking systems already in use, a slight change in regulations concerning a different type of permissible fixed skirt, commonly called a rubbing strip, was enforced from mid-season.

Contemporary fixed skirts are made of plastic material and chosen according to their effectiveness in terms of sealing. In 1981 they were defined as 6cm wide and 5mm thick as a maximum and were bolted directly along the lower part of the outer side pods edges. A big problem was that skirt wear makes the handling unpredictable.

The rules changed for 1982, banning the jacking system altogether and introducing a new length of rubbing strip, this time 10cm wide; in a way we have completed a full circle.

Rubbing strip or sliding skirts assembly calls for regular maintenance. In some cases mechanics have been appointed solely for this task.

Air Box

The purpose of the air box is to channel air over the engine's inlet trumpets. The air box was first introduced by Matra Sport in the early 1970s, and right away was adapted on all cars. Looking back a few years, it will be noticed that the air boxes were much too big for the service they rendered. However the ugly air box fitted to the first Ligier Formula One car (JS5) was without doubt the most efficient of all because of its very high position and well studied profile. This meant that it disturbed the rear aerofoil a little, but above all engine output was improved.

At one stage air inlets were so large that enormous turbulence very much reduced the effectiveness of the rear aerofoil which led to the necessity of using a steep angle of attack to obtain the downforce required. Furthermore, as 50cm^2 of air inlet is sufficient for the engine on certain cars, the air box was in some cases a useless object. A very effective sort of air box was used on most Ferrari T series cars, using large N.A.C.A. ducts incorporated in the bodywork at cockpit level. By this means a high pressure air flow to the engine was achieved.

For a few years air boxes disappeared on ground effect cars only to reappear in 1981 with more logical design (Williams FW07, McLaren MP4).

N.A.C.A. Ducts

The N.A.C.A. duct is a device invented by the American National Advisory Council for Aeronautics during their space studies. It is a design at once both complicated and straightforward. Its shape is of a relatively restricted section which becomes larger. The most important aspect is that, in order to get a maximum effect, it must be designed to accurate specifications of layout and must be placed in the region of a laminar air flow, parallel to the "local" air flow – failing that, the N.A.C.A. layout does not work. Basically, the N.A.C.A. duct

Airbox seen on the 1981 Williams FW07.

provokes a laminar friction of air which creates a wake of air particles which progressively accelerate, creating a maximum air entry into the opening. The N.A.C.A. duct design is used a great deal on Formula One racing cars for cooling oil, water through radiators and other accessories inducing heat, such as turbos, and even for cooling the driving area of the cockpit for the driver's comfort.

Chapter 9

Tyrrell P34

The main peculiarity of this creature was the fact that it had four directional 10 inch diameter front wheels and two conventional rear wheels of 13 inch diameter. By using "mini" front wheels and a full "sports car" nose, the frontal area of the car was reduced thus improving straight line speed. A second advantage was a gain of about 20% on the tyres contact patch, improving grip and braking performance through the tyres. Against that, there was 20% more rolling resistance because of the larger tyre contact patch plus the extra overall weight due to the additional mechanical "items" of the front suspension and brakes.

After traditional winter testing, the car appeared at the 1976 Spanish Grand Prix. Endless development took the car's weight from 590kg to more than 650kg (the minimum weight for Formula One cars being then 575kg) and reinforcing and modifying the suspensions (including longer wheelbase) added to this. Later, during its first season in service, a mini computer (called a "black box") was fitted to the chassis in order to record all the movements of the suspension, the reactions of the car, etc. The "black box" was to be retained on later Tyrrell Formula One models.

During its two years of racing, the P34 received different chassis, suspension geometries, track, wheelbase and the entire bodywork was changed, which changed its appearance and it ended up quite an attractive looking Formula One car. This intensive and hard work brought quite a few good race results, the car winning the Swedish Grand Prix and only missing some others because of minor mechanical failures or circumstances such as bad weather. Credit should be given to Team Tyrrell for its efforts to change the aspect of Formula One way of thinking, but the overall performance of the P34 was not convincing and Tyrrell went back to a conventional design with just four wheels.

The following descriptions of the P34 are based on one of the latest versions raced up to the end of 1977.

Chassis

The P34 was a unique car in that it ran four wheels on the front and two on the rear. The difference in the wheels on the front was, other than the fact that there were four of them, that an effort was made to enclose them into a 140cm wide bodywork and to this end the front of the monocoque was fairly narrow relative to other Formula One cars. Because of this, the monocoque was almost a two part monocoque, the front part attached to the rear part of the monocoque, near the front roll over hoop instrument panel area, so the chassis came wide up to the instrument area and then narrowed and went forward to the pedals and master cylinder area. Because everything was so tight and close fitting, there was a general problem of accommodating fire extinguisher bottles, twin master cylinder, front wheel arrangement, batteries, and air ducts to brakes and so forth. Basic complications were finally overcome and the car was raced for 1½ years.

The inner skin of the car was a single piece from the rear to the front of the monocoque in 18 gauge L72 and the outer skin was 16 gauge L72 but sometimes the inner and outer skins were made in NS4 which is a softer more resilient aluminium. The main panels and inner skin was formed from one sheet. Each lefthand and righthand side was made out of separate sheets in 16 gauge. The monocoque, in turn, was pre-drilled and before riveting it was processed by the edging process and the sheets were glued together with Epoxy resin or an Araldite compound, depending on what was needed to be used to join the skins together before riveting. The riveting was always done with solid rivets, upset riveting like on any Formula One car. Titanium was used on the monocoque on front roll over hoop. Some other bracketry was also made in titanium. Rigidity was required in the chassis, so the top skin of the chassis from front roll over hoop leading forward to the brake pedal area was covered by a 5mm magnesium plate. It was not really very heavy but it gave it a lot of rigidity, and it was all riveted with deep set rivets.

The fuel was in three main tanks and a fourth collector tank on the left hand rear. All tanks emptied into the collector pot from which it was supplied to the engine through a felt filter. Communication between tanks was by flat valves. The breakaway coupling was designed by Tyrrell and that was at the end of the collector pot system. The shape of the car was triangular so that the outer corner for 10mm was full of expanding foam to provide the deformable structure. On top of this was a layer of about four walls, which covered the regulations. A Lucas HP fuel pump was used for the initial start of the engine, as on many other cars. The P34 had some hereditary characteristics from the previous Tyrrell Formula One cars. It had an external complete hoop at the back, attached to the chassis and the engine and leaving a gap between the engine and the chassis into which area the oil tank was located. The advantage of this is that it is a roll over hoop and also a rigid structure (because it's continuous steel) taking all the forces and also the radius rods loads.

Front roll over hoop and steering column layout, note the brake balance adjustment cable – Tyrrell P34.

Rear Suspension

Rear suspension was a typical conventional Formula One type with parallel links at the bottom and top, adjustable top link on the top, and the toe-in was adjusted by the rear lower link and the gearbox sump, which served both as the attachment point for the inner inboard pick-up of the lower link and an oil sump for the gearbox. Very convenient; if ever the team wanted to change the suspension geometry it just changed the sump. The suspension loads

Rear suspension (left hand) – Tyrrell P34.

Engine top plate and top suspension radius rod pick-up on the rear roll over hoop right hand side – Tyrrell P34.

were taken out by a cross beam attached to the engine bell housing by means of stays and radius rods. There were twin parallel radius rods leading forward, attaching to the previously mentioned full hoop.

The magnesium uprights housed two, deep groove bearings. Wheel shaft was of EN24 or equivalent, CV joints with the stub flange, both double plunge. Two CV joints accommodated the new tyres of large, 27" diameter, giving roughly a rolling radius of 13", whereas the gearbox always stood at 10" so that there was a 3" incline outward and therefore the two CV joints were needed to get the necessary plunge.

The brake calipers were standard Lockheed, mounted on dural block, the dural block in turn mounted to the FGA 5 speed gearbox. The brake discs were inboard attached to the gearbox. The roll bar was attached to the top cross member which in turn was also holding the top link, therefore it had double usage. The cross member took the load of the damper because it was also attached to the cross beam on the top. The rear wing had two or three different configurations. The rear wing on 007 had a central aerofoil sectioned pylon which had rubber bushes bedded into the mounting point on the bottom and was attached to the gearbox on a steel frame. It was decided to try dural plates instead of the central pylon on P34 and the twin dural plates attached to the side of the FGA box, (the box had two flat mounting bosses) bolted directly into it and without the aid of sound block rubber bushes, and it was quite successful as a wing.

The gearbox had five speeds and the ratios of the crown wheel pinion were 8/31 and 9/31. Basically, the car was on steel springs with caliper springs to take up the initial drooping condition.

Cooling System

The cooling system had two radiators positioned longitudinally, which means along the axis of the car, situated in front of either rear wheel within the 140cm regulation and the principle of that was that air rushing by would meet the tyre, build up its pressure and would either go outside the tyre or inside the tyre, depending on how much was there and whatever went inside the tyre had to pass through the Matrix and therefore cooled the water.

Brake cooling ducts were of the snorkel type where there was a moulded fibre glass shape surrounding the inner CV joint and projecting air between that and the disc. Its

Water and additional oil radiators mounted alongside the engine – Tyrrell P34.

Tyrrell P34 safety accessories and batteries located in the nose box.

face pointed forwards, laying flush over the rear anti roll bar, and ducted air from that position into the brakes. The 1977 model had an all-encompassing body which had ducts feeding the brake cooling system that was also successful as a coolant.

The first system didn't have the all-encompassing body and therefore the car just had rectangular shaped ducts facing forward which passed the air into the disc, but on the later P34 with the all-encompassing body they wanted to smooth the air out around the car so they had N.A.C.A. ducts which were flush mounting to the body and therefore didn't present a disturbance to the air.

Oil System

The conventional oil system was as per DFV requirements; an oil cooler in the front was tried which worked and then two oil coolers under the wing, which also worked. The arrangement stayed like so up to the withdrawal of the car from racing. The oil piping was typical Tyrrell rubber stressed pipes of different sizes. The Lucas M35 starter motor was mounted on the left hand side of the gearbox and later on replaced by an air starter CP type.

Electric System

The electrical loom was made by the mechanics. When the car had a starter motor, a Varley battery was used which sat in front of the front master cylinders, but later, with an air starter system, small batteries of six volts from a motorbike were used, as on many other cars. A master switch controlled the whole system and that was the Solenoid type as opposed to the Citron type which was commonly used by other teams. The solenoid system is that you put a nominal amount of electricity through the solenoid winding, the primary winding, which would energise the plunger and the plunger would pull up and energise the secondary system, which was the main power supply to the whole car. The ignition system was conventional. In fact, it wasn't necessary to do anything except change the "black box" now and then.

Safety System

The fire extinguishers were the mandatory 5kg for the cockpit, located under the driver's knees, and later on forwards, in front of the pedals, and a secondary bottle of 2.5kgs, also under the knees and later on, on the seat tank. An air bottle was attached to the seat top panel, under the bodywork. A hook on the outside, or a loop, was a machined piece of dural which was attached to the roll over bar on the rear so that it could be activated by a pull rod by a marshal on the track and there was a push button on the instrument panel which also activated the fire extinguisher and the safety system. The weight distribution shift made by moving the fire extinguisher bottle was nominal but noticeable by the driver. Finally, a six point standard Willans seat belt was used.

Dashboard

The dashboard has two Snip pressure/temperature indicator instruments, one indicated the oil pressure and temperature and the other fuel pressure and water temperature. The rev counter was surrounded by a steel ring, and three points of the ring were attached to the instrument panel. Three points of this same steel ring were attached to the rev counter via rubber connections, thus the instrument was insulated from the instrument panel.

Wheels

Both front and rear wheels were Tyrrell designed and machined and were cast by Kent Alloys. Front and rear had a single nut. The rear had a large aluminium spin-on nut. The front had "K" nuts or steel nuts on pins; the pins were ½" and that was the only mounting system required. The wheels were a smaller diameter, 10" as opposed to the standard 13" diameter.

Steering System

Steering was by a double universal joint system because the steering column was offset to the left. The reason for this is that you have two pedals for the right foot and one pedal for the left foot, and to accommodate three pedals in an adult male foot area you require 12" – to pass a 1" diameter steering column through this area you require an offset. The offset (if there is any) varies from car to car and because of this you require two universal joints, although some people get away with one by actually inclining the angle of the steering wheel.

The steering box was a Tyrrell design with magnesium outer casing and a steel inner, with Renault road car ball and cup knuckle joint, bought off the shelf from any Renault dealer. It was a very good joint and its life was substantially increased by Tyrrell because it took out the plastic cup and replaced it by different material cups and lapped the joint in so that there was a nominal amount of friction and the steering felt very light. Outboard to the track rod was a regular rose joint in a yoke attached to the upright. The ratio available was all the way from 10-1 down to 6-1. There was never a fixed ratio; it was changed according to driver preference or to suit a circuit. Monaco would require 8-1 because the driver would want to be able to turn quicker. The initial thought was that with four front wheels it would be a heavier steering arrangement but as the drivers started to get used to the car they found that they didn't need anything special; in fact they could use exactly what was used on a two wheel car and still get the same feedback.

Steering was so arranged that a single rack and pinion activated all four wheels. This was done by having the rack and pinion activate the front pair of wheels; the track rod was attached to the front part of the front wheels and there was a slave track rod on the rear part of the same front wheels which worked on a swing arm, which in turn operated the rear pair of front wheels. Thus any right hand turn on the front right wheel was duplicated again with another right hand movement on the rear of the front front wheels, so that there were literally three track rods per side of the car. Of the three the first was the primary track rod activating the front pair of the four front

Front suspension, braking and steering layout – Tyrrell P34.

wheels and the other two were the slave for the second pair of wheels. The roll bar was connected to a beam attached to the two bottom wishbones and it was a proportionate type roll bar; you could increase or decrease the proportion of the anti-roll bar reaction by moving the bottom part of the drop link forward or aft on the beam. That beam was made out of a piece of sheet metal and formed over.

Corner weights were usually set-up by putting the front two wheels on a platform and then taking that platform and mounting it on a single scale.

The gear lever was still inside the inner skin area but because the body was fairly low, the lever and the knob stood proud and a bulge was visible. Molak joints were used for the gear shift, three at the most.

Front Suspension

The top wishbones were a machined piece of dural which had castor adjustment on it and inboard and outboard were rose joints. The bottom wishbone was fabricated from steel sheet metal with a single rose joint on the outside and two on the inside; two bushes on the inside were bedded in to the monocoque.

Uprights were machined in dural originally and later were made of magnesium. The original included the brake caliper in its design; it was part of the upright with Lockheed pistons into it. It was a very tidy assembly and a lot of people used the system at that time. It had to be accurately machined.

Dampers were special dampers made by Koni for this project, they were very tiny, short stroke, narrow diameter ones which fitted into all this very small area and were literally shrunken versions of a standard damper. Springs, in turn, were not the standard 2¼ inch ID type but Tyrrell design springs, all in steel and obviously a whole set of ranges was available, as required.

The original roll bar on the P34 was a two piece one because of the construction of the monocoque. Down the side of the driver's legs there were two box sections, roughly 4 inches wide that were part of the monocoque and because they were so arranged a formed roll bar couldn't be fed through for installation or replacement.

The way round this was to split the roll bar in half and put mating flanges on the roll bar with a six bolt arrangement. They took the two halves and fed them from inside the car outwards, and after they had lined them up they were just bolted together, thus forming a continual roll bar with a very heavy flange in the middle. This was then mounted onto a dural box, that was the original. Apparently, it became very

difficult for the mechanics to make a quick change or to modify the bar and because there were only three positions; soft, medium or hard, on the bar, because of the limitation of space in that area, it was replaced by a regular roll bar mounted on top of the monocoque above the driver's feet. Aluminium dural links were used with two rose joints on a single shear.

The front brake discs were small and in special cast iron, machined by Tyrrell. They were both driven by a nuts and bolts assembly and rolled on a belt which in turn held the bearing and it was all a single unit arrangement. The bell internally held the bearing and externally held the disc. Because the forward front wheel was directly in front of the rear front wheel it tended to absorb all the incoming air, so the rear wheel wouldn't get enough and therefore there was a flexible hose to the front wheels, flexible hose to the rear wheels and if it was a very hot circuit a snorkel type ducting was used to the rear set of the front wheels.

The clutch was worked hydraulically. Two master cylinders worked the front brakes, there was a single master cylinder for the rear brakes and single master cylinder for the clutch, each having its own reservoir. Some pedals were titanium, others were steel, sometimes light gauge. The brake balance could be set by the driver from the dashboard.

The front nose had flaps on or off depending on the requirements of the circuit. No wings; it was a full width nose (115") fixed high all the time with Dzus fasteners on the top.

Bodywork

The bodywork was all fibreglass, reinforced where required. Two plastic windows were placed about the height of the dash panel so the driver could see the front wheels and their position on the track. This arrangement was interesting from the spectators' point of view, because they could see the movement of the driver's arms. Finally, the bodywork was fixed by a series of Dzus fasteners.

Specification

Chassis
18–16 gauge L72 aluminium with titanium dash and rear roll over hoop.
Weight: 72lbs (32.5kgs)

Front Suspension
Machined dural top wishbone with thrust link – Fabricated bottom wishbone – Inner-outer ball joints – Original machined dural uprights with incorporated brake calipers then changed to cast magnesium uprights – Outboard springs-dampers combination – Special short stroke Koni dampers (4) – Steel springs – Steel single tubular anti roll bar acting on 2 "corners" of each side through a link and a steel fabricated member connected on both bottom wishbones – Rose joints – Tyrrell rack and pinion steering system with various ratios ranging from 6–1 to 10–1

Front Brakes
Outboard Lockheed/Tyrrell single caliper per wheel – Ventilated 9 inch diameter discs – ⅝ inch Lockheed master cylinder – ⅞ inch clutch master cylinder – Ferodo DS11 pads

Rear Suspension
Bottom parallel links attached to gear box – Single top links to cross beam – Twin radius rods to roll over hoop – Magnesium uprights – Tubular anti roll bar – Outboard spring Koni damper combination

Rear Brakes
Inboard Lockheed brakes – 10.5 inch ventilated discs – Single caliper (4 pistons) per wheel – Ferodo DS11 pads

Transmission
Hewland FGA (5 speed) – Standard Hewland locking differential – Ratio 8/31 – 9/31 – Tyrrell drive shafts – Serck gearbox oil cooler

Water Cooling
Twin Serck radiators – Aluminium hoses and piping – Capacity 3 gallons approx.

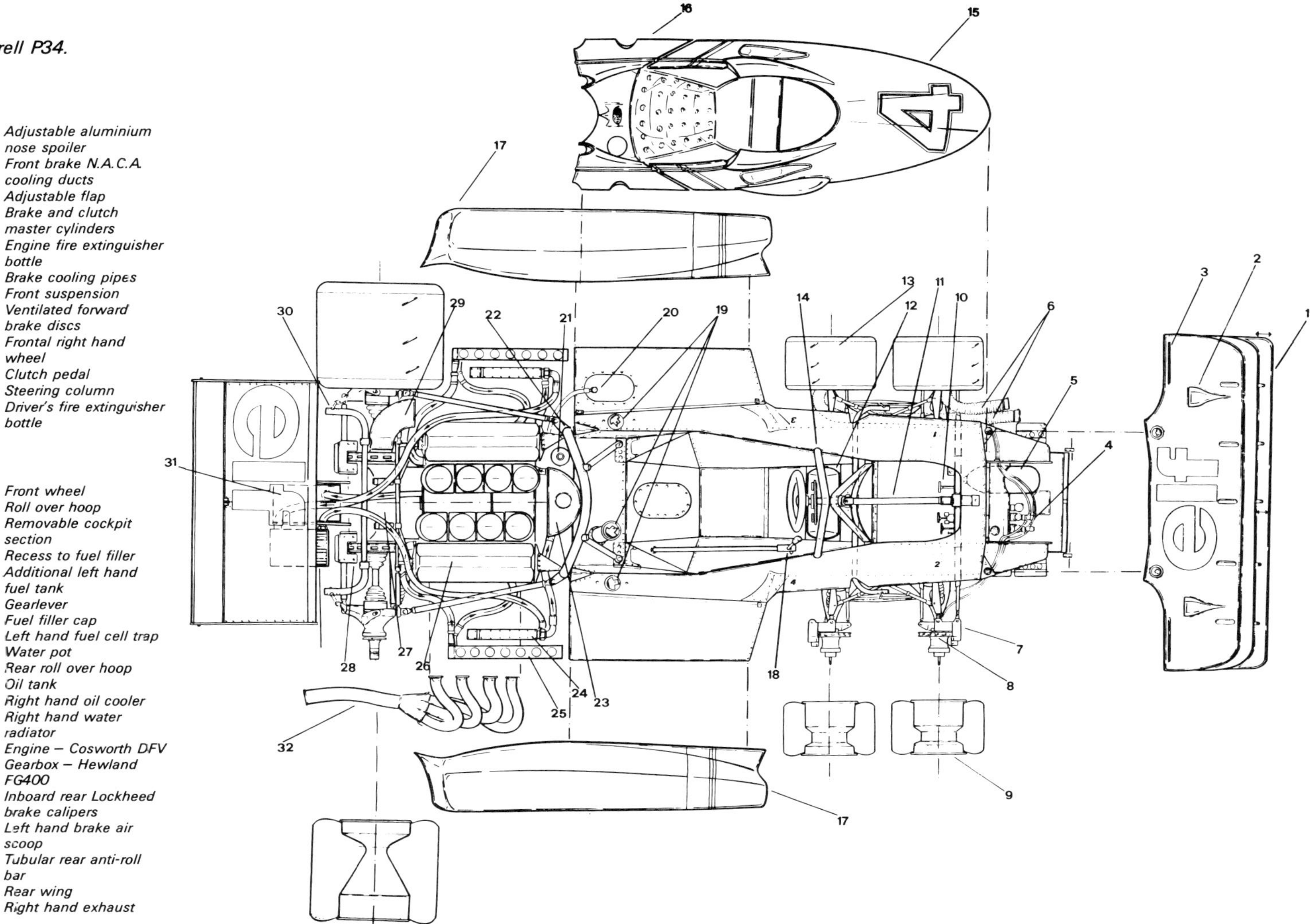

Tyrrell P34.

1) *Adjustable aluminium nose spoiler*
2) *Front brake N.A.C.A. cooling ducts*
3) *Adjustable flap*
4) *Brake and clutch master cylinders*
5) *Engine fire extinguisher bottle*
6) *Brake cooling pipes*
7) *Front suspension*
8) *Ventilated forward brake discs*
9) *Frontal right hand wheel*
10) *Clutch pedal*
11) *Steering column*
12) *Driver's fire extinguisher bottle*
13) *Front wheel*
14) *Roll over hoop*
15) *Removable cockpit section*
16) *Recess to fuel filler*
17) *Additional left hand fuel tank*
18) *Gearlever*
19) *Fuel filler cap*
20) *Left hand fuel cell trap*
21) *Water pot*
22) *Rear roll over hoop*
23) *Oil tank*
24) *Right hand oil cooler*
25) *Right hand water radiator*
26) *Engine – Cosworth DFV*
27) *Gearbox – Hewland FG400*
28) *Inboard rear Lockheed brake calipers*
29) *Left hand brake air scoop*
30) *Tubular rear anti-roll bar*
31) *Rear wing*
32) *Right hand exhaust*

Oil System
Twin Serck Oil coolers originally mounted on nose later mounted under the rear wing – Oil tank located between chassis and engine – Rubber stressed piping – Alloy fittings – Capacity 2½ gallons approx.

Fuel System
3 Marston fuel cells – Collector tank – Breakaway coupling on collector tank – Lucas HP pumps – Total capacity 42 gallons

Accessories – Safety
Graviner fire extinguisher, 5kg, under driver's knees – Graviner 2.5kg on nose frame – Medical air bottle – All electrically activated – Safety arrangement according to F.I.A. regulations – 6 point Willans safety harness – 2 Smiths dual pressure temperature gauges and rev counter – Originally Varley 12 volts battery, Lucas starter motor later replaced by an air starter system using the two 6 volt motorbike batteries for the general electrics

Bodywork
Entirely made with fibreglass fastened with quick release Dzus fasteners – Aluminium rear wing

Wheels – Tyres
Tyrrell design rims cast by Kent Alloys – 10 x 9 inches front (x 4) 13 x 18 inches rear, Goodyear Tyres

Engine
Ford Cosworth DFV

Dimensions
Wheelbase: 96.5 inches (245cm) Front axle (approx.)
78.5 inches (199cm) Rear axle (approx.)
Track: Front 48 inches (122cm) approx. same as for both front axles
Rear 62 inches (157.5cm) approx.
Total Weight: 620kg

Chapter 10

Ligier JS 7/9

Frenchman Guy Ligier has been involved in many forms of sport, including rowing, rugby and motorcycling and has won a number of French Championship titles in the various disciplines. In 1960 he discovered motor racing, first as a driver and then, in 1969, as a sports and racing car manufacturer.

Ligier spent most of his career alongside Jo Schlesser his great friend, who was killed during the 1968 French Grand Prix at Rouen circuit at the wheel of a Formula One Honda. Ligier's dedication to motor sport led him to compete in many international meetings, driving at first Formula One and Formula Two cars and later various makes of long distance G7 sports cars, including versions of his own JS (Jo Schlesser) Series, in which he distinguished himself.

In 1974, Ligier's dream came true when he signed an agreement with Gitanes (a brand name of Seita, the French tobacco concern) to build an all French Formula One car. A third member of this agreement was Matra, which was to supply its V12 engine for three consecutive seasons.

The agreement included the transfer from Matra to Ligier of engineers/draughtsmen and experienced mechanics, led by the engineer/Team Manager Gerard Ducarouge. All had been with Matra Sport since its debut in motor racing and became the head of Team Ligier from the beginning of its participation in Formula One.

Incidentally, the Matra aerospace Company "tested" its V12 on the Shadow DN7 in 1975, and fitted it to the first Ligier JS5 Formula One car in 1976. Driver Jacques Laffite showed the team's potential by collecting 19 World Championship points during the first year. The 1977 season, with a new JS7 was less successful due to engine problems, nevertheless Laffite won the Swedish Grand Prix and that, for the record book, was the first Grand Prix won by a French driver with an all French Formula One car.

Good preparation and driving resulted in an amazing race finish record, in 1978, when Ligier, like many other teams, was left behind by the Lotus wing car. Team Ligier was conscious that "ground effect" was the answer but its financial situation and an announcement from Matra that it was to end, once again, its involvement in Formula One, made things complicated.
A decision had to be taken on which engine to use for 1979. The Cosworth DFV was rightly chosen, in spite of a contact with Alfa Romeo, and so the JS11/JS15 ground effect car was designed around the "standard British power unit", coupled with the Hewland FG400 gear-box. The late Patrick Depailler joined Jacques Lafitte for the second drive and having won the first two races of the season with amazing ease, it seemed impossible for Ligier to lose the Championship but things started to go

wrong after Monaco when Patrick Depailler injured his legs during his leisure time. Gitanes intervened, insisting that a French orientated driver should replace Depailler, and Jacky Ickx was chosen. Sadly, his ability and experience weren't enough to fill the gap and added to this, accidents, mechanical failures, handling problems and finally the Ferrari T4 of Jody Scheckter destroyed the team's chance for the World Title.

In 1980 as expected, the main effort went to the exploitation of aerodynamics. Mechanically the major change was at the rear end of the car, where the brakes were put outboard for aerodynamic reasons, to obtain a better airflow exit at the back of the car. The chassis was kept in its original form, in the typical Matra way of building a light and rigid monocoque.

Didier Pironi joined Lafitte and they had become the car/driver combinations to beat by mid season. However, thereafter failure befell Ligier due to all sorts of misfortunes and misjudgements, and the Williams 007 and Alan Jones didn't help the team either.

In 1981 Matra surprisingly returned to Formula One with its familiar V12, externally "narrowed" in order to comply with ground effect requirements and this unit was fitted to the new JS17. Talbot also joined in and consequently the set-up became known as Team Talbot-Ligier. In the annual driver "re-shuffle", Pironi joined Ferrari and Jean Pierre Jabouille signed for Ligier, leaving Renault Sport after many years of association. Unfortunately, Jabouille's nasty crash in the last race of 1980 had left him with badly damaged legs and he found himself in the role of Team Technical Advisor. He was also appointed Team Manager when Gerard Ducarouge was dismissed. Patrick Tambay filled the vacant seat up until the end of the '81 season when Eddie Cheever was signed.

To the Ligier "resume", it should be added that the French government plays a major role as far as the financial situation is concerned.

Technically the Talbot-Ligier Team is always on the ball, but whether it will ever take the World Title is a different story.

The following technical details are based on the conventional JS7/9 of 1978 which used the Matra V12 engine and overall well illustrates the French approach to racing car design and technology.

Chassis

All the sheets employed for making the chassis are AU4G, in thicknesses varying from 8/10, 1.0–1.5mm, according to the area concerned. Before being riveted, all the panels are treated somehow then they are both bonded and riveted together. The chassis itself is also reinforced by a large number of fabricated rectangular and square steel frames (15 CDV6 in 8/10 – 1mm – 1.2mm) placed at the level of the driver's feet and knees. At the back and front of the chassis, the bulkheads receive the suspension and engine pick-up points, and thus take different loads. Chassis rigidity is increased by extra diaphragms equally divided, on the right and left hand side of the chassis, from the rear bulkhead to the dashboard level. This method of building the chassis is very highly renowned at Ligier, its thinking being to try to achieve maximum chassis rigidity for road holding as well as for driver's safety. The roll over bar is riveted at the top of the central fuel tank, with two extra bars bolted to the top of the engine cylinder heads.

The dashboard roll over bar is similar to the rear one but is riveted onto the chassis inner skin and at the top dashboard section. The naked chassis weighed 50kgs.

Fuel System

The JS7/9 has seven fuel tanks, all made by 'Superflexit', six alongside the driver and a central one housed right at the back of the monocoque. This unique arrangement comes from a Matra technique which has been kept all the way through the different Ligier JS Formula One cars as well as on the JS11/15 ground effect car. Each tank is connected to the others by a non-return valve. The idea is to empty, under acceleration, the front tanks first, rearwards, to arrive in the central tank.

The fuel system has no high pressure pump used for the initial start of the engine, instead three low pressure pumps fill up a small catch tank, consequently building up a certain inner pressure.

On the dashboard, a button governs an electro-valve which lets the fuel go into a little jet located within each engine inlet. Since there is not a collector pot as such, the engine is fed from another fitting of the catch tank, through a mechanical fuel pump to the metering unit; in fact similar to the Cosworth DFV fuel installation.

The fuel returns from the engine, goes directly into the central fuel tank and into the tank where the pressure is kept constant. However, as the amount of fuel returned is always greater than the feed, an overflow is added to the catch tank emptying into the main tank.

Dashboard Area

The dashboard controls are kept to a minimum: a Smiths engine tachometer and small Jaeger pressure and temperature gauges. A peculiarity of the controls is in the fact that one gauge indicates oil pressure while the other shows water temperature, both being electric. Oil temperature and fuel pressure can be checked by pressing a switch called "commuteur", which erases the normal oil pressure and water temperature, showing instead fuel pressure and oil temperature. The installation seems to be rather complicated since twin indicator gauges are available. However, once again, the idea has been picked up from the Matra generation. The rest of the dashboard controls comprise different electric switches and press buttons. The gauges themselves are rubber mounted on a single aluminium plate, to absorb the vibrations. Still around the dashboard, the steering wheel is bolted to a single column which is connected to the rack's pinion by an 'Apex' joint.

The steering column turns on a spherical joint, bolted to a fabricated steel box.

Dashboard and controls area. (Photo Nicolas Hollenwerger).

Vertical slots allow the setting or height of the steering wheel to be adjusted according to the driver's needs. The ignition switch is located to the left hand branch of the wheel.

On the right hand side of the cockpit, we find a gear lever fabricated from $^{4}/_{10}$mm steel sheet. From the lever to the gearbox, the gear linkage is made of steel tube and the different sections are joined together by a universal joint. The chassis inner skins are covered by the driver's foam seat, nicely finished with a cotton cover.

Safety

Safety starts in the fuel system where a non-return valve, placed in the lower part of the chassis and connected from the fuel catch tank to the engine mechanical pump, can interrupt the fuel flow if the engine separates from the chassis in an accident or when it happens during an engine change. The fire extinguishers are "standard"; a 5kg one for the driver and a 2.5kg one for the engine, both made by Ligier. The fire extinguishers can be set off by a mechanical arrangement; by pulling a handle from the

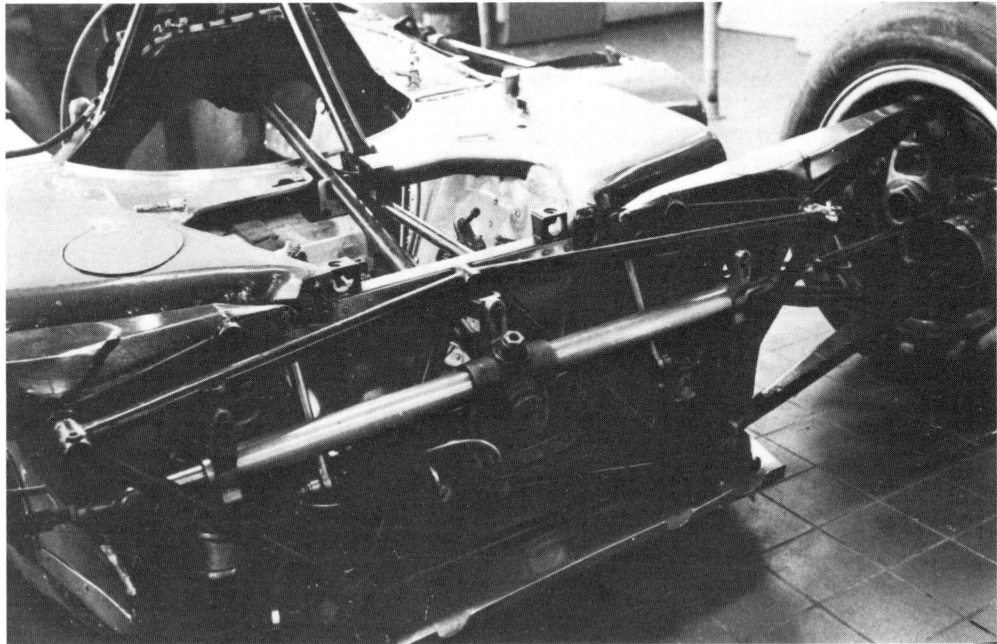

Steering suspension and brake arrangement. (Photo Nicolas Hollenwerger).

dashboard or from an external handle on the left hand side of the car. A cable acting on a trigger perforates simultaneously both bottle heads, then the bigger extinguisher empties into aluminium tubes drilled with numerous holes along the top area of the cockpit, spraying the driver's chest, legs and feet, and the small bottle empties in a similar manner with the piping finishing on the upper part of the engine, around the different parts of the fuel accessories.

The action of pulling the handles also instantaneously cuts all electrics passing through the master switch, stopping the different fuel pumps and other electrics functioning and cutting the ignition which obviously will stop the engine running. At the same time the "life bottle" will discharge its contents of oxygen into the drivers helmet for about 20 seconds. For weight distribution reasons the main fire extinguisher and life bottle are mounted on supports under the driver's knee bridge. The small bottle is located at the front end of the chassis between the inner and outer skin, at ankle level. Finally a Willans six point seat belt completes the safety layout which complies with the FIA safety rules.

Pedal Board

The pedal board is made entirely of aluminium, the clutch and throttle pedals being fabricated. The latter is connected to the engine guillotines by means of a small steel cable. The brake pedal is machined from a solid aluminium block. The brake balance is adjustable from the dashboard. The clutch is also controlled by a cable acting directly on the clutch fork on the gearbox. According to Ligier, this mechanical arrangement is lighter and more reliable than the hydraulic system, therefore master-cylinder pipeline, slave cylinder, etc., are not needed, thus avoiding possible oil leaks. On the left hand side of the clutch pedal, the lightened foot rest can be adjusted, as can the two other pedals, according to the driver's needs.

Steering System

The steering system is quite conventional. The box is machined from a solid block of magnesium. The rack and pinion are, of course, made of steel, then are heat treated before assembly and run on double ball bearings.

The box is entirely located on a frame hung from the front end of the chassis and supported by four double slotted aluminium blocks, which allow the bump steer adjustment to be made simultaneously for both wheels, since the track rods pick-up points on the uprights are fixed. The track rods are 15CDV6 steel tubing, terminated on both ends by titanium ball and socket joints bolted on the rack from a clevis and in sandwich, between two machined aluminium plates on the pivot. The whole arrangement, with a rack and pinion ratio of 11/1 and a large steering wheel, undoubtedly offers a light and easy steering movement.

Front Suspension

The top suspension arms are bulky 15CDV6 steel rockers, hinged on a pin going through the rack frame to the front end of the chassis. The inner part of the rocker takes the spring-damper combination (in turn bolted to a pick-up point) as well as the anti roll bar links, which act on a leverage to the interchangeable, fixed anti roll bar, also connected to the frame via double bearings. The outer part of the rockers have an old fashioned adjustable joint assembly going through the upper section of the uprights.

The bottom wishbones are made of two parts. The front part is fabricated 15CDV6 steel, picking-up on the rack's frame at the front and anchored at the lower end of the upright at the other end, where the wheel camber angle can be altered. The rear part of the wishbone is simply an aluminium S.A.R.M.A. bar bolted to the outer end of the front one, and buried into the chassis on the other end, and allowing castor angle adjustment. The complete wishbone swivels on machined titanium joints.

The uprights are cast aluminium, machined at the Ligier workshop for time and financial reasons. Steel axles, receiving a hard treatment process after being machined, and rolling on two ball bearings,

Front suspension and brakes layout. (Photo Jean Damon).

are kept apart by two aluminium spacers. The interesting thing about the stub axles is that the inner part acts as bearing tracks which obviously have only an external cage, tight fitted into the upright. The lot is closed and secured by a large titanium nut screwed onto the outer part of the axle, running freely without play. Externally the wheel is fixed onto the outer flat surface of the stub axle and is driven by four titanium pegs.

The brake discs are grooved on their outside circumference and are symmetrically drilled all around on both surfaces. The discs are held on their bells by a series of small bolts and are fitted free on to the axle.

A single unit, four piston, Girling brake caliper is bolted to the rear of the upright and secured by lockwire. The forward section of the uprights is also designed to take the outer track rods and the brake scoops.

Finally, the brake master cylinders are supported by the rack's frame, which also serves as quick lift jack point and nose support.

The brake pipelines are made of copper tube and run from the master cylinders along the chassis. From there the lines are joined with Aeroquip hoses to the calipers, in order to follow suspension movements.

Back end of chassis with water cooling system, oil and fuel accessories.

Water Cooling

The water is cooled by two Chausson aluminium radiators positioned slightly in angle alongside the engine and supported by an aluminium tube frame.

The general plumbing comprises aluminium pipes connected to the radiators and water pump with rubber hoses and jubilee clips.

On the forward part of the bodywork, surrounding the radiators, an air "activator" is added in order to guide the air flowing alongside the car, as much as possible to the cooling surfaces of the radiator which is also protected with a stoneguard. After passing through the radiators, the air is nicely ducted out at the back of the car by a deflector.

Oil Cooling

Oil cooling comprises two aluminium radiators located within the bodywork at the dashboard level. At the front of the side bodywork panels, the air coming from the inlet is ducted to the radiators and escapes to the top surface of the bodywork (the layout can be compared to a ground effect car where the cooling system is incorporated within the side pods). The plumbing is comprised in the main of aluminium pipes, high pressure resistance rubber hoses and union fitting, all metric sizes. It seems that because of the length of the Matra V12 engine, the oil tank could not be between the engine and the chassis and, as it was a crowded design, room was found on the left hand of the chassis at the driver level.

Oil level could be checked by removing a little trap, Dzus fastened to the top of the body.

Transmission – Rear Suspension

Transmission is by a Hewland FGA five speed gearbox, greatly modified by Ligier, in

Rear suspension and wing arrangement.

fact, the main casing, including the clutch bell housing, was entirely re-cast in Italy to Ligier drawings, in order to incorporate an oil sump in the main case.

The oil lubrication system was also improved and included an oil cooler placed between the wing support plates.

The rear suspension layout is in the standard fashion with two radius rods, two bottom parallel links and a single top link. All the bars are of the S.A.R.M.A. aeronautical type.

The uprights are likewise made of cast magnesium. The stub axles are machined and later treated like those at the front and run on a double ball bearing assembly. The wheels are also driven by four titanium pegs bolted and locked by a central aluminium nut, secured by a quick release clip.

The unusual gearbox crossbeam is of aluminium, machined entirely by outside contractors. It is fixed to the side plates of the gearbox and reinforced by a small triangular sub-structure for the pick-up points of top link and shock absorbers, consequently taking the suspension loads. The anti roll bar is also attached on each sub-structure and connected at the bottom of each upright by two small rods made of AU4G aluminium.

The bottom parallel links are anchored to the gearbox bell housing and onto the uprights, crossed by a simple pin-clevis which also serves as a bottom radius rod pick-up point. The top radius rod is also held onto the upright at a single point, both rods running onto the inner part of the chassis rear "bulkhead".

The drive shafts are the Glenzer Spicer type, made wholly of steel, with splined semi shafts sliding into each other, the end of the shafts attached via cross joints. The spline grease is sealed by a plastic ring retained on the outer semi shaft. The cross joints, in their housing, are inserted with a press fit on the inner part of the axle. On the gearbox side, the cross joint housing holds the drilled brake disc bell onto the gearbox drive shaft by four bolts, all being locked at a specific tightening torque.

However, the ventilated Lockheed discs are mounted free on their disc bell. The brake arrangement is completed either side by a single Girling four pistons caliper, the piping being of Aeroquip type.

Koni shock absorbers are anchored on the sub structure, at the top, and on the lower part of the uprights. Titanium rear springs complete the combination.

The rear wing is supported on two thin machined aluminium plates, bolted to the cross beam and gearbox back cover. The wing plates also serve as a quick lift jack point. According to Ligier, the type of wing mount was retained following intensive tests in the wind tunnel, since it turned out to be the most efficient.

The wing surface is made of 0.5mm AU4G aluminium, glued and riveted to five diaphragms, themselves made from AU26 which is a specific aluminium which lends itself well to being stamped out. All the work is carried out at Ligier and represents about thirty hours of labour. The wing incidence can be altered degree by degree from the twin drilled plates incorporated in the wing.

A Gurney flap is added to the main wing end plates and is also adjustable. The single front wing is made in the same manner and of the same material; it rests on the nose and can be adjusted, like the rear one. The gearbox oil cooler is located between the wing support plates and a red light is situated beneath the cooler. The rear end is completed by an electrical socket in to which is plugged the slave battery to start the engine externally.

Electrics

The electrics are basic and are designed and loomed at Ligier. The engine at first used a Marshall electronic ignition box but this was later on replaced by a Magnetti Marelli system. The same has been done with the starter motor, bolted directly to the engine. A 12V Varley battery operates the whole system.

Bodywork

The large bodywork is made entirely of fibreglass and is fixed by means of Dzus fasteners and pit pins. The air box is hidden under the engine cover.

Specification

Chassis
Aluminium sheets with fabricated 15CDV6 steel bulkheads – Steel roll over bars – Weight 50kg

Front Suspension
Fabricated 15CDV6 steel Top rockers, bottom wishbones half the same material as above, the other half S.A.R.M.A. bar – Tubular anti roll bar – Cast magnesium uprights – Inboard Koni shock absorbers spring combination – Ligier rack and pinion steering system – 11 to 1 ratio

Brakes – Front
Outboard AP Lockheed 26.4 cm ventilated discs – single Girling caliper – Ferodo DS11 pads – Girling master cylinder ⅞ inch – Brake balance adjustable from cockpit

Rear Suspension
Bottom twin parallel S.A.R.M.A. bars, Top single S.A.R.M.A. bar – Twin S.A.R.M.A. radius rods – Magnesium uprights – Tubular anti roll bar – Outboard Koni shock absorbers-spring combination – Anti roll bar (full) 15mm

Brakes – Rear
Inboard AP Lockheed 30cm ventilated discs – Single Girling calipers – Ferodo DS11 pads – Girling master cylinder 0.7 inch

Transmission
Ligier/Hewland FGA 5 speed gearbox – Glenzer-Spicer drive shafts and cross joints – Salisbury self locking system – Ratio $^{8}/_{35}$ – Borg and Beck dry disc clutch

Water Cooling
2 Chausson water radiators – Aluminium piping – Capacity 14 litres

Cutaway of the Ligier JS7/9. (Courtesy Gitanes).

Oil System

2 Serck aluminium coolers – Fabricated alloy tank – Total capacity 16 litres

Fuel System

7 Superflexit tanks – 225 litre capacity – Ligier design fuel circulation system

Safety – Accessories

5 and 2kg fire extinguishers and medical air bottle (F.I.A. norms) – Smith tachometer – Jeager electric gauges – 12v Varley battery – Magnetti Marelli starter motor and electronic ignition

Bodywork

Aluminium front and rear wings – Bodywork made entirely of fibre glass

Wheels and Tyres

Speedline rims – Front 11 x 13 inches – Rear 19 x 13 inches
Goodyear tyres – Front 10/0/22,13 – Rear 16/2/26, 13

Dimensions

Wheelbase: 280cm Rear Track: 151.1cm
Front Track: 172.5cm Weight: 610kgs

Chapter 11

Matra V12 Engine

The Matra phenomenon is simple yet complex. The name of Matra has been linked with motor racing from 1964 to present day in an on/off way. Matra is a French government owned Company which produced all sorts of transport machinery, but its main field is the construction of military missiles (Engins Matra) and other armaments and this employs about five thousand people.

Originally, a small group of men decided to get the name of Matra known around the world and they resolved to do this through motor racing. So when the small firm "Rene Bonnet" found itself in difficulty with its motor racing activities, Matra bought the lot and thus "Matra Sport" was created.

The first Matra racing car, the MS5 was a Formula Three car with a chassis design based upon rocket body building techniques and two cars were first entered for the 1965 Monaco meeting. After problems and frustrations, Jean Pierre Beltoise gave Matra its first win at the Reims circuit and in the same year he took the French Championship. A few months later Matra management spread rumours about a French Formula One car and sketches were drawn. However, Formula Two was the next logical step. The MS7 Formula Two car was an improved version of the MS5 which appeared in 1967 and immediately proved to be very competitive. The assault was launched with two cars for Beltoise and Henri Pescarolo. 'Matra International', Elf sponsored and managed by the Ken Tyrrell Organisation, entered two more cars for Jackie Stewart and Johnny Servoz-Gavin. Later these cars were handed to the John Coombs Team to release the pressure on Team Tyrrell which was running Formula One car as well.

Throughout '67, '68 and '69 the two teams dominated Formula Two and shared the European titles. In 1967 the government gave extra financial support and the go-ahead for an all French Formula One car. In 1968 Matra International was supplied with an MS10 chassis powered by Ford DFV, Jackie Stewart won three Grand Prix and lost the World Championship to Graham Hill in the last race of the season. The Dunlop shod MS10 used a full monocoque with tubular structure freeing the engine from suspension loads.

In France, in the meantime, the 3000cc Matra V12 engine was installed in a modified Formula Two chassis and testing began in the Spring of 1968. The engine proved rather large and heavy, although Beltoise managed to bring a few good early results home. His car, called MS11, had a full monocoque, but the engine was completely unstressed, as was common at that time. The overall uncompetitiveness of the car forced Matra, in 1969, to withdraw temporarily to re-think their concepts. However, in the same year, Matra

International (Team Tyrrell) continued using the MS10 until a new chassis appeared, the MS80.

The MS80 was very different to the MS10, keeping practically nothing except the Cosworth DFV engine, which was bolted directly to the chassis to form the rear end of the car, a fashion started by the Lotus 49. The basic principle of the chassis remained unaltered but it featured a bulbous monocoque forepart, concentrating fuel weight on either side of the cockpit, which explained its pot-bellied appearance. The car also carried new suspension and new front and rear wings. Later the general aspect of the car was altered by the lower wing imposed on Formula One by new regulations. During 1969 the car received a certain amount of modification, orientated mainly towards aerodynamics in general and at the end of the season, the combination Matra and Jackie Stewart and Team Tyrrell took the World Championship Title.

The MS84 was another Matra project which appeared in 1969. Four wheel drive was very much in fashion and like Lotus (63) and McLaren (M9A), Matra produced its own version. The Matra MS84 looked like the MS80 but had a tubular chassis in order to simplify the installation of the Ferguson transmission system. The main peculiarity of the car was that the engine and gearbox unit was turned around so that the gearbox was in front. The transfer box was on the output end of the gearbox and two shafts went from there to the front and rear differential, with a torque division of 25% to the front and 75% at the rear. The overall concept was quite complicated, and suffered from handling and traction problems. Jackie Stewart did some development in practice sessions but preferred the conventional MS80. French driver, Johnny Servoz-Gavin raced the car without the success hoped for by Matra. However, the MS84 was quickly developed to become, initially at least, the most competitive of the FWD cars. 1969 was the last year of the Tyrrell-Matra collaboration and from then on Tyrrell built its own car to be driven by Jackie Stewart.

In 1970 Matra Sport returned to the Formula One team line up. The object was to race an all French car. A totally new chassis design approach and the revised V12 engine put the team in better shape, but without really worrying the opposition. Its product, the MS120, had a flat and rectangular chassis. Its sides formed fuel tanks, designed with a negative angle of incidence, which helped to give aerodynamic "downforce" at high speed. The general aerodynamics and the suspension geometry had been totally redesigned and the car had a distinctly different look from other cars. Drastic changes to the chassis were reported as it became the MS120B of 1971 and the MS120C of 1972.

The MS120C featured new suspension geometry as well as revised details around the driving area (cockpit), rear wing surface and full nose, which got larger. For the first time, an airbox placed right over the engine inlets was used on a Formula One car.

In 1973, the MS120D received a different monocoque. It lost the angular look of the previous models to return to a rounded shape with a pot-bellied appearance. Weight distribution and suspension and aerodynamics were revised and this gave some happier moments to the team. However, it failed to win a Grand Prix other than the Argentinian Grand Prix, 1971 non-championship race won by Chris Anon, and in 1974 Matra Sport abandoned the Formula One scene altogether. The vast racing programme of Matra had included sport prototypes, from 1966. In contrast to Formula One, the sport prototype designs gave Matra an unprecedented success around the world. After numerous long distance race wins, including the Le Mans 24 Hours, and two World Championships of Makes titles, Matra announced its retirement from motor racing for "good", at the end of the '74 season.

Despite its retirement, Matra never lost contact with racing and in fact Matra technicians continued to develop the V12. In 1975 under the influence of racing driver Jean Pierre Jarier, Shadow designed a 'DN7' chassis to fit the V12 engine.

The DN7 was designed and built very hastily. It appeared that the car was much

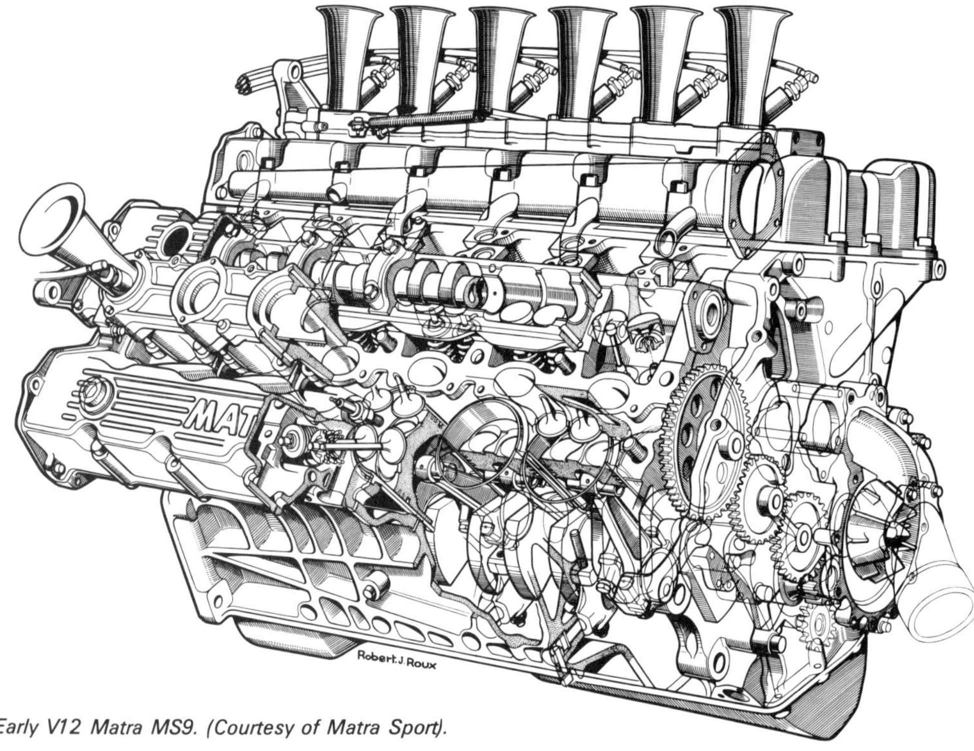

Early V12 Matra MS9. (Courtesy of Matra Sport).

too heavy since it had to carry more petrol to feed the V12 than a DFV required and it also had bad balance and weight distribution which was the cause of a poor handling and after only two races in Europe, the Matra-Shadow collaboration came to an end in September 1975.

It was certainly a very good experience for Matra to look into racing again to see what was going on, since a French Formula One project was under way at the Ligier workshop. The Ligier JS5 made its debut at the Brazilian Grand Prix with a V12 Matra engine at the back! This French connection lasted from 1976 to the last race of the 1978 season, with much success thanks to Jacques Lafitte, Ligier's only driver, who gave Matra its first official Formula One victory at the 1977 Swedish Grand prix, as well as many good results.

Financial reasons this time forced Matra to retire from Formula One, so Ligier had to fit the Universal Cosworth DFV to continue. On the other hand, with the demonstration of the Lotus 78, and the coming of ground effects, the Matra V12 engine would have been a little inconvenient because of its overall length.

At the beginning of the 1981 season, the Ligier-Matra association was reformed, under the Talbot banner.

Over the years since its first run, the V12 Matra engine received drastic changes and incessant development, as is briefly described below. Note that in the period 1967–70, Matra technicians created a flat 12 engine after Ferrari introduced its own flat 12. However, the Matra design did not go any further than a mock-up. Research on a supercharged single cylinder engine was carried out and was similarly abandoned after a short period of time.

Matra V12 Development

MS9

On December 19, 1967 the V12 ran for the first time on the dynamometer and it was later fitted on the MS11 chassis raced at the Monaco Grand Prix in 1968. Cylinder block and cylinder heads were made of AS9KG (NF) using a conventional ignition system. The inlets were placed on each bank of cylinder between the twin cam shafts. A power output of 390hp at 10,500rpm was not competitive enough for Formula One but was acceptable for long distance sports car races. Lack of smoothness and high fuel consumption caused it eventual withdrawal from Formula One, but development was carried on for use in the MS650 sports car.

MS12

Ironically, right from its debut, the MS9 engine was recognised by Matra engineers to be an old fashioned design. Also, apparently it suffered overheating which was impossible to cure. From then new cylinder heads were designed with inlets and exhaust valves inclined at 33° angle so the inlets appeared on the middle of the "V" and the cam shafts were covered by a single cover. The bottom end did not change but the engine was nominated MS12 and fitted to a Formula One chassis as well as on the 650 Prototype. Later on the engine was withdrawn from Formula One and fitted only to another sports car, the MS670, which won the 24 Heures du Mans in the hands of Graham Hill and Henri Pescarolo.

MS71

In the middle of 1971, the V12 had new cylinder heads and the valve angle was reduced to 15°. New lightened pistons improved torque due to a better air intake. Problems were found with the oil system, especially in the scavenge area. The MS120B Formula One car received the MS71 motor but handling problems were encountered.

MS72

This time the oil system was put right. For the last time the engine was seen on the MS120B and C Formula One car and in a Sport Prototype car. In 1973 Matra Sport stopped its activities in Formula One to concentrate only on the World Championship for Makes. It won virtually all the races and consequently the World Championship with the 650B chassis.

The power output of this MS72 engine was close to 450hp at 10,700rpm with a set of bigger valves for the short races.

MS73

In 1974, new cylinder head and piston design raised the power to 480hp at 11,200rpm and the team won for the second consecutive year the World Championship, as well as the 24 Heures du Mans. As we know, 1975 was the end of all Matra activities in motor racing but the engine was developed further to go in the Ligier car from 1976 to 1978. Finally, in 1978, the bottom end of the motor was shortened by 27mm to fit the Ligier JS7/9 chassis. The MS78 had a competitive output of 500-510bhp at 11,800rpm and this, combined with an excellent chassis and driver, put Ligier among the top runners, but the firm decision from the Matra management of retirement from racing put an end to the "screaming" V12, although the chances of a comeback were not ruled out.

Two years later, Matra returned once more to Formula One. During the two years of inactivity, research had been centred on ground effect chassis requirements. The main work was concentrated on narrowing the overall engine, in particular repositioning the oil pump mounting and other accessories. Intense work was also carried out to improve the fuel consumption by the adaptation of an electronic fuel metering system, but other than that the overall specifications remained very much the same as at the end of 1978

In 1981 the MS81 notched up three more wins for the V12, making a total of four in Formula One. 1982 saw Ligiers continuing with the V12 awaiting a turbo-charged V6 Matra engine.

The constant development and change

Matra MS81 modified to fit the Ligier JS17 Formula One car.

in design of the V12 engine was brought about by the fact that Matra never intended the V12 to be a commercial enterprise, unlike the Cosworth DFV engine. Basically, the engine had been a matter of national pride, encouraged by the French government.

It should be noted that any engine number or title is based on a modification of the previous engine and refers to the year it has been raced. For example, the engine which powered the Ligier JS7/9 was the MS78 but its basic characteristics are from the MS73, the one described below.

Engine Block

The general appearance of the engine block is rather conventional, but, nevertheless, it represents a very handsome piece of casting and machining. The engine block is made from AS19KG cast aluminium (French norms) and the front and rear of the engine are designed to take the various accessories. The lower part of the engine has two sections. The upper one is close to the crankshaft, having large grooves for the bob-weights and is very smooth in order to reduce to a miniumum aerodynamic turbulences created by the crankshaft assembly when running. It also recovers returned oil. The lower section, being the sump forming labyrinths/baffles to calm the oil, is connected to the scavenge pumps. The block is finally closed by a simple cover, maintaining the other two sections by a series of screws on each side of the block.

In the block water channels are provided around the cylinder liners and the water and oil joints are sealed by "O" rings.

Crankshaft

For reasons of balance two types of crankshaft have been used, called, consecutively, 6W and 4W.

The block and crankshaft during assembly process, note the distribution main pinion. (Photo Jean Damon).

The original 12 cylinder crankshaft, 6W, caused imbalance at high speed was later replaced by the new 4W design, as advised by the British engine bearing manufacturer, Vandervell. The 4W was a lot lighter, thus allowing a higher rotation speed. This enabled Matra to continue its engine development and to win the 1971 Le Mans 24 Hours. However, despite this success with the 4W, problems arose in 1978; these were related to the cylinder blocks and not, as at first thought, to the crankshaft. The cylinder block cracked due to the greater stresses on the main bearing caused by the speed of the engine and consequently Matra reverted to the 6W crankshaft, which was more expensive to make because of its overall design but did not pose any problems as far as the block was concerned. The diameter of the 6W and 4W crankshaft main bearings were the same.

From the point of view of the torsion of the crankshaft, Matra did not have any positive way of checking it. However, it was determined that the critical period for the 6W crankshaft was around 15,000rpm, tested on the dynamometer. For the 4W it was a higher rate. It appears that crankshaft breakages occurred on the test bench, this time due to the fact that the engine was mounted rigidly on the Froude dynamometer, which created a great inertia.

The crankshaft is made of nitrided steel (French norms) and is machined from solid. It revolves on seven main bearing caps assembled by means of two vertical bolts, therefore in the direction of the stresses and by means of two lateral bolts, thus avoiding any distortion of the bottom end of the engine. This type of assembly is peculiar to Matra as no other racing engine has shared this principle. Two con rods are mounted and bolted on each pin. Matra used titanium con rods and developed a method of protecting the faces, as slight seizure was observed on the faces that ran together on the pin at high speed. Matra continued to apply this method on the later steel con rods.

On the timing gear side the main pinion is a press fit on the nose of the crankshaft and secured by cotters. On the other side seven bolts hold the engine flywheel to the end of the crankshaft.

Strange as it may seem, a braid cotton seal and rubber seals were used for oil-sealing at the ends of the crankshaft. Knowing that braid cotton is as old as the invention of the automobile and in view of the rubber seals absorbing 4bhp at 12,000rpm, the latter system was retained on all engines. The drawback of the braid is that when assembling the crankshaft in the engine, it is so tight that it is difficult to turn it. Once the engine has turned over on the test-bench there is no longer friction and no leakage of oil. Although the braid is not a modern means, it appears to be very efficient. Tests were carried out on the test-bench without braid and no difference in power was observed.

Final assembly of the crankshaft into block, note the two con rods mounted on each pin. (Photo Jean Damon).

Partial view of the liners. (Photo Jean Damon).

Liners

The cylinder liners are made from neutralised forged steel. It was found at the beginning that the cylinder liners had too fine a finish; a coarse finish was tried and finally a compromise was arrived at. All these options were tried in order to minimise the wear of the liners. The liners press fit in the block, cold and "float" in their housings at the operating temperature of 90°C, and are sealed by means of "O" rings at the base. Although there are several methods of assembly used by various engine builders, Matra favoured the above method because the problems encountered in sealing materials with different rates of expansion were overcome. On the latest engines the sealings between cylinder liners and cylinder heads are ensured by circular gaskets similar to the Cooper joints as used on the Cosworth DFV and Ferrari 312 Boxer engines.

Con Rods

The steel con rods are machined from the solid. For balancing, the con rods were sorted out in pairs, but as they were machined almost entirely in the same way they were always of the same weight within the tolerances. The con rod belts were always tightened with a torque wrench, except in the latest engines where the tightening was effected by stretching the bolts. The principle of tightening by stretching is that the bolts are tightened with the tightening-torque stress being determined at the start, which in fact is a very accurate dispersion of the tightening torque. This being an accurate operation, it becomes a laboratory rather than garage assembly and certainly takes quite a long time to complete.

As Matra engines are built in small numbers and only they and Ligier use them, the stretching method is advantageous. For the Cosworth DFV engine, for example, it would be extremely time consuming as Cosworth engine production is quite considerable and the firm also produces other types of racing engine.

Con rod, piston with its rings and gudgeon pin. (Photo Jean Damon).

Bearings

The bearings are of a standard type made specially by the British Vandervell Company to dimensions determined by Matra. The shell is made of steel and has a layer of indium lead. In the rods, the bearings are held by a stop. The total longevity of the bearings in the 24 Hours Le Mans was 30 hours, including a test. In Formula One they were changed after 1,200km (approx 850 miles) for safety reasons.

Pistons

The pistons are forged in aluminium, like all conventional pistons. The gudgeon pins are forged steel and mounted free in the piston and con rod and held in position by two circlips.

The first engine (MS9) had the pistons with the head forming a ridge. The pistons used now have a flat head with four pockets necessary to give clearance to the valves when fully opened. The up-to-date pistons have two "L" shape compression and one oil scraper rings, although two piston rings have been tested in the past to measure the loss or gain in power.

At 12,000rpm the piston speed is approximately 20 metres per second. But, despite this speed, wear on the piston rings is very small. Nevertheless, they are changed during a general rebuild.

Cylinder heads with valve guides and their springs. (Photo Jean Damon).

Cylinder heads with inlet exhaust valves, seats and manifolds. (Photo Jean Damon).

Cylinder Heads

The cylinder heads are made from the same material as the engine block, that is to say AS19KG (FN). The design of the combustion chamber is similar to that of the Cosworth, Ferrari and other Formula One engines. The valve seats, made of aluminium-bronze and copper-nickel, are dipped in liquid nitrogen before assembly and can be replaced by (oven) heating the whole cylinder head to a pre-determined temperature. The valve guides are likewise made of bronze and the valve stems are sealed by a small rubber seal which is held against the stem by a little spring, as in a normal circular oil seal. The valve head diameter is 27.2mm for the exhaust and 33mm for the inlet. It can be seen from a photograph that there is a small space between the two valves. The spark plug housings are made up of threaded bronze inserts to take 10mm racing spark plugs.

Each valve is held on its seat by two springs made of OTW 60 (FN) for the inlet and OTW 70 (FN) for the exhaust. The quality of the springs can vary, according to the supply. For this reason they are checked one by one, before assembly. The springs are tested on a small test-bench made specially by Matra. They are on test for approximately six hours at 14,000rpm. The inlet down-draught forms part of the cylinder head. The gases enter through a single manifold which, at a certain distance, is divided into two small orifices emerging onto each inlet valve. For the outlet of the gases, the slides are mounted on small rollers with an adjusting stop at the end of the travel, full opening. Idling is effected by a small hole situated in the centre and corresponding to the centre of each manifold on the slide. For safety reasons the slides are returned by a large spring mounted on the fuel metering unit control rod.

The injectors are screwed onto the outside of the inlet trumpets secured by 3 nylock nuts.

Inside the "V" of the assembled cylinder

A cam carrier with exhaust camshaft. (Photo Jean Damon).

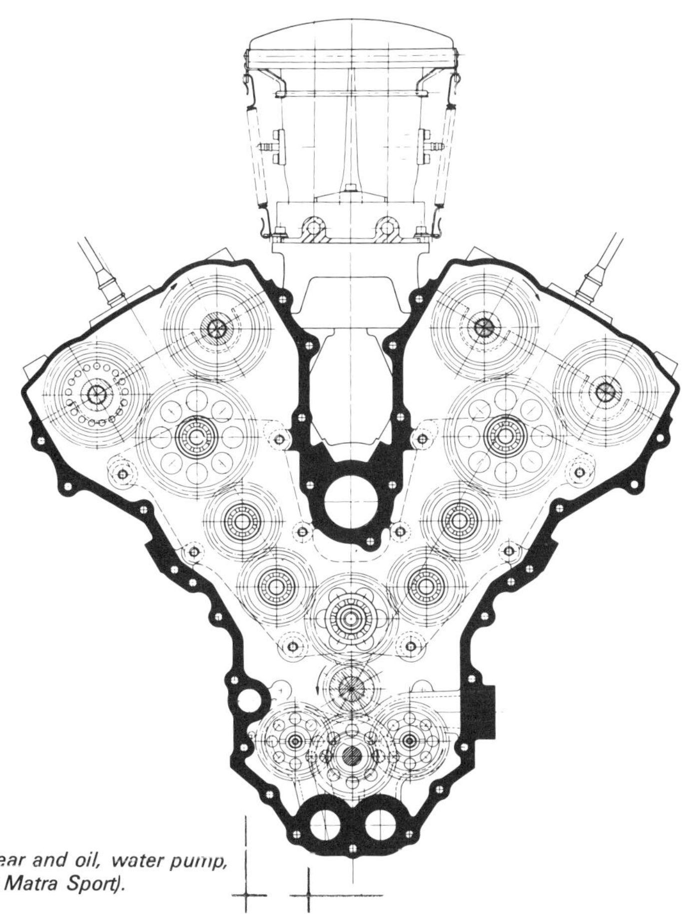

Layout of the timing gear and oil, water pump, driving gear. (Courtesy Matra Sport).

heads an enormous water channel, made of magnesium, passes through the whole length of the engine and is held in place by a series of 6mm bolts. This pipe communicates with the orifices of the block and cylinder heads for the water circulation and is directed towards the radiators, mounted alongside the chassis, by an unusual aluminium tube in the form of a Ram's horn, screwed to the central water channel.

Camshaft and Timing

The camshafts are made of hardened steel, Rockwell 55, and are machined at Matra. The cams push directly the buckets housed in the carriers and the operating clearance is provided by shims lodged between the valve stems and the inside of the buckets. Each camshaft is maintained in its seating by seven plain bearings. The assembly of the whole of the timing gear train represents a very nice piece of machining. The front of the engine is completely enclosed by a cover made of cast magnesium and having the "Y" shape of the engine. Looking at a photograph, two gearwheels can be seen driving the oil pressure pump and two scavenge pumps; higher up is the black gearwheel driving the water pump and in the middle of these two is inserted the main timing gear mounted above the crankshaft. Still higher there are three free gearwheels covered by a machined aluminium plate and finally right at the top, the spaces left by the camshaft gearwheels. Each gear rotates on two bearings, either needle or roller and the visible holes are covered by a small round piece of plastic. All the gears are made of case-hardened steel, therefore they are tough and durable. Generally the same gears are used over again. The clearance between each gear is adjustable. This clearance is governed by choosing the appropriate gear, all varying by a 100th of a millimetre. The camshafts are assembled in "standard" fashion, the setting of the timing being made on one shaft at a time and the operating clearance being adjusted beforehand.

For the timing setting the camshaft driving gear has a series of asymetric holes (the same number of holes is found on the camshaft flange, less one which after setting gives a stagger of 2.5° on each hole). A pin is inserted through the gear and camshaft flange in the appropriate holes and is locked by a large central nut. Finally, the engine is closed at the top by a single magnesium cast cover on each cylinder bank.

Water and Oil

On the left, outside the bottom of the block, there is the enormous oil filter, above which is the housing provided for the starter motor. At the front of the motor, on top, the water pipe, in the form of a Ram's horn, is connected to the central tube. Higher up on the right hand cylinder head the engagement of the revolution counter is driven mechanically, directly by the exhaust camshaft and is held by two small screws. On the left hand cylinder head the alternator, covered by an aluminium shell, is driven by the timing gear and can be clearly seen. Towards the bottom of the cylinder heads, in the centre of the "V", there is a 12 bladed water pump covered by another water pipe made of aluminium. Finally, right at the bottom of the block, the oil pressure and oil scavenge pumps forming a single piece are attached directly to the timing cover and engine block.

Fuel System

The fuel system is made entirely by Lucas, with the exception of the feed and return of the fuel which is incorporated in a small bottle placed inside the main petrol tanks of the car and is made by Ligier. The

The oil sump forming lower part of the block showing labyrinth/baffle with connections to scavenge pumps.

Ignition and fuel metering units arrangement. (Photo Jean Damon).

mechanical pump, identical to that of the Cosworth engine, is placed on the end cover of the left hand cylinder head and is driven by the inlet camshaft. The mixture is adjustable by turning and eccentric pin which passes through the cam which is connected to the slides by a small rod. The two slides are driven simultaneously by a spindle mounted on a bearing and are supported by a small block made of magnesium mounted to the bottom of the cylinder head. An electronic fuel metering control system has replaced the Lucas system.

To start the engine, as explained in the Ligier JS7/9 chapter, the car did not have a high-pressure pump, but a small fuel tank lodged in the main petrol tank, under slight pressure. A button on the dashboard activates this pressure, making it possible for the petrol to emerge into the bell-mouths via the small jets. Actually Ligier retained the same system on their cars equipped with the Cosworth engine and, later, on the 1981 Ligier-Matra JS17.

All the machining of the engine is sub-contracted, except for the camshafts and blocks.

Camshaft driving gear with the series of staggered assymetric holes. (Jean Damon).

Ignition

The ignition was originally of the Ducellier type, modified by Matra. The ignition pick-up formed part of the engine flywheel. With the new 1978 JS7/9 Formula One car, Ligier reduced the ride height of the chassis and the flywheel pick-up system could not be re-used because of this modification. In its place an electronic ignition system made entirely by Magnetti Marelli was used, but apparently this latter did not prove as accurate as the Ducellier system. Its distributor is placed at the rear of the right hand cylinder head and is driven directly by the inlet camshaft. The routing of the spark plugs cables leaving the distributor, together with the injection pump pipeline to the injectors, represents a tidy, well thought out job.

Specification

Configuration: V12 60°
Capacity: 2993cc
Bore: 79.7mm
Stroke: 50mm
Compression Ratio: 11.5 to 1 (approx)
BHP Rating: 525 (approx) at 12,200rpm
Torque: 33mkg at 10,000rpm
Valve Lift: 9mm
Firing Order: 1-11-5-9-3-12-6-8-2-10-4-7
Cylinder Configuration:

Front

6	12
5	11
4	10
3	9
2	8
1	7

Rear

Cylinder Block
Cast aluminium (19kg) bearing type general assembly

Crankshaft
Nitrided steel machined from solid.
Revolves in 7 main bearings, 4 con rod pins

Liners
Neutralised forged steel and finish in constant contact with water

Con Rods
Steel machined from solid

Pistons
Forged aluminium with 2 "L" shape compression and 1 oil scraper rings

Cylinder Heads
Cast aluminium (19kg) 2 (27.2mm) exhaust valves 2 (33mm) inlet valves per cylinder and assembled with double springs – 1 spark plug located in the middle of the combustion chamber

Carriers
Cast aluminium machined – Takes camshafts and buckets

Camshafts
(4) hardened steel Rockwell 55 – Each revolves on 7 bearings

Slides
Steel – Sliding on a series of rollers called back by a single large spring mounted on metering unit control rod

Manifold
Cast aluminium alloy – Inlet trumpets press formed with steel injector location and starting jets

Injection System
Lucas indirect injection shuttle metering system – Fuel pressure: 10K/cm^2

Ignition System
Originally Ducellier-Matra later replaced by a Magnetti Marelli system – Alternator Speed Limiter – Marshall spark plugs

Water System
1 large water pump

Oil System
1 Pressure pump – 2 scavenge pumps
Pressure: 8kg cm^2

Weight
170kg including starter motor

Chapter 12

Lotus 79

Lotus has always been the "innovator" in Formula One technology and certainly not concerned by design solutions of other teams apart, perhaps, from using little points through which performance can be improved. On the other hand, Team Lotus sometimes has been racing in the "dark" – victims of its own creative development. The situation became desperate in the mid seventies after some "misses" including the Lotus 76 and 77 but some serious thinking led the design department away from current standards.

Research into ground effect started back in 1975. The idea was to use the airflow under the car to create a downforce, thus loading the tyres to increase cornering power. The Lotus 78 was the first product of this research, and the first real "wing car". Basically it had a conventional chassis (three fuel cells, inboard brakes, outboard spring-damper, and side mounted radiators) and two large "aerofoils" mounted upside down alongside the chassis, producing that famous downforce. Of course, it wasn't as simple as that, but once the right principles had been achieved, work carried on with "details" such as venturi section, centre of pressure, trailing and intake edges etc., (see aerodynamics).

The attributes of the car were clearly noticeable on long corners where the ground effect system was at its most effective. The cost of the increase in cornering power was the diminution of straightline speed.

Originally, sealing of the side pods was done with brushes, later with plastic rubbing skirts and finally with rigid panels which were the "real thing" (see aerodynamics). The car won five races in 1977 and without a doubt would have taken the World Championship if many engine failures hadn't cost valuable points.

The Lotus 79 was another step further ahead of the 78-concept, exploring and using the venturi effect, with more downforce and less drag. This was effected by a slender chassis, rethinking of weight distribution, side pods as wide as possible with different sections, engine and gearbox enclosed, more effective skirts etc.; in fact everything to get smooth air flow under and above the car, which at the time, gave the car an appearance of being aerodynamically "clean".

Although performances of the 78 didn't seem to be conclusive evidence, the superb 79's amazing demonstration convinced everyone that ground effect was the way to go. In 1978 the car won seven Grands Prix each with embarrassing ease. Of course, everyone else copied the 79, which rapidly changed the face of Grand Prix racing.

Chassis

In order to obtain a maximum venturi surface, the chassis was very narrow, holding a large single fuel tank just behind the driver's shoulders.

The whole monocoque was formed of L72 16–18 gauge aluminium bonded and riveted together with small steel brackets, except for the anchorage points areas.

Still at the rear, the roll over bar was also made of aluminium and bolted at the top of the fuel-housing tank. For aerodynamic reasons, the roll over hoop was covered with an aluminium sheet riveted to the tubing. From the dashboard onwards, up to the nose frame, the chassis contained several aluminium bulkheads, closed by an aluminium sheet and forming a pitching dome with two large holes for access to pedals and dashboard control areas.

During its time in service, the chassis received minor detail changes, mainly in search of weight saving. The chassis was elongated with a small built-in aluminium monocoque nose frame which held the battery and wings.

The wings were fabricated from 24 gauge L72 aluminium filled with polystyrene foam and closed by two small end plates. They could be adjusted independently of each other.

The slim monocoque alone showed the way in ground effect design chassis building that the majority of teams were going to follow.

The dashboard was as normal with two temperature pressure indicator gauges and a tachometer, all Smith supplied and mounted on a panel recessed on the knee bulkhead. The hoop itself contained all the switches except for the ignition switch which was placed in the centre of the steering wheel.

Still within the cockpit area, on the left hand side there was a non-adjustable gear linkage made for each driver which apparently caused a few problems when the drivers had to switch from one car to another. The rest of the linkage was made of ⅝ inch 18 gauge T45 steel tubing, the two sections connected with apex joints.

Safety

The compulsory deformable structures around the fuel tank were of the standard 10mm thick honeycomb section bonded inside the tank bay.

The mandatory two fire extinguisher system was installed, the small one of 2kg capacity, mounted alongside the fuel tank area and supported by a large aluminium bracket. The large extinguisher of 5kg capacity was placed inside the cockpit area, underneath the driver's knees and the electrics master switch were closed by an aluminium panel forming bridge.

The life bottle was located on the fuel tank seat panel and hidden by the driver's seat.

The systems were entirely electrically powered from the dashboard and outside from the left hand side roll over hoop. Finally, a six point Willan safety harness completed the system.

Pedals Board

Nothing special about the pedals, which were made from 20 gauge 41/30 steel, heat treated, as well as the bracketry, bonded and riveted to the floor panel. For the driver, access to the pedals seemed easy enough despite a large recess for the inboard spring damper combination.

The two ⅞ inch brake and the 0.7 inch clutch master cylinders with the high plastic fluid reservoirs were located at the lower front part of the chassis.

Fuel System

An Aerotech made single fuel tank held 37 gallons of fuel. The engine was fed from a collector pot mounted centrally inside the main tank (incorporating a filter) with four remote pipe scoops in each corner of the tank, feeding the central collector pot.

The Bosch high pressure fuel pump was located right on top of the tank bay and served only to start the engine, the

Front section of the chassis. The nose tray contains front wing arrangement, brakes, master cylinder reservoir and battery – Lotus 79. (Photo Jean Damon).

Right hand front suspension and steering layout – Lotus 79. (Photo Jean Damon).

View of the dashboard. Note the rear anti roll bar adjustment lever and brake balance and adjustment knob both on the left hand side – Lotus 79. (Photo Jean Damon).

Front uprights and brake arrangement – Lotus 79.

plumbing being made of Aeroquip piping and fitting, complied with the Cosworth engine fuel system installation.

The Lotus 79 was the first of the recent Formula One cars to have a single fuel tank, which became a layout featured on all ground effect cars.

Front Suspension

The steering system included a Jack Knight rack and pinion housing with a 7/1 ratio, bolted stressed as part of the monocoque and placed just above the driver's legs and behind the front wheels. The racks' end ran on a bearing aluminium block bolted to the rear rocker plate. The aluminium track rods picked up on the rack and uprights from a clevis. The steering column was a single piece of tubing made to suit the driver, with a titanium muff-coupling connected to the pinion. The whole column was supported by a ball bearing at the dash hoop. The uprights were magnesium casting with the axle running on large diameter double row angular contact bearing of Lotus' own manufacture. The top section of the upright took the outer rocker bearing, crossed by a single pin forming also a clevis at one end for the track rod pick-up point.

The lower part took the wishbone's ball joint in double sheer with an added aluminium plate bolted underneath the upright. The ventilated 11 inch diameter brake discs were solidly bolted to their belt, freely sliding onto the "axle" drive pegs. The twin AP Lockheed calipers which replaced the original Lotus calipers were held to the uprights by two studs for each caliper. The inside face of the uprights was designed to accept a small fibreglass brake duct, ducting air through the centre of bearing and out through the eyes of the disc. The wheels were held on by a single nut-washer fixing which had a ⅝ inch UNF thread and was driven by six drive pegs. For an easy wheel fixing, the axle stud had a conical aluminium spacer added to it so the wheel centre could be guided and centred to the drive pegs.

The lower wishbones were fabricated from 20 gauge 41/30 steel, heat treated and anchored to the chassis in double sheer and on to the uprights with a large rose joint where wheel camber angle could easily be altered.

To reduce air turbulence (drag) the brake pipes ran inside the rearward wishbone tube. Again, this clever idea was retained on a few other Formula One cars. At the top, the suspension rockers were also fabricated of 41/30 steel, heat treated, pivoting and crossed by a steel pin on twin aluminium plates, themselves bolted directly to the monocoque and reinforced by a thrust bar. The outer end of the rocker articulated on a single rose joint taken in sandwich onto the upright. The whole design was aimed to steer the wheels from lock to lock without restriction. The inner side was assembled to the spring top platform and connected to the rocker on needle bearing and taking the damper rod from where the rebound setting could be accessible.

The anti roll bar was fitted on twin aluminium blocks and was connected to the rockers by two aluminium rods. The roll bar leverage was operated by a rigid aluminium lever on the left hand side and by a rotating blade on the right hand side; consequently its stiffness could be changed from the dashboard by the driver, according to the cars handling and without stopping at the pits. The shock absorbers and titanium spring combination were located in the driver's foot well, riveted to the monocoque, the dampers bump setting being accessible from a hole specially made for the purpose at the lower part of the chassis.

Rear Suspension – Transmission

Originally the Lotus 79 was fitted with a Lotus Getrag gearbox. A major fault within the gearing forced Lotus to design a new rear end to fit the "standard" Hewland FG400, this being modified and machined by Lotus in order to take the bell housing, also forming the oil tank. The bell housing bolted directly to the engine was designed to contain only 1.5 gallons of oil which, surprisingly, seemed to be enough to feed the engine oil system. The development of the Getrag gearbox was continued on other models of Lotus Formula One cars.

At the top of the gearbox, a catch tank came to be bolted and it was protected from the exhaust heat with a stainless steel shield. It received the oil return pipes from the engine, scavenge pump, cooler radiator and also acted as an oil tank filler. For the oil inlet it went from the bottom left hand side of the bell housing to the engine's oil pressure pump. Internally, the clutch mechanism was cast into it and was used co-axially on the gearbox input shaft with the necessary pipe work inside the bell housing. Such a system did not require a clutch fork and the free play was not adjustable as the bearing was facing the clutch's pressure plate constantly with little hydraulic pressure, consequently always turning at the engine speed.

Obviously the whole bell housing required a rather long input shaft going from the gearbox to the clutch discs and sealed from the gear box and engine with rubber seals.

This system was something else that Lotus pioneered. The other modification that the Hewland gearbox received was to the side plates which had the inboard brake half calipers cast into them, the other half of the caliper being a separate casting which was bolted on them and of Lotus design and manufacture.

The ventilated discs were supplied by AP Lockheed, and had Ferodo pads. Aeroquip supplied the steel braced pipe work. The arrangement was quite impressive, since the four calipers were enormous, giving the impression of tremendous braking power. However, less impressive was the fact that the lower part of the shock absorbers picked-up on the external half of the calipers; a hazardous

The rear end. Note the right hand brake caliper and its damper pick-up location – Lotus 79. (Photo Jean Damon).

layout, but it certainly was "different", and it worked. The lower suspension wishbone picked up on a machined aluminium plate sandwiched between the main cage and bearing carrier of the gearbox. Oil cooling was via a single oil cooler placed on the left hand side of the chassis above the engine oil radiator, but this necessitated a rather long pipe run from the gearbox oil pump to the cooler; this was for the reason of better air flow around the back of the car. The air operated starter motor was mounted alongside the bell housing on the left side. This air starter was based on an air drill system with the casting and gearing manufactured by Lotus and a small onboard bottle was placed at the back of the chassis on the right hand side, cable operated from the cockpit in case an emergency start was necessary, but usually operated from outside. The back of the gearbox carried the usual red light, quick lift point, oil filter etc., and all in machined aluminium plates.

The suspension top rockers were fabricated of 41/30 steel, heat treated pivoting on a single pin from the cross beam at the rear end and a tubular frame bolted to the gearbox engine. The inner part of the rocker attacked the inboard Koni shock absorber titanium spring combination directly; further out a bush received the anti roll bar blades. The outer part moved on a ball bearing and bolted in double sheer on top of the upright.

The rear part of the rocker had an aluminium link with double rose joint left and right handed for toe-in or toe-out adjustment and joined to the upright.

The lower wishbone was also made of 41/30 steel tubing, picking up to the lower part of the gearbox and connecting to the upright where the wheel camber adjustment could be altered by lengthening or shortening the large rose joint locked by a double bolt squeezing its own threaded bush.

The uprights were fabricated in the same way, and from the same material as the top rockers. The steel axles ran on double angular contact bearing designed by Lotus; similar to the front layout but this time it was machined on the outside of a

General view of the back of the chassis without engine or transmission and engine oil cooler is on the left hand side – Lotus 79.

constant velocity joint. The wheel pin was the ⅝ inch UNF single pin, washer and nut arrangement with six drive pegs, at the front end. Steel drive shafts were connected to the gearbox output shafts by a Lobro type joint which had an inner/outer tracks ball system, holding also the brake discs against the gearbox output shafts by a series of ⅜ inch UNF nuts and bolts. The wheel axle was also connected to a Lobro type of constant velocity joint designed by Lotus and produced by Ransome/Hoffman/Pollard, specifically for Lotus' racing department. On both sides, the joints and grease were protected with a rubber cover, the whole design representing a very neat arrangement.

The adjustable roll bar was connected to the cross beam by two double rose joints. The right hand blade rotated on 90° travel from a cable worked from the dashboard, while the left hand blade was kept in only one position. Finally, the gearbox cross beam was made of 41/30 steel tube, heat treated as well. Originally it was formed with a single machined aluminium plate, later it was made from steel tubes. Details to the anti roll bar mounts also changed according to changing needs, mainly due to the change from Lotus-Getrag to Hewland gearbox.

Water-Oil Cooling

The water system had a large single radiator mounted on the right hand side of the chassis. The original Marston had been replaced later on by aluminium Serck coolers of six or four rows according to the ambient track temperature, and the cooler was joined to the engine's water pump by two 1¼ inch diameter aluminium pipes connected with a rubber and jubilee clip combination. Changes appeared later on within the water pipes running from the bottom to the top of the radiator.

The system was filled up from an aluminium water pot located right at the back and on top of the chassis fuel tank. It also received the usual air bleeding pipe from the radiator. The water filling pipe

joined directly to the engine right hand water pump. Both pipes were dash 10 Aeroquip pipe and unions.

The oil cooling system initially had a single Marston, later a single Serck radiator mounted on the left side of the chassis, opposite the water cooler. Its positioning required rather long plumbing running to the bell housing oil tank. Both main radiators were secured to the sides of the monocoque by a tensioned wire arrangement which actually clamped the radiators onto the chassis. The method was later replaced by a single aluminium rod on each radiator.

The fibreglass air exit ducts were in one piece for each radiator, separate from the rest of the bodywork and consequently easy to adapt, sealing pretty well the surrounding of the radiators.

Electrics

As on most British Formula One cars, the electrical system of the Lotus 79 was reduced to simplicity; no fuses at all and only a small 12v YUASA battery was used, thanks to the air starter system. The wiring was of B.I.C.C. green fireproof cable with Rotax switches, the loom being formed at Lotus. Finally, a Lucas electronic ignition designed for the Cosworth DFV set-up was located between the "V".

Bodywork

The Lotus 79 had side pods on the venturi principle, in which air entering up front was accelerated to exit cleanly at the rear of the car. The wing sections were designed and made by Lotus and bolted to the side of the monocoque. They were full length, one piece, made of fibre glass, one for each side, and had a small stone guard in the aperture at the front in order to protect the radiator. Underneath each side pod was a pair of "Vortex generators", which were small aluminium devices made to accelerate the air under the car. The side pods extended rearwards alongside the top section of the engine, supported by an aluminium frame on each side of the monocoque and enclosed by an undertray, so improving the air flow exiting at the back. The movable skirts, mounted freely in each side pod wall, sealed the venturi "U" section air chamber against the road surface to enclose the low pressure area, (see ground effect system). They were made from what became the popular honeycomb material for great strength and light weight. The lower part of the skirt, constantly rubbing the ground, was a combination of plastic strip and ceramic tube section for longer life. As skirts are very important items of a ground effect system, they required constant servicing. The skirts dropped with their own weight on plastic "rollers" and stayed in contact with the ground as the chassis ride height changed. A little retaining device prevented the skirts falling out if the car became airborne, or when the whole car was lifted up on jacks at the pits.

Apart from the side pods, the rest of the bodywork was made in three fibreglass sections. The upper surface, which included the chisel nose and cockpit, enveloped the entire top engine area and extended right to the back over the gearbox with the exhaust tail pipes emerging through an opening in the middle of it. Rear brakes cooling operated from a N.A.C.A. duct cast on the engine cover

The rear wing had an unusual arrangement in that what was known as a rear deck, of fibreglass, also picked up off the side pods, resting on the suspension cross beam and at the back of the gearbox where two large side plates held the aerofoil, the latter constructed in the same way as the front wings. Finally, flick-ups were added to fair in the rear wheels, improving the air flow around the rear wing. The entire top bodywork sections were held with Dzus fasteners.

Note that the majority of nuts and bolts are of metric size.

Indeed a superb looking car, masterfully engineered.

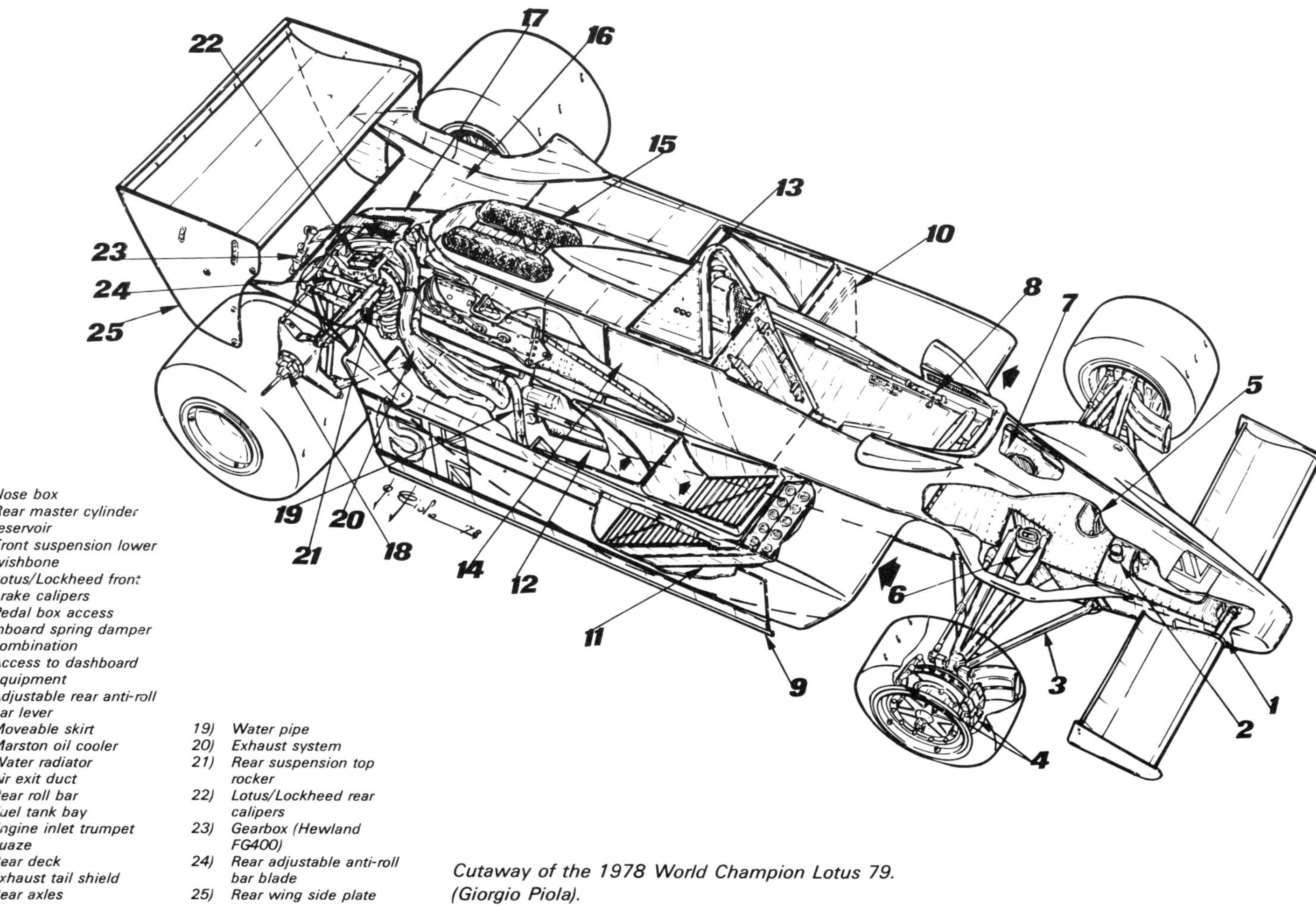

1) Nose box
2) Rear master cylinder reservoir
3) Front suspension lower wishbone
4) Lotus/Lockheed front brake calipers
5) Pedal box access
6) Inboard spring damper combination
7) Access to dashboard equipment
8) Adjustable rear anti-roll bar lever
9) Moveable skirt
10) Marston oil cooler
11) Water radiator
12) Air exit duct
13) Rear roll bar
14) Fuel tank bay
15) Engine inlet trumpet guaze
16) Rear deck
17) Exhaust tail shield
18) Rear axles
19) Water pipe
20) Exhaust system
21) Rear suspension top rocker
22) Lotus/Lockheed rear calipers
23) Gearbox (Hewland FG400)
24) Rear adjustable anti-roll bar blade
25) Rear wing side plate

Cutaway of the 1978 World Champion Lotus 79. (Giorgio Piola).

Specification

Chassis
L72 18–16 gauge Aluminium sheets – Weight 80lbs.

Transmission
Lotus Getrag
Hewland FG400 – Five speeds
Lotus drive shafts – Lotus/Ransome/Hoffman /Pollard constant velocity joints.
Borg & Beck clutch – Pressure plates, twin dry discs

Rear Suspension
41/30 steel fabricated uprights – 41/30 steel top rocker arms – 41/30 steel bottom wishbones – Inboard Koni shock absorber – Titanium springs – Adjustable anti roll bar – Track 68 inches – Goodyear tyres 17–18 inch – Speedline wheels – Dimag rims

Front Suspension
Cast magnesium uprights – 41/30 steel top rocker arms – 41/30 steel bottom wishbones – Inboard Koni shock absorber – Titanium springs – Jack Knight rack and pinion – 7/1 ratio – Adjustable anti roll bar – Track 64 inches – Goodyear tyres, 13 inches – Speedline wheels – Dimag rims

Brakes
Outboard front – Inboard rear – Lotus/Lockheed calipers – Lockheed ventilated discs – Ferodo DS11 pads

Wheel Base
108 inches

Oil Cooling System
One Marston or Serck aluminium radiator, capacity two gallons (approx.) – Valvoline lubricant – Aeroquip pipes and unions

Water Cooling
One Marston or Serck 4–6 row aluminium radiator – Capacity 2½ gallons (approx.) – Aluminium piping

Fuel System
One Aerotech fuel cell – 37 gallon capacity – Bosch high pressure pump

Accessories
Smiths gauges – 12 volt YUASA battery – Dreadnought extingushers – Life bottle

Engine
Ford Coswoth DFV

Total Weight
1270lbs (577kgs)

No. of Cars Built
Five (1978–1979)

Formula One World Champion 1978 – Driver, Mario Andretti

Chapter 13

Ford Cosworth DFV Engine

Much has been written and discussed about the Ford Grand Prix engine since the moment it was conceived, many of these stories being inaccurate. For the sake of abbreviation and for more details about the creation of the DFV engine, readers are advised to refer to the book *The Story of the Ford Grand Prix Engine* by Blunsden and Phipps.

Originally, when the 1.5-litre normally aspirated Formula came to an end in 1966, Coventry Climax ceased its activites in this field, leaving Maserati, fundamentally with a very old-fashioned and heavy underpowered engine, BRM with its complicated and unreliable H16 and the Australian Repco engine, which Brabham used exclusively, as Grand Prix engine suppliers. This meant that the situation was very restricted as regards the choice of an engine to use for the new 3-litre Formula One.

It was then that Ford appeared on the scene, sponsoring Cosworth Engineering in the production of the Formula Two 1600cc (FVA) and the Formula One 3000cc (DFV) engines. Lotus were also involved in this project and were at first the only team to be supplied and supported.

In the meantime, Lotus used the BRM H16 with which only Jim Clark won a Grand Prix, taking the USA Grand Prix in 1966. Other teams gambled, such as McLaren, with the Alfa Romeo and Serrinissima engines, but without success. McLaren also struggled with the BRM engines until they were able to purchase a Ford Cosworth DFV, while others carried on with Maserati or Repco, until the DFV was available to them.

The Ford Cosworth Formula Two engine saw the light of day at the end of 1967 and immediately proved to be competitive, equipping most of the Formula and dominating it almost without any opposition, except that provided by the BMW factory. The DFV Formula One engine was designed so as to be compact, in order to fit the layout of the chassis and to be rigid enough to support the chassis, gearbox and suspension and cornering loads; in other words, to act as a stress member.

At the end of 1966 the engine was running on the dynamometer and in April of the following year it was officially presented to the Press in London and handed over to Lotus.

It was intended that the new Lotus 49 DFV should make its debut at the 1967 Monaco Grand Prix but first appeared later at the Dutch Grand Prix, in the hands of Jim Clark and Graham Hill. In spite of many troubles with the new car Graham Hill managed to set fastest time in practice. During the race, he had to make a pit stop with engine trouble. Clark was running among the leaders and eventually took the lead and, despite engine trouble during the

late stages of the race, managed to win from Jack Brabham. It was the beginning of a long series of victories which made Cosworth famous throughout the Motor Racing world. Today Cosworth Engineering is a notable and established firm which produces many different types of racing engines from Formula Two to the supercharged DFX which is equipping most of the American U.S.A.C. cars. It has also won the 24 Hours of Le Mans, and is still very much in use in today's Group C cars.

The first DFV gave 400bhp at 9000rpm, but like anything new, little problems arose, especially with the timing gear layout. Later on during the '70s big problems made themselves known with the crankshaft, which were due to a manufacturing defect.

Building and racing a Formula One car to the minimum weight imposed by the rules is of constant concern among constructors. Understandably there are still difficulties to overcome. Nowadays the application of light materials such as carbon fibre eases the problem at the cost of high expenditure. Knowing that, back in 1977, Cosworth came up with the theory that a saving in engine weight would have an appreciable effect on the overall weight of the car, thus providing better lap times.

The idea was debatable, since the performance of a Formula One car doesn't depend only on being within the weight limit but also on a number of other factors. Nevertheless, Cosworth produced a small series of engines with block and cylinder heads made entirely of magnesium which notably reduced the overall unit's weight. This was then loaned to leading teams under a mutual agreement that the engines would be rebuilt by Cosworth only (the cam covers were "sealed"). This series was called Development Engines.

On the track, the theory certainly worked, perhaps not to the extent of giving a full second a lap, but an appreciable fraction of a second. Was this due to the weight reduction or to the better engine power output? It's difficult to say. Ironically, or unfortunately, the lighter units weren't too reliable and were dropped at the end of the season for the more conventional design. Rightly, credit should be given to Cosworth for their worthwhile effort.

The DFV has won more than 150 Grand Prix and is still winning races (1982). Turbo charging seems to take a greater emphasis every year and could in time seriously threaten the life of the DFV.

There is little that can be done to improve the power output of a 3000cc Cosworth normally aspirated racing engine in its present form, except that if a desmodromic valve gear system could be adapted it would raise the rpm limit and, above all, improve the breathing, therefore efficiency at the top end of the speed. The idea would, of course, require a lot of work and development before use, but it's not impossible. (The desmodromic valve gear system is a complex mechanical arrangement of levers rockers cams to close the valves which would eliminate the use of the conventional springs). The system is old, like the automobile, and is used in motorcycle racing and for road bikes by Ducatti.

The DFV has remained very competitive since its first appearance and powers the majority of Formula One cars, while the turbocharged cars have yet to achieve a satisfactory reliability.

The following descriptions of this superb V8 is based on 1982 versions.

The Block

The block is aluminium with a five main bearing crank. Three main bearings are formed by the sump and two are formed by caps. Front bearing, centre bearing, rear bearing; the main caps are the sump. The early ones were formed by five sump bearings. The caps are aligned with one dowel either side and the caps are tightened regularly so that the gap between the cap and block is kept square; when achieved the dowels are locked, the feeler gauge is slid out and both sides are slowly torqued. A hole underneath the metering unit is to allow for any leakage such as fuel or water going through the right hand bank just underneath the cylinder.

The Ford Cosworth DFV block and liners, note the vertical grooves.

Liners

The eight cast iron liners are in constant contact with water. In case of a blow-up the liners can be changed by keeping the standard bore and machining its location in the box to accept a bigger external diameter liner. The inner bore is perfectly straight, the outside of the liner has on its bottom two "O" rings, the top flange rests on the counter bore and is sealed with sealing compound. The sequence of putting the liners in the block is that first the block has to be cleaned and prepared, together with the liners, all marked for correct position within the block. The block is then heated to 150°C to receive the liners. The liner must be a certain distance down from the top of the block and the sealing between cylinder head and block is secured by a Cooper ring, located in a recess formed between liner and the cylinder block. At normal running temperature the liners are tight in the block. Grooves machined on top of the block at the edge between the liners give an indication of any leaks from head gasket and cylinder head.

Crankshaft

The crankshaft is steel forged and finished at Cosworth. It is of single plane shape, very similar to a four cylinder engine; on one end a boss takes the flywheel with eight ⅜ inch UNF bolts, on the other end is the location for the timing gear. The crankshaft revolves on five main bearings. No. 2 and no. 4, hold the crankshaft in position. Originally the engine was giving a reading of 85–90psi oil pressure, then Cosworth modified the oil pump and achieved an oil pressure of 100+psi, which does not change engine speed. The latest modification was a new crankshaft but the same pump as before with a relief valve modification to run at a lower pressure, 60psi but with a better oil feed. The crankshaft has five journals, four pins and two con rods mounted on each pin next to each other, like any Formula One engine. On the timing gears side the crank gear drives the series of gears, the main pinion is mounted press fit and located on one dial. The oil sealing on each end of the crankshaft is made simply by a conventional

The crankshaft mounted on block – Ford Cosworth DFV.

The liner, con rod and piston showing valve pockets and gudgeon pin – Ford Cosworth DFV.

oil seal retained on the flywheel side by a retaining ring and on the front of the engine the oil seal is pushed in the front timing gear cover and secured by three little screws.

Con Rods

The con rods are steel forged and in the piston end there is a mixture of soft metal alloy (Vandervell lead indium shells), while on the big end is just a plain shell bearing held by a cup and two ⅜ inch UNC high tensile steel bolts. The tightening is conventional. The outside of the con rod is shot peened for extra strength.

Pistons

The pistons are forged aluminium by Cosworth and retained on the con rod by a gudgeon pin, itself retained by two circlips. Between the gudgeon pin and circlips are dished synthetic washers. With such an assembly the gudgeon pin is free between the con rod and piston. The piston crown is pocketed to give clearance to the valves and is machined after a dummy assembly to give correct clearance between piston and cylinder head, as recommended by Cosworth. The pistons have three rings; two compression and one oil scraper.

Cylinder Head

The cylinder head is aluminium with aluminium, bronze and copper nickel valve seats and guides which are easily replaceable. There are four valves per cylinder, and a central spark plug hole.

On the front of the cylinder is an idler gear which drives the camshaft pinions mounted on a roller bearing on a steel pin which protrudes from the cylinder head. All valves are assembled with double spring; the length of the springs are governed by the shims underneath, to set all springs at the same height and rate. The springs are held to the valves by a top cap and two retainers, in the conventional way. The valves are different material because obviously the exhaust valve has to cope with the heat while the inlet valves can run much cooler. The valve stem is sealed to the guide by a rubbery seal which is held against the valve stem by a little spring as in a normal oil seal, and that in turn is held on to the guide by the bottom spring platform. The stem of the valve is round and

Cylinder head (shown upside-down) with valves – Ford Cosworth DFV.

parallel where it runs in the guide but where it runs through the port it's a lot thinner to allow better gas flow into and out of the combustion chamber. 10 studs hold the cylinder head to the block, four smaller studs on each outside edge which stabilises it. Seen from the top the inlets ports are oval to begin with and end as two passages with a very thin and sharp wall between them. The walls are very smooth for minimum turbulence. The size of the inlet valve is 1.36 inch (34.5mm) and 1.14 inch (29mm) for exhaust. The exhaust outlets have roughly the same shape but a smaller diameter than the inlet. The exhaust pipes are held to it by four ¼ inch UNF studs, assembled to the engine and sealed by an asbestos and foil gasket.

Cam Carrier

The cam carrier is of aluminium and is retained by studs which also retain the cam bearing caps and eight cap screws. The cam carrier carries the tappet brackets and cams in its own assembly and a small shim is located between the valve stem and

Same as preceding picture but correct way up. Note the inlet ports – Ford Cosworth DFV.

Cam carrier with camshaft, inlet and exhaust valves, spring, cup and bucket – Ford Cosworth.

tappet bucket and that governs valve clearance. Buckets and shims are steel.

Camshaft

The steel camshaft rests on plain shell bearings and five caps. When the camshaft location is machined, all caps are mounted blank and the assembly is line bored to produce a perfect straight alignment of the bearings and caps. The caps are numbered to avoid incorrect replacement. The inlet and outlet cams are the same shape, but cannot be wrongly installed because the difference in distance between the lobes due to the different diameter of inlet and exhaust valve heads. At the front and rear of the front bearing is a shoulder which prevents the camshaft from moving.

On the back of the engine a small magnesium plate is held to the cylinder head by four ¼ inch UNC bolts cap heads and a 5/16 inch UNC cap head with a big washer. Another magnesium plate is bolted to the cam carrier in a similar manner and these seal the rear of the cylinder head and cam carrier.

To lubricate the cam an oil passage passes through the cylinder head from the block to the centre camshaft bearing and the camshaft being hollow the oil passes to the other bearings as well. At the end of the camshafts a bung prevents the oil escaping. The cam cover is also cast magnesium bolted to the carrier by a series of twenty-two 10/32 inch UNF cap heads around its edge and down its centre are ten 5/16 inch nuts and washers.

The front of the cam cover is designed to form part of the engine mounting. Four 5/16 inch bolts secure an engine plate to the cam cover and this is in turn bolted to the chassis by a single ⅜ inch UNF bolt. At the bottom of the sump is bolted an aluminium mounting block which is designed to be bolted to the chassis by two ⅜ inch studs coming out of the chassis.

Looking inside the "V" the manifold main body is bolted to the cylinder head by four UNF bolts per cylinder and sealed to the cylinder head by a ⅛ inch Tufnel spacer. This spacer also prevents heat being transferred into the inlet manifold from the cylinder head. In the manifold body is a drilling from front to rear which forms part of the fuel system itself. The fuel is passed through the manifold in this way so that the incoming air which cools the manifold keeps the fuel cool before it returns to the fuel tank.

Manifold and slide arrangement – Ford Cosworth DFV.

Slides

The slides rest on a series of ball bearings and rollers. The slide movement is from front to back. The guillotine travel is limited by little plastic stops so that a minimum amount of throttle opening can be maintained, and also when fully opened the throttle slide/guillotine is in exactly the correct open position in alignment with the holes in the manifold. The guillotine is returned by two little springs located on the back of the manifold and supported by two little plastic plungers. The way in which these springs are mounted results in them both acting upon the same point on the guillotine and provides a constant pressure. These springs are also aided by two additional springs mounted to suit different throttle pedal/cable arrangements.

The manifold top encloses the slide and bore arrangement by a series of $^{10}/_{32}$ inch UNF cap heads, and it also supports the throttle control rod and trumpets. The trumpets are mounted on two "O" rings and are retained by a steel ring which is screwed to the manifold top. These are conical in shape and the fuel injector is located in the trumpet itself.

Metering Unit

One of the most beautiful components of this engine is the metering unit, distributor and alternator assembly. The metering unit and electrical assembly are both connected to a small gearbox which obtains its power from the distribution gears via a small quill shaft. Because the ignition and the fuel injection are combined in this way the timing of the ignition and fuel injection can be accurately set in relation to each other. The whole unit is located inside the "V" and the front of the metering unit is supported by a little aluminium mount bolted to the block. The amount of fuel injected is controlled by a fuel cam which is linked to the throttle slide by a control rod assembly; this means the air fuel ratio can be accurately maintained.

When the engine is built the ignition timing can be adjusted by moving the distributor base plate in relation to the distributor body. Looking from the front of the engine the layout of the timing gears follows the shape of the engine. The crankshaft gear drives the first compound gear which in turn drives the second compound gear. The second compound gear provides the take-off point for the metering unit/ignition assembly drive and carries on the timing gear to the cam shafts via idler gears. The second compound gear is a very complex assembly being made up of a hub by 12 miniature torsion bars. This method of construction of the second compound gear means that it is also, in effect, the vibration damper for the engine.

At the end of the line are the cam shaft gears, these are bolted to the cam shaft by three cap screws and the holes in the gears through which these cap screws pass are elongated so that the gear can be moved in relation to the cam shaft. This allows the cam shaft timing to be accurately set.

These gears are enclosed by a cast magnesium cover on the engine and also two smaller magnesium covers on each cylinder head assembly. These are all machined accurately to provide an oil tight cover. Originally a damper was fitted on the end of the crankshaft to absorb the

Distribution 2nd compound gearing as mounted on block – Ford Cosworth DFV.

Magnesium distribution front cover. Note the fuel pump on right hand side and two pulleys at the bottom driving the left hand water pump and oil pressure pump, and right hand side driving 2nd water pump and oil scavenge pump – Ford Cosworth DFV.

vibrations. Later on another type of damper was fitted for the ignition timing and then this unit was eliminated and the compound gear damper was introduced.

On each corner of the cast cover is a pulley on which runs a toothed belt which is driven once again by the second compound gear. These pulleys provide the power for the engine's ancillary equipment. On the left hand side is the mechanical fuel pump, the water pump for the left hand bank and the oil pressure pump. On the right hand side is the water pump for the right hand bank and the scavenge pump. This draws used oil from the sump to the tank. In the original construction twin eccentric rotors were used but later these were replaced by twin lobe type rotors. Incorporated in the pump is a centrifuge fan and also a special valve which helps to separate the air from the scavenged oil. Between the rear of the water pump and the front of the scavenge pump is a small clutch assembly which will slip at a pre-set load and this prevents damage to the rotors should blow-up debris get past the scavenge filters into the pump. This clutch also helps to prevent the toothed drive belt from being strained when the oil is cold. Therefore, before any attempt is made to start the engine it is recommended that the engine is heated by a form of external heating such as a hot air blower. This prevents any damage to the engine and also makes it easier to start.

On the bottom right hand side of the sump is a passage cast into the sump which passes to the left hand side. This arrangement makes it possible for the scavenged oil to be piped back to the tank from either side of the engine, to suit the design of the car.

The water pumps are identical in their construction apart from the fact that they are handed and cannot be interchanged left and right. The impeller is contained in the aluminium housing of the pump body and its shaft is supported by two ball bearings which are pre-lubricated and sealed. Water is prevented from escaping by a seal both sides of the impeller. The vanes of the impeller were first made in a spiral formation but now are straight; this gives increased flow rate. Water from the pump is passed through an aluminium tube and this is secured to the block by a small cast aluminium elbow. The tube is sealed to this elbow and to the pump outlet with conventional rubber "O" rings.

Oil Pressure Pump

The oil pressure pump receives its power through an Oldhams coupling from the rear

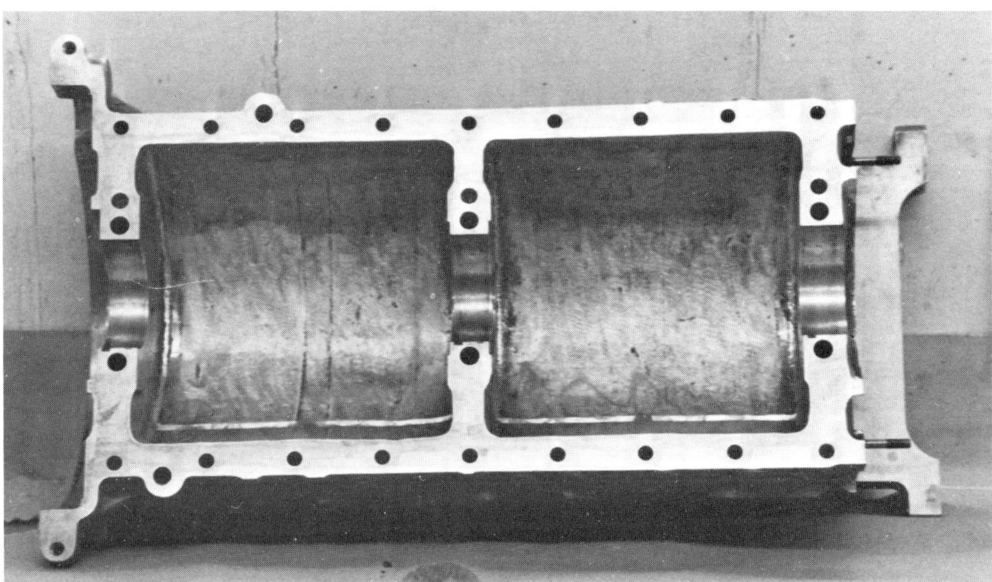

Crankshaft bearing cups' sump – Ford Cosworth DFV.

of the left hand water pump. The pumping mechanism is the conventional eccentric rotor type. The oil pump body is mounted to the engine and contains the rotor, the pressure relief valve and oil filter in one assembly. The oil is passed from the pump to the engine via a pipe and excess oil from the pressure relief valve is bled into the scavenge system.

Engine Oil System

Oil is drawn from the tank and into the oil pump and there it is pressurised and is pumped through the filter, out of the pump and into the cylinder block via a small steel tube. It passes through oil ways in the block to the crankshaft assembly, the cylinder heads and camshaft assemblies and a small amount is directed onto the compound gears through a small jet. The "used" oil returns to the sump and is then scavenged by the scavenge pump and returned to the tank via the oil coolers. The air which is separated from the scavenged oil is returned to the oil tank through its own pipe due to it carrying a very small amount of oil. The oil tank is vented to a catch tank which is in turn vented to the atmosphere.

The car's oil tank should allow for an approximate consumption of six pints during a Grand Prix race of an average 200 miles.

Water System

Water can be introduced to either water pump as these are connected by a passage contained in the sump. It is driven by the impellers into the cylinder block and passes around the liners and through the cylinder head and leaves the engine through an outlet at the rear of each cylinder head. The water then returns to the radiators, is cooled, and then is drawn into the water pumps again. Water circulation is constantly maintained in this way. The belt and pulley arrangement is protected by a thin aluminium cover.

Fuel System

The original layout of the fuel system is fairly simple and starts from the fuel tank of the car. The petrol (five star) is sucked by the electrical high pressure pump through a filter which goes to a non-return valve or by-passes the mechanical engine fuel pump

The Lucas ignition distributor, fuel metering unit and its drive rod – Ford Cosworth DFV.

then to another filter and the metering unit which distributes the petrol to the cylinders through injectors.

For the return to the tank, the petrol comes out of the metering unit through a relief fuel pressure valve. The fuel enters the right hand manifold, comes out on the back of it to go to the left hand manifold by a simple line to the front of it, goes through this manifold and comes out to the collector pot.

Lucas Fuel Injection System

The Lucas fuel injection systems equip saloon cars and most racing engines, especially those in Formula cars. Originally designed for sports cars, the Lucas unit was adapted to the Ford Cosworth DFV engine and gave the performance required. The obvious simplicity of its design brought reliability which contributed greatly to the success of the DFV engine.

The DFV engine used the indirect Lucas shuttle metering system; this is generally accepted as the most convenient and is almost trouble-free. The unit is compact and facilitates installation to meet the accurate demands of engine design. A separate electric pump is mounted on the chassis and is governed by a switch on the dashboard. When switched on, the pump sucks the petrol from the tank, sends it around the system; the petrol is then pressurised because of its flow and by a relief valve which is accurately designed to keep the pressure constantly at around 110psi. This pressure also helps to minimise vapour lock which can occur very easily today because of the complete enclosure of the engine to meet the wing car design, and is worse in hot atmospheres such as in South America.

The pressurised fuel is fed to a metering unit which combines a metering distributor with a mixture control. A piston driven by the shaft, coming from the distribution located inside the metering, sends the correct amount of fuel at the precise time to each cylinder of the engine. The amount of fuel injected is determined by the travel of a small free piston or shuttle operated by the fuel pressure. This ensures that each injection is matched in quantity while the low mass of the shuttling piston contributes to the rapid response of the system; the engine accelerates or decelerates.

The mixture control assembly, which is a simple fuel cam mounted on the front of the unit and liaised to the slides of the engine by a little rod, receives a signal from the engine proportional to the amount of air going through the inlet. When opening, the slide determines the travel of the shuttle and sends the quantity of petrol to be injected. Like so, the engine, under different conditions of load and speed, receives the exact amount of petrol to match the quantity of air admitted. The metered fuel reaches the engines cylinders through the injectors located on the outside of the "trumpets" which atomise the fuel as it enters the air stream. The shuttle or fuel cam is mounted on an eccentrical pin, going through it. On one side the pin has a notched shoulder to keep it in a steady position. On the other side a spring retained by a circlip keeps the pin in position. The pin has five positions and initially, to start the engine when cold, is set in full rich position and for easy starting (infact it acts as a choke) then, when the engine reaches the running temperature, the pin is re-set to the position required to meet the specification given by the engine builder for normal running. Another factor to take into consideration for the petrol mixture is that there is a set of different fuel cam profiles available to suit given circuits, depending on their height above sea levels. There are two other settings to be respected, which are the gap between the cam and the piston; slides closed and fully open

Electrics

There is little to say about the electrics except that in between the metering unit and the distributor assembly there is an alternator of a sufficient power to keep the battery charged. The current regulator is incorporated inside a "box" in aluminium which contains the complete electronics ignition system. This box is located at the back of the inside of the "V" and can easily be changed by disconnecting the wiring coming from the unit and undoing three clips. To avoid the tiny vibration of the box rests on three rubber blocks, located on two plates supported by the manifolds.
clips. To avoid the tiny vibration of the engine, the box rests on three rubber blocks, located on two plates supported by the manifolds.

Specification

Configuration: 90° V8

Capacity: 2993cc (182.64cu. in)

Bore: 3.373 inch (85.6mm)

Stroke: 2.555 inch (64.8mm)

Compression Ratio: 11 to 1 (approx.)

Bhp: 480 (approx.) at 10,500rpm

Torque: 245;b.ft. at 8,500rpm

Valve Lift: 0.410 inch (less tappet clearance)

Timing: Inlet: 102° ATDC
Exhaust: 102° BTDC

Firing Order: 1–8–3–6–4–5–2–7

Cylinder Configuration:

Front
5 1
6 2
7 3
8 4
Rear

Cylinder Block: Cast aluminium alloy. The general assembly is bearing type

Crankshaft: Steel forged finished at Cosworth. Turns on five main bearings hence "bearing type". Positioned between the block and the sump

Liners: Cast iron steel in constant contact with water

Con Rods: Forged steel (spot pinned)

Pistons: Cosworth forged aluminium with two compression rings and one oil scraper

Cylinder Heads: Cast aluminium alloy, two 1.14 inch (29mm) exhaust valves x two 1.36 inch (34.5mm) inlet valves per cylinder assembled with double springs. One spark plug per cylinder located in the middle of the combustion chamber

Carriers: Cast aluminium alloy takes the buckets and camshaft

Camshafts: Four steel, each turns on five bearings

Slides: Steel sliding on a series of ball bearings and rollers called back by two guided springs

Manifold: Cast aluminium alloy inlet trumpets pressed formed steel with injector location

Injection System: Lucas indirect injection shuttle metering system. Pressure 110psi approx. Injection Timing at 30° ATDC

Ignition System: Lucas ignition with current alternator assembly system and Thyristor engine speed limiter. Setting 35° BTDC

Spark Plugs: Champion R56 or equivalent

Water System: 1 water pump on each bank

Oil System: One pressure pump, one scavenge pump

Weight: 165kg

Chapter 14

Ferrari T4

The T4 was the first ground effect Ferrari Formula One car. Despite a large gearbox and boxer engine, which were not ideal for ground effect concept application, Ferrari somehow managed to get around the problem to produce one of the most competitive cars for 1979. The efficient combination of the team, drivers, good rubber, powerful engine, preparation and the total reliability of the T4 gave another World Championship to Ferrari. A total of five wins (including three one-twos) and numerous place finishes was sufficient to give Jody Scheckter the Drivers' title, with team mate Gilles Villeneuve runner-up.

During the time it was in service, the T4 received numerous alterations in every respect, especially in the field of aerodynamics. The T4 was replaced by the T5 which, although an improvement on its predecessor, and the last of the "T" series, was to be a real disaster for Ferrari in the 1980 season, due mainly to many engine failures.

As turbocharging seemed to be the way to go in Formula One (without sliding skirts), Ferrari entered the 1981 season with a brand new concept of car, 126C with a turbocharged V6 engine.

Ferrari is part of, and is financed mainly by, the Fiat Group. At its Maranello Headquarters, chief designer Mauro Forghieri is responsible for the racing department and is, naturally, constantly in touch with Mr Enzo Ferrari. They are the ones who make the decisions. There is a department for future projects, controlled by Mauro Forghieri. The racing department is divided into a machine shop, a spare parts store, a large engine assembly area, four Formula One engine test benches, a gearbox assembly department, four bays for car preparation, a parts inspection office and other administration offices which arrange race schedules, hotels, travel etc.

Ferrari organisation owns its own private circuit, located near the main factory and called Fiorano, where constant tests and developments are carried out, all monitored by a television and computer centre, which is a great advantage.

To return to the subject of the T4, let's see how this "jewel" is put together.

Chassis

The Ferrari monocoque looks a little untidy when compared to most of the British designs, almost as if it has been designed as it is built up around the suspension and engine gearbox unit. However, considerable improvements were to be seen on the following T5 and turbo 126C Formula One cars in this respect.

The T4 monocoque is entirely formed from aluminium and is reinforced with fabricated square section aluminium

The T4 without left hand side pods, note the height of the fuel tank.

stiffener tubing, extending from the front end to the rear bulkhead, to which the engine is bolted directly. Ferrari think that this system has the advantage of being stronger than that employed on their previous models, and it also offers the advantage of being easily repairable, but above all it does not lose its rigidity characteristics. Right at the front a cast magnesium "bulkhead" is riveted to the aluminium bulkhead and takes the various master cylinders as well as the anti roll bar and front legs of the lower suspension wishbones. The pedals are supported by cast magnesium bracketry riveted to the chassis floor panel. The rest of the chassis holds all the necessary pick-ups for the various components. Again, these pick-ups are made of either magnesium or steel and are riveted or bolted onto structures for maximum rigidity. The roll over hoop is formed entirely of titanium tubing with 2 extra legs extending forward with an aluminium panel riveted to the inner panels and top frame section.

The fuel cells are located right at the back of the chassis, looking like a single bay with two "step outs" on either side of the chassis. At the driver's shoulder level, an angular aluminium panel is riveted to the tank bay and cockpit skins which again offers extra rigidity and protection around the centre of the car. The rear roll over hoop is formed in the same way and from the material, but the two legs extend rearward and two side aluminium panels close the hoop, also riveted to the tank area. The right hand panel houses the intercommunication box and the left hand panel houses the safety and emergency devices. Note that riveting is not opposed by Ferrari. However, in concept the T4 chassis seems to be thoroughly rigid and safe.

Fuel System

Three fuel cells made by Superflexit and Pirelli are located behind the driver's seat. They comply with the F.I.A. regulations. The two side tanks empty into the central tank by means of a one-way valve system. A collection tank is buried inside the main cell and feeds the metering unit through a safety fuel valve placed right at the back of the chassis. Although the T4 was the first Ferrari ground effect car and thus required the chassis to be as narrow as possible, an ideal design wasn't achieved because to carry the capacity of fuel necessary to feed the greedy boxer engine the designers were forced to locate the extra small capacity fuel cells on each side of the main one, and thus ended up with two "step outs", as mentioned before.

The rest of the fuel system is designed in accordance with the engine's fuel feed requirements and forms a labyrinth of piping and Teflon tubes.

To start the engine, the necessary fuel pressure is attained by an electric pump which also acts as a mechanical pump, driven by the left hand bank cam shaft, as soon as the engine fires.

Safety

The safety system in the main consists of the usual deformable structures around the fuel bay, a safety quick relief fuel valve, roll over bars and fire extinguishers. The latter, an exclusive Ferrari design made and fitted at the workshop, comply with the Formula One safety rules. Contrary to all other Formula One cars, the bottles contain a liquid chemical mixture. Both bottles of 5kg capacity for the cockpit area and of 2.5kg capacity for the engine area are mounted under the driver's knees. A small medical air bottle, also an exclusive Ferrari design, is located on top of the central fuel cell panel and is connected to the driver's crash helmet by means of a flexible pipe.

In an emergency the extinguishers and air supply can be triggered off electrically from the dashboard, by the driver, and from the outside, where another switch, placed on the left hand side of the rear roll over hoop, can be switched on by a track marshal. The system also includes a Termo Sensor which automatically sets off the three safety bottles. The action of setting off the fire extinguishers also cuts off all the cars' electrical components. However, the extinguisher and air bottle have their own little battery placed in front of the dashboard and this is loomed separately to the car's electric circuit. Again, this is part of the F.I.A. safety requirements When triggered off, the extinguishers last about six minutes and the air bottle lasts 4½ minutes, which seems a lot safer than most of the systems carried on British and French cars, since theirs last less than one minute.

Driver safety is a great concern at Ferrari. In that respect, contrary to most other cars, their chassis is designed to allow their drivers to get in or out quickly. Another point is that the Ferrari cars do not have a detachable steering wheel since it is not considered safe. The standard six point safety harness is bolted to the chassis floor panel with the two shoulder straps attached to the fuel bay, just above the driver's seat.

Dashboard

The dashboard controls are arranged in simple fashion and comprise a central magnetic tachometer, two electrical dual gauges indicating water, oil temperature and oil and fuel pressure, an ignition contact and an oil pressure warning light. All these are inserted into a dash panel. On the left hand side of the dash area, another aluminium panel supports the high pressure fuel pump, rear red light, engine rpm limiter device, ignition switches and, finally the extinguisher button. Further back, on the chassis inner skin, a little lever controls the adjustable rear anti roll bar.

On the right hand side is the unique and traditional Ferrari gear-selection gate and its gear lever, as the primary linkage runs along the inner skin, up to the back of the chassis. This very nice and cleverly designed device ensures positive gear selection, thus avoiding a missed or wrong gear engagement.

Ferrari T4 dashboard and controls area. (Photo Jean Damon).

Front Suspension

At the front, the T4 has unusual wide tubular bottom wishbones, reinforced each side by a third tube welded at an angle to the flexing of the wishbone. The wishbone is anchored to a cast magnesium pick-up which is riveted to the chassis and, at the front end, to another cast magnesium "bulkhead", which also takes the brake master cylinders and anti roll bar. Externally, the wishbone is attached to the upright with an old fashioned ball joint.

The top section is even more crowded with tubes. The rockers are of tubular steel and are attached to the upright with a similar joint as the bottom wishbone. The inner part forms a "hat" section directly operating the spring damper combination, which is bolted at its bottom end to a steel bracket, riveted to the chassis. The rocker oscillates on a single pin mounted in double sheer, which goes through two lots of steel braces, half bolted and half riveted to the upper section of the chassis. The layout is reinforced by a link attached to the rocker pin clevis and to the chassis at the dash roll over hoop level. The uprights are another Ferrari magnesium casting and the steel axles revolve in double angular contact bearings. The wheels are driven by four pegs and are secured by a very large titanium nut. This solution was chosen in order to minimise the rim torsion when loaded during cornering. The anti roll bar is mounted on the cast bulkhead. The bar stiffness is adjustable. The left hand side has a steel fabricated lever linked to the "hat" of the rocker via a small aluminium link, connected through rose joints.

The right hand side is similar except that the lever has a steel blade rotating at 90° maximum angle and operated by a cable and knob from the cockpit.

Steering is by the conventional rack and pinion system, entirely made by and at Ferrari. All parts are bolted to the floor panel, just under the driver's legs. Each end of the rack is supported by an additional little trap, which acts as supports. The aluminium track rods have rose joints and link the rack to the uprights via clevises and double sheer plates on the wheel side. The steering column, forming a steep angle, is made from two sections, joined with a universal joint. The primary column is connected to the pinion's rack and the secondary column is supported on a boxed bush bearing and takes the steering wheel from a splined flange with three bolts. The central part of the steering wheel is padded for driver safety and is embellished with the Ferrari rampant horse emblem. The steering wheel is adjustable for depth and height. The rack system and fire extinguishers are entirely covered by the one piece fibreglass driver's seat.

Front Brakes

Cast magnesium brake and clutch pedals are mounted on their own bracketry which is riveted to the floor panel. The brake balance is adjustable, but not from the dashboard.

A cast bulkhead supports the Lockheed brake and clutch master cylinders, two fluid

Front suspension and brake arrangement, note the anti pitch hydraulic system (centre). (Photo Franco Lini).

reservoirs, (one feeding the front brakes, the other feeding rear brakes) and clutch slave cylinder. The ventilated discs are mounted floating on their own bell and are driven by the wheel drive pegs. Only one four piston type caliper is mounted on each upright. The calipers are fed by Aeroquip type flexible piping, running along the front leg of the bottom wishbone. A fibreglass brake duct is bolted directly to the upright and guides the air into the disc channels.

Rear Suspension

The rear suspension layout is composed of a bottom tubular steel wishbone anchored to the lower part of the gearbox and to the upright, where the ball and socket joint can be altered length-wise in order to set the wheel camber angle. On either side, a "wishbone" style top rocker is semi-fabricated with steel sheet and tubing and is located between two cast "supports", which are part of the gearbox casing. Out board it picks-up on the rocker on a single point, inboard it compresses the spring damper combination directly. The front section has a small link also fixed to the upright and this is used to set the toe-in. The hollow uprights are, of course, made of cast magnesium and incorporate the axle, running on a double ball bearing assembly. As at the front, the wheels are driven by four drive pegs.

The entire suspension uses ball and socket joints. None of the bolts are taken from the shelf, but are specially made at Ferrari's.

The anti roll bar is very short and only the left hand blade rotates. To obtain the stiffness desired, as the right hand one is fixed, two "levers" are connected to the onboard section of the rockers through two aluminium rods and rose joints. The anti roll bar is adjustable from the cockpit. The system works from a cable acting on a lever, this pivoting on the gearbox casing and in turn moving the left hand blade.

Rear end of the T4. Note the anti dive hydraulic system connected to the front cylinder. (Photo Franco Lini).

Transmission

The five speed gearbox is placed transversally in relation to the engine axis, (the T in T4 stands for Tranversial) and this has the advantage of providing a shorter gearbox, (see the transmission chapter). The logic for this unusual layout is to improve weight distribution around the centre of gravity. Gearbox and final drive are located within the layout and it is composed of a first train of gears receiving the movement from the engine, a second train of gears, which in turn transmits the movement to the crown wheel and pinion and thence the wheels. Gear engagement is operated with dog rings, similar to the Hewland design, which allows a very quick gear change. The oil pump is located within the box and is driven by the second train of gears. Differential crown wheel is straight cut machined, as is the pinion which really, in this case, is simply a gear located onto the second train of gears. The differential also has a self-locking device.

Because of its general design, the change of ratio necessitates partially dismantling the gearbox, and removing the brakes to allow this.

The final drive is by drive shafts with Lobro/Ferrari tracks and ball joints bolted, on the outside, directly onto the wheel axle, and on the inside, to gearbox final drive shafts. The inboard brake discs are sandwiched between the joints and the gearbox shafts.

A small gearbox oil cooler rests on top of the bell housing, this being part of the gearbox unit "V". The starter motor is bolted on the lower right hand side of the gearbox. The clutch slave cylinder is placed in front of the cooler. The movement from the engine to the gearbox is transmitted through a Borg and Beck clutch with twin dry discs.

Brakes

The rear inboard brake assembly is supplied by AP Lockheed. As on the front, the ventilated discs are assembled floating into

General view of the Ferrari T4 during practice session.

their bell and are mounted next to the gearbox. Two large calipers (four piston type) are placed at the back of the discs and are bolted directly to the gearbox casing. The brake lines and unions are all the Aeroquip flexible type. Each side has an air cooling duct which blows air into the central disc channels. Strangely enough, these ducts are pointed downwards, where the air passing the venturi system is at a low pressure. The ducts are placed very close to the exhaust pipe and tails, where the heat generated certainly doesn't help brake cooling! One can assume that Ferrari must have had their own reasons for doing it that way. Ironically, Ferrari had problems with brake temperature during their winning season of 1979.

Water – Oil Assembly

Like any other "ground effect car", the water radiators are mounted on either side, alongside the chassis, at cockpit level. The engine's water pump feeds each radiator, channelling the water through the lower part of the cylinder heads' cast covers and returning it from each radiator to the top of the same covers, to enter the engine through the heads. The water runs into aluminium pipes, nicely formed and placed either side of the chassis. All connections are made with rubber shells and circlips and the temperature "dip stick" is placed on the return neck. Each radiator has an air bleeding Teflon line ending in a water pot placed at the back of the chassis. This pot also receives air bleeders from the engine itself. Water filling is through the pot which is connected to the engine only by a small rubber tube of about Dash 10 (10mm bore) so it must take a fair amount of time to fill the system.

The oil system starts, of course, from engine pump which leads into the filter, then to a large oil cooler on the right hand side. The lower neck of the cooler receives the oil from the engine which then passes through the radiator and enters the tank from the top. The tank is rubber mounted alongside the right hand side fuel tank bay and feeds the engine oil pump from its bottom part. The catch tank is built within the tank and all is hidden by the bodywork. Oil circulation is by means of aluminium and rubber braced pipes with similar unions to those used on the water system. Water and oil radiators are protected with stone guards. The battery is found under the oil tank.

Bodywork

The side pods are bolted to the monocoque venturi sections; side sections are joined together by a series of Dzus fasteners for quick removal. The sliding skirts are located in a "V" section built into each side pod and covered by an external panel. These skirts rub on the track on single-length hard wearing rubber strips. They are pressed to the ground by a series of boxes inserted in the internal panel and acting as sprung devices; a lot more complicated than other Formula One car systems. The radiators also act as bodywork supports. The top section of the bodywork entirely envelopes the car from the front right back to the rear of the engine, with the rear section slightly raised to guide the airflow around the rear aerofoil.

Various N.A.C.A. ducts provide air for the engine inlets, to cool the gearbox oil and, right at the front, to provide fresh air for driver comfort. The radiator air exit is through "louvres" on either side of the car. Other accessories include a tinted plastic screen and, of course, mirrors which are incorporated in the bodywork. The bodywork is completed by a small nose cone, supported by the top section and the front wing frame. The idea is to allow a maximum airflow to the side pods. Again, this piece of bodywork is secured by Dzus fasteners. Underneath, the engine is enveloped by an "undertray", for better air flow exit.

At the front, a single piece wing is mounted ahead of the nose cone and supported on a titanium frame. The wing is adjustable on a central fulcrum and also readily detachable, complete with the cone which can be quickly replaced as a complete unit in the case of damage, or different aerofoils can be rapidly substituted. The wing has small end plates and riveted on each end is an adjustable lip. The rear wing is supported by two vertical aluminium plates with several adjustment points and these are bolted to another cast magnesium box, itself attached to the back of the gearbox. Two end plates complete the wing. The wing's shape and position varies from circuit to circuit according to the cars' handling and to the Ferrari way of thinking.

Apparently construction of the front and rear aerofoils is a unique, secretly guarded process! However, looking at either wing it can be assumed that first it is formed in a "V" shape with hard aluminium sheets (i.e. L72) for rigidity. As it is put together in two sections, these sections have to be riveted flush somewhere and as the wing has to be supported by something pretty strong to cope with the load, it has to be a large diaphragm. The end plates are riveted, most probably, to smaller diaphragms on either side; perhaps there are two aluminium tubes crossing the three diaphragms. Extra rigidity is obtained by injecting expanding foam.

Specification

Chassis
Steel frame – Aluminium sheets

Transmission
Ferrari transversal five speed plus reverse gearbox-weight 55kg –Lobro/Ferrari drive shafts – Constant velocity joints – Borg and Beck clutch (twin dry discs) – Agip lubricant

Rear Suspension
Cast magnesium uprights – Steel fabricated top rockers – Tubular bottom rockers and wishbones –Inboard Koni shock absorbers and steel spring combination – Adjustable anti roll bar – Track 160cm – Speedline rims – Michelin tyres, 18–19 inches

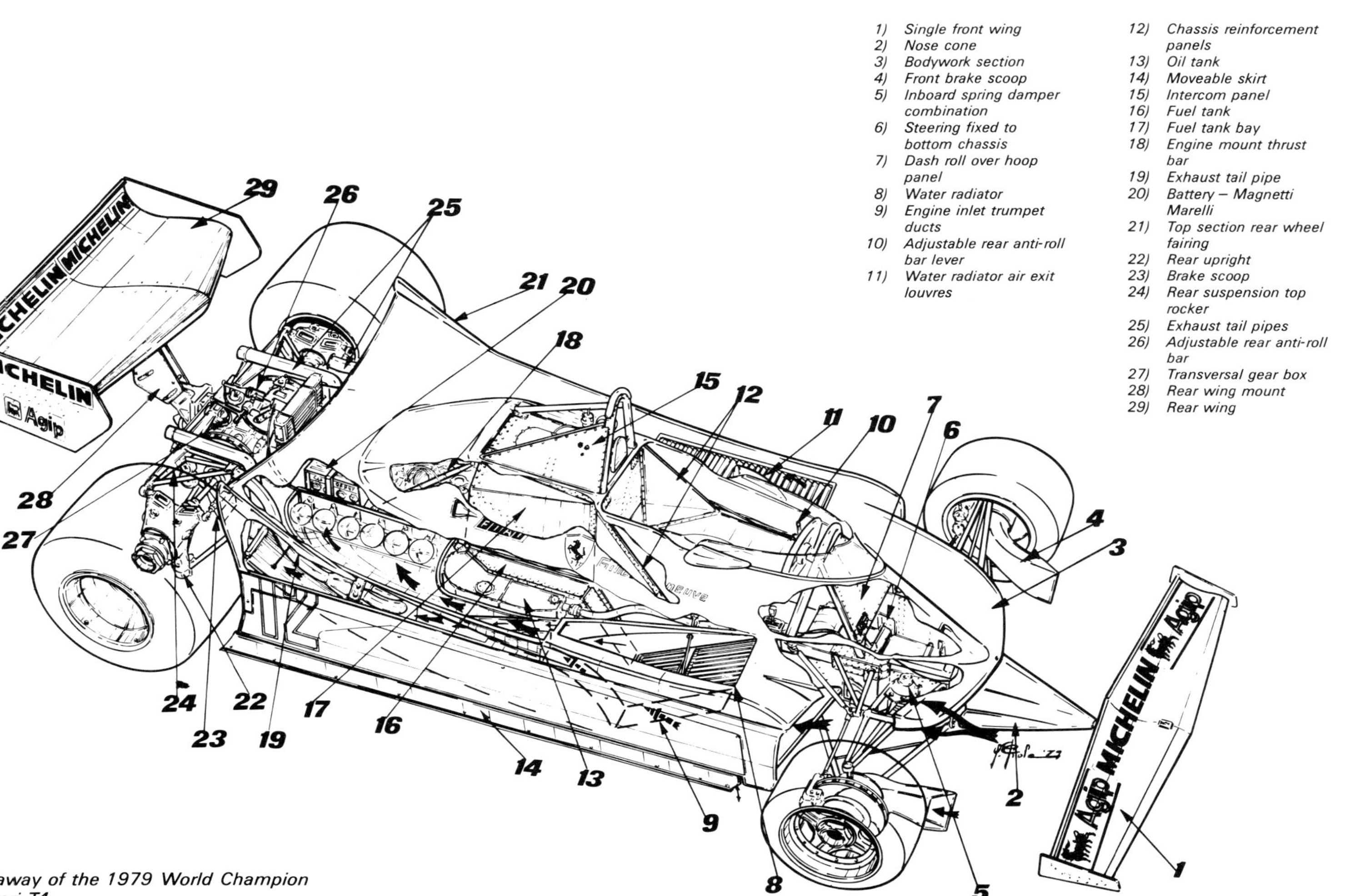

1) Single front wing
2) Nose cone
3) Bodywork section
4) Front brake scoop
5) Inboard spring damper combination
6) Steering fixed to bottom chassis
7) Dash roll over hoop panel
8) Water radiator
9) Engine inlet trumpet ducts
10) Adjustable rear anti-roll bar lever
11) Water radiator air exit louvres
12) Chassis reinforcement panels
13) Oil tank
14) Moveable skirt
15) Intercom panel
16) Fuel tank
17) Fuel tank bay
18) Engine mount thrust bar
19) Exhaust tail pipe
20) Battery – Magnetti Marelli
21) Top section rear wheel fairing
22) Rear upright
23) Brake scoop
24) Rear suspension top rocker
25) Exhaust tail pipes
26) Adjustable rear anti-roll bar
27) Transversal gear box
28) Rear wing mount
29) Rear wing

Cutaway of the 1979 World Champion Ferrari T4.

Front Suspension
Cast magnesium uprights – Tubular top rockers and bottom wishbones – Inboard Koni shock absorbers and steel spring combination – Ferrari rack and pinion steering system (ratio 10/1) – Adjustable anti roll bar – Track 170cm – Speedline rims – Michelin tyres 12–13 inches

Wheelbase
270cm

Brakes
Front outboard AP Lockheed ventilated discs and single calipers – Ferodo DS11 pads – Rear inboard AP Lockheed ventilated discs and single calipers – Ferodo DS11 pads

Oil Cooling
2 Serck aluminium radiators – Agip lubricant – Aluminium braced rubber piping – Capacity 8 litres

Water Cooling
1 Autokhuler aluminium radiator – Aluminium piping – Capacity 9.5 litres

Fuel
Pirelli/Superflexit three fuel cells – Ferrari/Lucas – injection system – Capacity 190 litres

Accessories and Safety
Borletti gauges – 12V Varley battery – Ferrari fire extinguisher – life bottle – Willans six point safety harness – Magnetti Marelli – master switch

Engine
Ferrari 312 12 cylinder, 180°V – Lucas indirect fuel system – Magnetti Marelli starter motor and electronic ignition

Total Weight
596kg

1979 Formula 1 World Champion: Jody Scheckter

Chapter 15

Ferrari Flat 12 Engine

The Ferrari Boxer engine was designed for both the 312B Sports Prototype and Formula One car. The first time the flat 12 engine was fired up was in 1969, a few weeks before the Italian Grand Prix at Monza, when Mr Enzo Ferrari wished to introduce the new 312B Formula One car. But the unit failed during testing due to piston and crankshaft defects. Consequently, it was re-designed and returned only during the early stage of the following season. From 1969 to early 1970 all sorts of endless modifications were reported, such as revised valve angles, new inlet manifolds, revised cam profile and also different types of crankshafts, different casting, new location of accessories, etc. After curing the problems encountered in 1969, progress was made towards the overall engine weight saving as well as a reduction of fuel consumption, improved reliability and performance. The power output was then 400hp at 12,000rpm. In the mid '70s Ferrari ended its Sport Prototype programme to concentrate solely on Formula One.

In designing a flat 12 engine, Ferrari's aim was to reduce the car's centre of gravity and keep the engine's internal frictional losses to within reasonable levels. However, in theory, of course, the faster the engine runs the more power it should develop, but with a high speed racing engine the frictional loss increases rapidly with speed, thus reducing the theoretical power output gain. To try to overcome this, the large crankshaft ran on two plain shell main bearings, in the middle, and a ball bearing on each end. The result was a short and light arrangement, frictional losses being thereby kept to a minimum. According to some rumours, in order to reduce the inertia, tests were carried out with "weightless" crankshaft bobs, still with two con rods, mounted next to each other on one pin.

The increase of the power output since the first appearance of the unit was: 1969–70 – 460bhp; 1971 – 470bhp; 1974 480bhp; 1976 – 490bhp/500bhp and from 1977 to 1980, 514bhp.

Although the Ferrari Boxer engine did not conform to the requirements of a ground effect Formula One car, in 1979 the flat 12 engine went from strength to strength with a near faultless finish record and an amazing reliability – giving another World Championship title to Ferrari (previously the team had won in 1975 and 1977 with Nikki Lauda). By contrast, in 1980 the season began badly with failures, due mainly to revised oil system and cylinder heads. Sadly, 1980 was the last season for the Boxer engine, which was replaced by a new, compact 126C V6 turbocharged engine.

The Ferrari 312 Boxer engine was the best compromise for weight, fuel consumption and performance of all 12 cylinder conventional racing engines designed up to 1980. Furthermore, racing car enthusiasts or connoisseurs will appreciate the superb exercise of this cast monument of engineering complexity.

The following brief description of the unit is based on one of the latest versions, seen in 1979–1980.

The Block

The block is made from a mixture of light alloy, based on aluminium. The block is formed by two large shells, assembled together with a series of nuts and bolts placed in the longitudinal centreline all around and with two nuts and studs at the top and bottom faces on either side of the unit. The oil and water passages are cast in each shell and connected to each other.

Crankshaft

This is produced from a block of steel, forged to shape, which is then machined in order to cut the "fibres" of steel for greater reliability in mechanical wear. It is heat treated before assembly. It revolves on four main bearings and its six pins each receive two con rods, arranged at 180° angle. The crankshaft front ends drives the alternator, ignition distributor and fuel metering unit by a disposition of gears and pinions, positioned at a 90° angle. At the rear end the crankshaft has a main pinion which drives the rest of the timing gear system. The small "flywheel" is bolted on the crankshaft through a rubber damper in order to absorb the vibration. The unusual prominent starter ring is taken in sandwich between the clutch pressure plate and the plates and circular disc ring, the whole lot being bolted to the flywheel.

Liners

The liners are made from light alloy, fitted free at top and bottom and sealed with "O" rings. The upper area is cooled by the water and the lower cooled by the oil circulation. Sealing of the cylinder heads is effected by a typical Cooper ring.

Con Rods

The con rods are made of forged titanium material, finished at Ferrari, and receive a special treatment carried out by an outside firm. The big ends are connected to the crank pin by a plain bearing held by a cup and two high tensile steel bolts.

Pistons

The pistons are made of forged aluminium made entirely outside the factory. The pistons are retained on the con rod by a steel gudgeon pin, itself retained by a circlip on either side and free in the piston and a tight fit on the con rod. The piston crown is pocketed to give clearance to the valves when fully open and there are four rings – three compression rings and one scraper.

Cylinder Heads

The cylinder heads are of cast aluminium alloy and are sealed to the block by a series of 16 studs and a single conventional gasket for each head. The four valves, placed at a 20° angle, are of different materials since the exhaust valves have to cope with the exhaust temperature while the inlet valves run a lot cooler. Valve seats and guides are made of a bronze based material. Each valve has two springs and its stem is sealed with a rubber cup-seal. Because of the height of the cylinder heads, the inlet ports are long and are formed in one single section, the inlet and exhaust walls being very smooth for minimum turbulence.

The titanium exhaust pipes are held with three studs and are sealed with a thin aluminium gasket. Before delivery each engine has the exhaust pipe system, less the tail pipes, mounted to it, since the pipes run practically under the heads, where accessibility is restricted. This makes the job easier for the mechanics at the race track and is typical of Ferrari organisation. The cam shafts are part of the cylinder heads. They run on seven caps and bearings and directly operate the valves through the tappet buckets and shims which govern valve clearance.

Each manifold guillotine slides on a series of rollers on its two faces, is controlled by a small shaft and lever passing through the ignition system and fuel metering unit casting, and is supported on its end by two small cast mounts. Two small guillotines and the metering unit are connected to each other by a small rod, joined directly to the injection pump and tension springs to call back the guillotines. The manifolds are cast magnesium and are bolted to the cylinder head inlet ports. The trumpets are maintained by two small size nuts and studs. A coarse plastic gauze prevents any object being sucked into the manifolds. The injectors are mounted on the inner part of the manifold, this is in order to lower the fibreglass engine cover as much as possible.

Timing

The timing gear follows the shape of the engine, as with the Cosworth DFV and Matra V12, except that the 312 Boxer has less gears in total. The crankshaft gear drives two compound gears, which in turn drive a single large diameter second compound gear, driving the cam shafts. Except for the cam shafts, all the gears revolve on needle bearings located on the cylinder heads, blocks and timing covers.

Oil, Water and Fuel Systems

Oil lubrication is operated by one pressure pump, placed at the back on the right hand cylinder head and driven by the timing gear. The pressurised oil goes out of the pump into the oil filter, placed at the rear of the fuel metering unit, and then enters the front part of the block. The scavenge pump is located in the same casting as the pressure pump and returns the oil into the tank placed on the right hand side, along the cars fuel cell bay. The lefthand cylinder head exhaust cam shafts also drive a little scavenge pump which returns the oil from the heads into the block. The right hand bank inlet camshafts operate (through a gearing) the tachometer and another little scavenge pump.

The front end of the overall engine is a masterpiece of magnesium casting, which closes the block and partly contains the gears driving the unit's alternator, distributor and fuel injection pump, and the single water pump. Each cylinder head is closed by a cast magnesium cover. The water circulates to each other through a channel cast in the block's cover. On the left hand bank, the exhaust cam shaft drives the high pressure fuel pump through a gearing arrangement, and can also be elctrically operated to fire up the engine. The whole engine is fixed to the chassis by four studs, screwed on each side of the head covers. The fuel injection is indirect and is operated by a Lucas pump which works on the same principal as the one on the DFV Cosworth except that it is designed to feed 12 cylinders. The other difference is that there is not a fuel richness control notch, but a graduated semi-circular piece is bolted at the rear of the unit. The leverage on the fuel cam is equally marked, so indicating the position of the fuel cam in ratio to the guillotine opening stages.

The electronic ignition is designed and supplied by Magnetti Marelli, who also supply the large alternator. The loom is also formed by Magnetti Marelli, and is comprised of fuses.

A Varley 12v battery supplies the current and operates the electric Magnetti Marelli starter motor located at the front end of the gearbox unit.

The Ferrari 312 Boxer engine. (Photo Franco Lini).

Specification

Team Ferrari did not wish to divulge all of the engines' specifications therefore only the basics are available:

Firing Order: 1–9–5–12–3–8–6–10–2–7–4–11

Cylinder Configuration

Front	
12	1
11	2
10	3
9	4
8	5
7	6
Rear	

Bore: 80mm

Stroke: 49.6mm

Unitary Capacity (One Cyl.): 249.31 cc

Bhp: 515bhp at 12,400rpm

Torque: 33K/m

Height: 300mm

Length: 650mm

Width: 680mm

Total Weight: 180kg (with accessories)

Chapter 16

Renault RE 20

Introduction

The name Renault is familiar to all racing car fanatics, whatever their age. As early as 1906, a Renault won the A.C.F. Grand Prix at Le Mans. In 1973, the Alpine Renault Berlinettes carried off the World Rally Championship. In 1976 and 1977 the Renault Gordini V6 engine was awarded the title European Champion in Formula Two. The 24 Hours of Le Mans was won in 1978 by Renault.

Renault's participation in motor racing has always been well reasoned but its main reasons have considerably evolved along the years.

In the past, automobile competition was the test bench of *avant-garde* techniques, enabling specific qualities to be evolved for mass-produced cars, such as stability and braking.

The performance of certain mass-produced engines is still attributable to lessons learnt during competition. But the difference between a modern single-seater racing car and an everyday car is enormous. On one hand, this is due to the nature of competition which, by definition, makes technicians and drivers strive for performances which always go beyond that which has already been achieved. On the other hand, the rules allow the use of slick wide tyres on race cars, which have nothing to do with those tyres applicable to road cars.

On the same note, the present use of automobiles is subject to particular traffic conditions, speed limits, and other regulations and constructors are forced to develop cars with an emphasis on safety, comfort and economy. Thus, we can ask ourselves, what has pushed Renault after an extensive enquiry, to increase its effort in competition and especially to take part in competition of the highest level?

In order to undertake Formula One, Renault chose a unique turbo compressor solution. The F.I.A. (then C.S.I.) rules drawn up in 1966 authorised the use of either a 3-litre atmospheric engine or a turbo compressed 1.5-litre engine. Renault was alone in using the latter technique for several reasons. Renault had looked into the problem for several years and had found that turbo-charged engine offered several advantages:

1) The thermo-dynamic efficiency of a thermo-compressed engine is better than that of an atmospheric engine, thus consumption is reduced and its application to mass-produced vehicles is increasingly relevant.

2) The engines used in Formula One of which the general conception, six cylinders placed in a "V", corresponds

to the probable evolution of top-range cars. But in the case of the Renault Gordini V6, it is known that an ulterior motive was the basis of this conception: the possibility of using an existing engine for the basis of the Formula One engine.

Undoubtedly, Renault took a risk by taking part in Formula One with a new type of engine, but this risk is proportional to the positive result which should eventually be achieved.

Continuous development and research with its turbo-charged engine as well as aerodynamics and handling of its evolving chassis, proved more and more that Renault could be at home on any kind of circuit. 1981 proved the Regie and its turbo-charged RE30 to be one of the strongest threats in Formula One.

Renault employs 100,000 people and produces over 7,000 vehicles a day, is influenced by the success or defeat which is brought about by competition. At this level we can understand better the importance of the Renault undertaking and how it may have an impact upon the commercial success of the Company.

The RE20 explained in this chapter is the beginning of a sequence of different models based on the RE20/30. The cars were known as RE20, 23, 30, 31, etc.

The RE20 was the fruit of the development of the first Renault wing car which was put into service at the Spanish Grand Prix in April 1979, equipped with the single turbo V6 engine. A double turbo unit became available from the Monaco Grand Prix in May of that year.

Chassis

The chassis is constructed from the following materials: fabricated steel frames in 15DV6, panels in dural 2002 and carbon fibre panels. The various units are assembled by riveting, steel pop rivets being used for the assemblies lying flush, aviation type aluminium rivets with snap head and heated (stored at minus 20°C) for the assemblies glued with araldite.

A first bulkhead, in the front, supports the pedals, the master cylinders and the front attachment of the lower triangles, then there is a second frame, which supports the upper rocking levers, the rear attachments of the lower triangles and the lower attachments of the shock absorbers. Onto this frame is bolted the dashboard roll over bar. A third frame, at the back of the driver, supports the main roll over bar and is joined to the rear engine support frame by horizontal parts, also made of steel 15CDV6, which forms a rigid box inside which is fitted the fuel tank. The rear frame, mentioned above, therefore supports the engine by two lugs level with the cylinder heads (similar to the DFV Cosworth) and by a lower centre support (also similar to the DFV, although much larger).

The bottom of the body shell is made of dural 2002 reinforced by a honeycomb structure up to the level of the tank. The front panel (at the back of the driver) and the rear panel of the tank are also reinforced with a honeycomb structure. The left and right hand panels of the tank are made of carbon fibre. As for the lower panels, these are also the sides of the chassis, since they are in one piece up to the front frame supporting the pedals. The top of the tank includes a trap for putting it into position.

The rigidity of the chassis is obtained from two internal partitions which are riveted to the bottom on the one hand, and are closed at the top, to pick-up the external panel. The partitions divide at the level of the tank (back of the drivers seat) and extend as far as the front bulkhead. Inside these boxes are fitted the last stages of the cooling system. Level with the drivers elbows, so that he is free to move them, the boxes are provided with cut-outs and are closed up by two screwed in carbon fibre panels, which serve also as inspection flaps for the electrical installation. Also, through one of these boxes, the clutch cable and the medical air bottle, the battery for operating the extinguishers, and the various pipelines which travel from the front to the rear, are housed. The bending of the various metal sheets is rather complex and

Front of chassis and suspension – Renault RE20.

calls for some degree of precision in order that the assembly may be correct. The chassis weighs only 46kg. On each side of this bodyshell, thus formed, are bolted two aluminium fabricated frames which support the radiators and the side pods. The heat exchangers themselves fitted directly to the rear frame and contribute to the homogeneity of the assembly.

Dashboard

The dashboard roll over bar is made up in titanium tubing to a standard shape. It supports the dashboard, the steering column and the bearing blocks of the front anti roll bar. The dashboard is composed of an electronic engine revolution counter, a charged-air pressure gauge which indicates the turbo's air flow pressure, an oil pressure warning light, the ignition contact push-button, the press-button for the Rotel electric HP fuel pump, the push-button for the rear red light, the extinguisher controls, the starter button and a push-button for the brake distribution. The gear lever and linkage, on the righthand side, is fixed to the frame of the roll over bar and travels into the box, then onto the outside, along the fuel tank bay before going to the gearbox via several universal joints. On the lefthand box is situated the front adjustable anti roll bar control lever. The rear titanium roll over bar is riveted to the rear bulkhead and tank bay.

Cockpit Area – Renault RE20.

Front end area view of pedal box and fluid lines arrangement – Renault RE20.

Pedals – Steering

The clutch, brakes and throttle are fabricated in aluminium and are fixed to the front bulkhead. The rack and pinion steering system is placed above the driver's heels and is turned by a steering column made of steel and is divided by two universal joints made by Renault. The small rods are made of steel (fabricated) and the ball and socket joints are of the ADR (a branch of SKF) type.

Front Suspension

The upper rocking lever is fabricated of 15CDV6 steel (FN) as is the lower triangle and all attached to the chassis by ball and socket joints (ADR). The shock absorbers (inboard) are of the Koni or DeCarbon type.

The wheel camber adjustment is effected by the end ball and socket joint of the lower triangle; the castor angle is not adjustable, being fixed by the design office. The machining of the various parts is accurate to the point where the adjustment is always exact. The bump steer settings are made with a "Muller" gauge which is very accurate, (see photo, page 187).

As with the rear, the front uprights are cast magnesium, designed by Renault and built and maintained by SNR personnel only. The arrangement is of the "angular contact bearing" and steel type. The wheels are driven by four pegs bolted to the axle and are tightened by a single nut secured by a clip.

The anti roll bar, fixed to the stay rods of the front roll over hoop, is controlled by small bars and ball and socket joints fixed to the end of the upper rocker, level with the head of the shock absorber, and is adjusted from the cockpit.

Safety

The large R.O.T. fire extinguisher is fixed to the floor in a box, in the form of a bridge underneath the drivers legs, and feeds two jets, one each side of the front roll over hoop. The small extinguisher is fitted to the left hand side, underneath the radiator, and feeds two jets, one on each turbo. The medical air bottle is to be found in the left hand box. All the controls of these accessories are electric and the battery, independent of the car's electrical circuit, is also situated in the left hand box. The two switches, one on the dashboard the other at the foot of the rear arch, are accessible from the outside and cut off the electricity when they are operated and start off the extinguishers and the medical air bottle which connect to the drivers helmet with a flexible pipe.

Brakes

The master cylinders are Girling and are for the front as well as for the rear. Originally, the clutch was controlled hydraulically but the cable was subsequently taken up again as a more reliable and lighter system. Ventilated Lockheed discs, 274.4mm in diameter, are inside the wheels, on the hub bearers, at the front and rear. The Lockheed front calipers are of the four piston type and there is the possibility of mounting one or

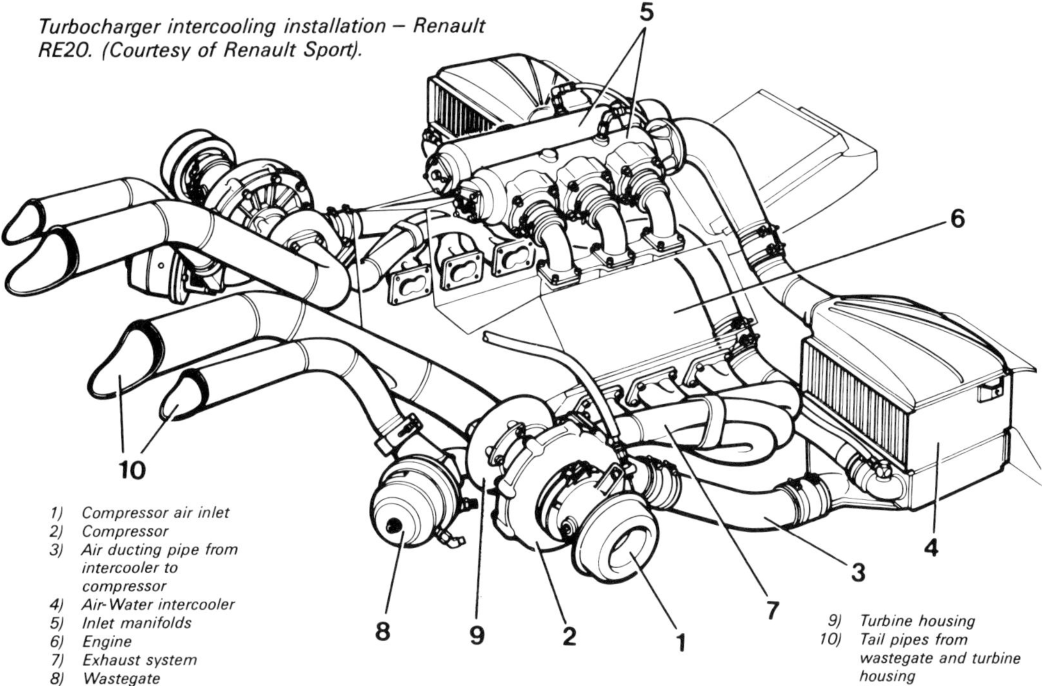

Turbocharger intercooling installation – Renault RE20. (Courtesy of Renault Sport).

1) Compressor air inlet
2) Compressor
3) Air ducting pipe from intercooler to compressor
4) Air-Water intercooler
5) Inlet manifolds
6) Engine
7) Exhaust system
8) Wastegate
9) Turbine housing
10) Tail pipes from wastegate and turbine housing

two calipers on the hub bearers of each wheel.

At the rear, the calipers are incorporated, for the internal part, with the uprights, the external part being Lockheed, which means that there are two two-piston calipers for each wheel. Later, new rear hub bearers were made to provide the possibility of mounting different and larger calipers. The braking on a turbo car is that much greater a problem in view of the non-existence of engine braking.

Water, Oil, Engine Compressed Air Layouts

The cooling on this type of car is quite complicated, because it cools three things: the water, the oil and the engine's incoming air. The water is cooled by two aluminium radiators fixed to each side of the chassis and located in the side pods. The pipelines consist of aluminium tubing, bent in one single piece (each pipe) and connected by Quinsons shells and rubber, there are no flexible hose connections. These radiators are combined and have one part reserved for the oil. The oil plumbing is also Quinsons.

The engine's compressed air is cooled in two heat exchangers placed also on each side of the rear end of the chassis, level with the fire resisting partition. These exchangers are, in fact, double air radiators; in effect, the air which emerges from the turbo at approximately 150°C passes into one part of the exchanger which is bathed with the water from the engine cooling system, causing the temperature to fall to approximately 110°C, then this air passes into the row of tubes of the heat exchanger which are swept by the surrounding air which causes the temperature of the inlet air to fall to within reasonable limits around 60°C.

The problem of the turbo engine is precisely its cooling. The colder the inlet air, the better the output and response of the engine. The incoming air is channelled into the pontoons by sleeves which feed the combined water/oil radiators and the exchangers. This air is evacuated via the

ducts and louvres on the top of the side pods for the water/oil radiators and via the rear of the exchanger, towards the turbos and the outside, for the heat exchangers.

The oil lubrication of the engine is of the dry sump type. The oil tank is situated within a bell housing placed between the box and engine and made of cast magnesium. It is closed at the top with an aluminium container forming also oil filler and catch tank. The oil discharged from the engine and the turbos, collected by the scavenge pumps, passes through the radiators and is subsequently returned to the tank and cooled, where it is again sucked up by the pressure pump and travels on to lubricate the engine and the turbine bearings. The whole plumbing is formed with Titeflex and Quinson unions. (note; Titeflex is light material, a high pressure piping greatly used in the French aeronautic industry).

Transmission

The universal joints are of the Glenzer-Spicer type, made specially for Renault. The drive shafts are steel castings machined and heat treated. The gear box is a Hewland FGA400 five or six speed box which receives various ratios of 8/31 or 9/31 crown wheel and pinion and which has been modified to improve the lubrication system by Renault Sport. A small oil radiator fixed in the rear aerofoil cools the gearbox oil. The clutch is a Borg and Beck, twin discs, as standard on Formula One cars.

Rear Suspension

The rear suspension is composed of an upper rocker lever arm fabricated in 15CDV6 steel sheet and rocking between a small tubular sub-assembly frame fixed to the gearbox lugs and the aluminium cross beam which is also bolted on top of the gearbox. The toe-in is adjustable from a small S.A.R.M.A. aluminium bar connected to the rocker and the upright.

The classic lower wishbone is also fabricated 15CDV6 steel and is anchored to the lower front part of the bell housing (oil tank), the gearbox and on the outer side on the upright, a large rose joint also allows wheel camber angle adjustment. All the ball and socket joints are ADR. The shock absorbers spring combinations are bolted to the lower part of the bell housing and upper rocker arm. Access is restricted, therefore making it difficult for the mechanics when altering the car's ride height or changing springs, for example.

As at the front suspension, bump steer setting is not adjustable since this is defined by accurate designing and machining of the different components.

The short anti roll bar, supported by "Nadella" type bearings, is placed on top of the cross beam and is controlled by small rods and joined to the upper rocker arms, level with the heads of the shock absorbers.

The huge uprights are cast magnesium, designed by Renault and made by "SNR". The stub axles and their bearings are of the "angular contact" type, totally assembled and prepared only by SNR personnel since the whole arrangment requires special equipment. This applies also to the front end axles and uprights. The rear wheels are driven by six pegs screwed onto the axle, the whole wheel being tightened by a single nut secured by a safety clip. The uprights are designed to act as brake half-caliper; the other, external, half-caliper is supplied by AP Lockheed. The air flow around the back of the car has been improved by totally covering engine and gearbox to the extent that a semi-circular fibre glass shell covers the outer drive shafts joints and is bolted to the uprights.

Fuel System

The single fuel cell and the fuel system arrangement are located within the chassis, in a special bay protected by a fire guard at the back of the rear bulkhead. The tank is French made by Superflexit, padded with

Rear suspension and brake assembly – Renault RE20.

foam material and contains about 210 litres. Inside this tank are immersed four (sealed) electric pumps and a tubular aluminium catch tank, fixed at the top to the inspection trap and going all the way down, for maximum capacity and in order to avoid fuel starvation. The four discharge pumps feed this catch tank and there are two other pumps fitted at the bottom for suction purposes. The first, electric, a Rotel gear-type pump, serves to provide the pressure necessary for starting, the second also a Rotel, driven by the crankshaft (mechanical) takes over as soon as the engine starts to turn over. The necessary pressure is low, from 0.8 to 1.8 bar, because the Kugelfischer mechanical injection system, driven by a camshaft, also supplies the injection pressure. The petrol only has to flood the head of the pump, at the pressure. mentioned above and at an adequate flow, for the system to function. This pressure is regulated by a valve in the tank return circuit. All the pipelines are made up in Titefex as are the oil feed and discharge pipelines, etc.

Starting

The starter operates pneumatically and is made by Renault. It can be operated from the cockpit and from outside. A small reserve of compressed air situated on the gearbox enables the driver to make two or three starts out on the track. The electrical installation is reduced to its simplest form. A small alternator on the engine supplies the necessary power to the pumps and for the ignition. A small dry battery (motorcycle type) is situated at the front end of the chassis. The transistorised ignition is by Magnetti Marelli. The ignition contact plate which contains the electronic part and the coil is situated on the tank and is easily interchangeable.

Bodywork and skirt system – Renault RE20.

Turbos

KKK turbos and their own waste gates are supported by a tubular frame and rose joints bolted onto different parts on either side of the cylinder heads. This is in order to try to avoid exhaust cracking which would result in the instant loss of exhaust gas pressure, leading to a loss of power. The exhaust system is entirely made from stainless tubing since that is supposed to resist heat better than steel piping. The whole system is made of separate pipes connecting to the turbos with special heat resistant clips. The four tail pipes run along the top of the gearbox.

Turbo Installation

In the latest installation, each turbocharger supplies its own bank of cylinders and has its own waste gate and throttle valve arrangement. The pressurised airflow coming from the turbos runs into large aluminium tubes, each entering two large inter-coolers which are located on either side of the fuel tank bay. These heat exchangers receive air from a large duct, the mouth being just under the large water cooler, the air entering directly through the side pod opening. From the inter-coolers, the airflow is also ducted through two large aluminium pipes running just between the front end of the engine and the back of the chassis' fuel tank bay. Having passed through the inter-coolers, the air is routed directly into the two cast light alloy manifolds placed above the engine, which duct the air in each cylinder independently through six down draught pipes to the ports, which also carry the fuel injectors. The waste gate is attached to the exhaust system and regulates the gas pressure driving the turbines (see turbo engine).

Bodywork

This is made outside to Renault patterns, from Kevlar material. The bottom parts of

Renault RE20. (Courtesy of Renault Sport).

the pontoons are in honeycomb while the internal skirt panels are made of Kevlar material to take all the inserts necessary for fixing the skirts, springs and the external panels of the skirts, these being in honeycomb. The whole length of the skirts is trimmed with ceramics. The springs which force the skirts down on the ground are long carbon strips which form two large undulations, from the front to the rear of the skirt, with a low point fixed to the middle of the skirt panel.

The nose is not integral with the cockpit, but rests on a tubular frame which also supports the front aerofoils (with adjustable leading edge flaps).

The rear aerofoil is fixed to a support, typically Renault, made of Kevlar material and anchored to the rear casing of the gearbox. Its fin is adjustable, in one or two parts, according to the circuit. The aerofoil support is adjustable for height by its fixing on the gearbox. The fins are made of aluminium sheet riveted onto the internal frames.

Indeed, a very nice modern Formula One car engineered by a professional automobile manufacturer.

Specification

Engine
Renault Gordini V6 90° turbocharged KKK

Chassis
Light alloy, Dural 2002 sheets – Carbon Fibre – Honeycomb panels with 15CDV6 – Steel fabricated bulkheads – Titanium tube roll over bars

Front Suspension
Top rocker arms, bottom wishbones all 15CDV6 steel fabricated – Renault cast magnesium uprights – S.N.R. axle bearings – Inboard springs – Koni/De Carbon shock absorbers combination – Adjustable anti roll bar – Renault rack and pinion steering system – Ratio 7/1

Brakes – Front
Girling master cylinders – AP Lockheed twin calipers – Ventilated discs 11 inch diameter – Ferodo DS11 pads

Rear Suspension
Top rocker arms, bottom wishbones all 15CDV6 steel fabricated – Renault cast

magnesium uprights – S.N.R. axle bearings – Inboard springs – Koni/De Carbon shock absorbers combination –Non-adjustable anti roll bar

Brakes – Rear
Renault/AP Lockheed calipers. Discs and pads same as front

Transmission
Hewland FG400 5 speed – Borg and Beck twin dry discs Clutch – Renault/Glenzer Spicer driveshafts and joints

Water, Oil and Air Cooling
Chausson/Seim aluminium radiators – Heat exchanger – Quinson fitting – Titeflex piping

Fuel System
Renault/Superflexit fuel cell 220 litre capacity – Rotel/Kugelfischer pumps – Titeflex piping and fittings

Instruments
Contactless/Ppoinsot – Magnetti Marelli ignition system

Wheels – Tyres
Gotti rims 13 x 11 inch – 15 x 11 inch Front 13 x 18 inch Rear Michelin tyres

Bodywork
Fibreglass – Kevlar body – Aluminium front and rear aerofoils

Dimensions
Front Track : 1720mm
Rear Track ; 1570mm
Wheelbase : 2860mm
Weight : 600kg

Chapter 17

Renault Gordini V6 Turbo Engine

Originally, the Regie planned to use the V6 configuration for its future mass production road cars, as well as for its different versions of racing models such as Prototype and Formula Two cars, where the configuration derived from. The arrangement, a "V" at 90°, was chosen in order to obtain a good balance and a harmonious proportion between length, width and height, making it possible to have a more accessible housing of the inlet and exhaust manifolds and a more practical attachment of the components and assemblies such as the fuel-injection pump. Furthermore, this choice notably lowers the centre of gravity of the engine and consequently that of the car.

Cylinder Block

The general line of the cylinder block is in the form of a "V" at 90°, which provides it with an arrangement of three cylinders on each side. Compressed air is admitted at the centre of the "V" and exhausted at the sides, over the gearbox. The block is made of GS Spheroidal-Graphite cast iron, the result of experiments carried out by the modern foundry of the State-owned Renault Company. This material was preferred to light alloy for two reasons:

1) On the one hand, in order to produce an engine strong and rigid enough to withstand high power output and to meet, in the best possible way, the requirements on mechanical and thermal strength.

2) On the other hand, in order to resolve the special problems that are raised by thin wall casting techniques; the wall thickness varies from 3.5mm to 4mm. In addition to this, the cast iron cylinder block does not create heat expansion problems.

For a racing engine, the only drawback of such a solution is that of weight; a little greater than that which can be obtained by using a cylinder block made of aluminium. But there is a limit to this, since the weight of such a finished engine does not exceed 135kg (without turbo assembly); that is to within approximately 10kg of that of rival engines.

At the top, the cylinder block receives the cylinder heads and at the bottom the bottom crankcase, both made of cast aluminium alloy.

Except for minor modifications to the layout of the crankcase stiffening ribs, the block has remained unchanged from its original design. The general assembly is of the "bearing "type.

Liners

The liners are made of nitrided steel. In the Renault tradition, wet liners are used. This offers the advantage that the cylinder wall

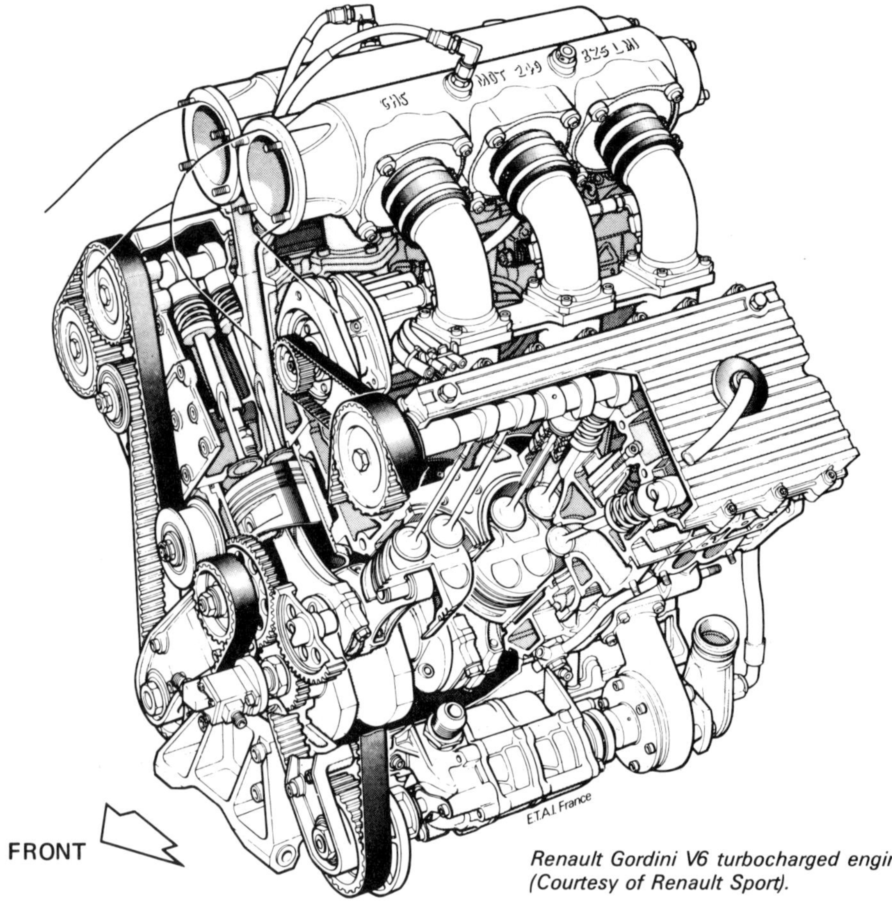

Renault Gordini V6 turbocharged engine. (Courtesy of Renault Sport).

surface can be freely chosen and water passages can be closely controlled. The liners themselves are in direct contact with the cooling water. This is the technique adopted for Renault sleeved competition engines, in order to be sure of a very satisfactory geometry.

In effect, at the upper part of the liners, very high temperatures arise, which creates very large thermal loads. Thus, the liner is fixed at the top of the cylinder block, but remains free whilst being guided at the lower part, which allows it to expand freely.

The block has a recess to support the liners which are sealed at their base with two "O" rings. The sealing to the cylinder heads is effected by means of composite metallic rings. As for oil and water passages, Viton "O" rings are used.

Crankshaft

The crankshaft is turned from solid steel and is nitrided with integral bob-weights. It revolves on four main bearings and has three crankshaft pins divided at 120° from one another, each one taking two con rods. Its assembly to the block is effected by bearing type assembly which forms a whole with the lower part of the cylinder block (similar to the Cosworth DFV). In this way, the unit is assured of a greater rigidity. The same technique is likewise adopted for the camshaft layout in the cylinder heads.

Con Rods

The con rods are forged nitrided steel. The big end is assembled to the crankshaft with

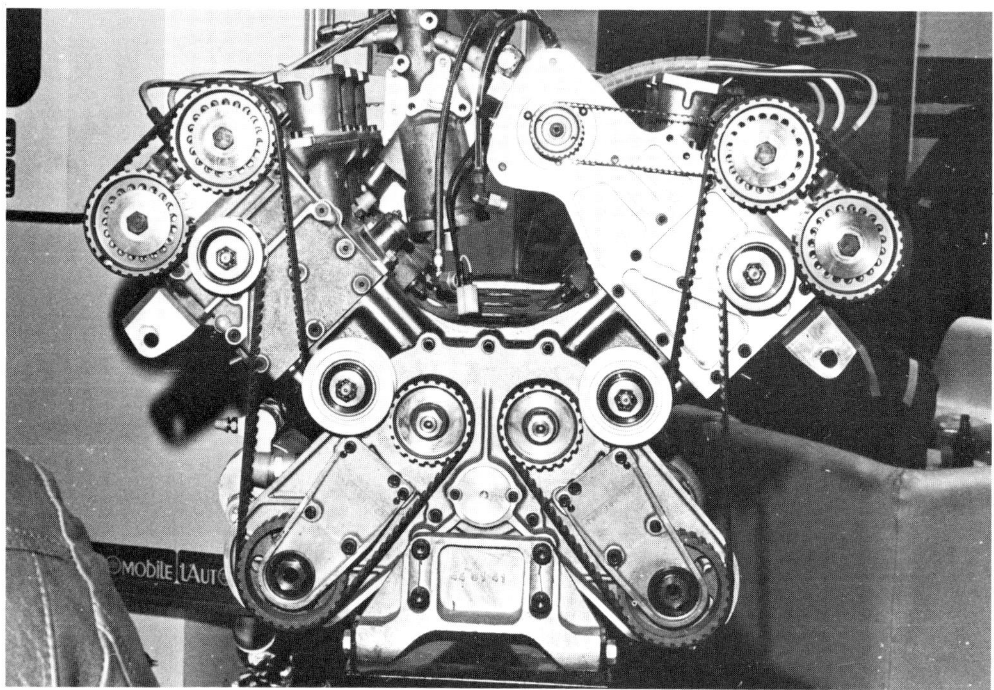

Front view of turbos installation without inlet manifolds – Renault Gordini V6 turbocharged engine.

"standard" plain shell bearing held by a cup and two high tensile bolts. The piston is held by a steel gudgeon pin, free in the con rod and piston.

Pistons

The pistons are made from forged aluminium alloy. The crown is pocketed to give clearance to the valves. (The average speed of the piston is 15.7 metres per second at 11,000rpm). Three rings are used, one "firing stroke", compression and oil scraper. It seems that major problems encountered in 1979 were due to piston failure. Although the pistons are cooled by oil jets from the main gallery, the pistons of a turbocharged and supercharged engine run at a higher temperature than those of a normally aspirated engine; this caused problems with piston liner running clearances. Added to this was an inconsistency of mixture which became over-rich (the Kugelfischer fuel injection pump is not sensitive to the density of the charge), as the temperature rose and with the high-incoming charge in the combustion chamber, any excess blow-by destroyed rings and pistons.

These problems were largely cured by fitting new large air-water intercoolers which considerably lowered the compressed air temperature before it reached the combustion chambers.

Cylinder Heads

The cylinder heads are made from cast aluminium alloy and include four valves per cylinder. The combustion chamber design is in effect "pent-roof" shape, but very much flattened. For this reason the valve angle in respect to the cylinder axis is of 10° for the inlet and 11.30° for the exhaust. Renault claims that the combustion chamber pent-roof shape creates turbulence of the gases and so assures a more flexible combustion. The cam carriers are also made of cast aluminium alloy and take two cam shafts (on each bank) which operates the valves

Rear view without turbos and inlet manifolds – Renault Gordini V6 turbocharged engine.

through steel tappet buckets and shims. Each cam shaft revolves on four bearings, shells and caps.

Fuel System

The indirect fuel injection is operated by a Kugelfischer plunger type injection pump system driven by the right hand bank's inlet cam shaft. The injectors are located on cylinder inlet ports connected to the two air collectors. Throttle is controlled by means of butterflies located at the inlet of each turbine, as slides apparently cannot be used because of the pressure of the compressed air.

Timing Gear System

These are driven from the crankshaft by means of a relay of three gears, then by two toothed belts which compared with a standard train of gears have the advantage of reducing the weight and of making it easier to replace them when necessary.

These belts drive the two camshafts of each cylinder head as well as their components on each side of the engine. On the left hand bank, the inlet shaft also drives the alternator.

Oil and Water System

Oil lubrication is effected according to a pressure pump which circulates the oil, going through filtered to the engine at a pressure of between 8 and 10kg/cm^3. The oil which drops back to the engine sump is sucked up by a scavenge pump, then after being cooled through a radiator it is sent back into the tank.

As for the water system, two centrifugal type water pumps circulate the water around the cylinder, each one supplying one row of cylinders. Oil and water pumps are mounted on either side of the lower part of the engine and are driven by the toothed camshaft belts.

Renault Gordini V6 turbocharged engine with drive (distribution) systems exposed. (Photo Jean Damon).

Ignition

The ignition is a Magnetti Marelli electronic system with impulses taken off by electro-magnetic pick-ups.

As for the Turbo's installation, this is described in the RE20 chassis chapter. Note that the latest model used "KKK" turbos which replaced a single Garrett AiResearch unit.

After many troublesome years in Formula One, in 1981 the V6 achieved the reliability so long sought.

Specification

Configuration: V6 90°

Capacity: 1492cc

Bore: 86 mm

Stroke: 42.8mm

Compression Ratio: 7 to 1

Bhp: 520 at 11,000rpm

Torque: 38mkg at 9,600rpm

Timing: Inlet: 100° A.T.D.C.
Exhaust: 106° B.T.D.C.
Ignition: 40° B.T.D.C.
Injection: 40° B.T.D.C.

Firing Order: 1–6–3–5–2–4

Cylinder Block:
GS Spheroidal-Graphite cast iron – General assembly is "bearing type"

Crankshaft:
Solid steel nitrided turned from solid – Turns on 4 main journals – Has 3 pins, each one taking 2 con rods

Liners:
Nitrided steel – Water cooled – Suspended type

Con Rods:
Forged nitrided steel

Pistons:
Mahle Boetze forged aluminium alloy, with 1 "Firing stroke", 1 compression, 1 oil scraper piston rings

Cylinder Heads:
Cast aluminium alloy – 4 valves per cylinder – Integral aluminium alloy camshaft carriers – take camshaft buckets and shims – Valve inclination 10° inlet, 11.30° exhaust – Each valve with double springs.

Camshafts:
Four Steel, each turns on 4 bearings – Camshaft and pumps driven by 2 toothed belts

Injection System:
Indirect injection system – Kugelfischer plunger type injection pump – Throttle incorporated in each compressor

Ignition System:
Magnetti Marelli electronic ignition alternator

Water System:
2 centrifugal water pumps each one supplying 1 cylinder bank

Oil System:
1 pressure pump – 1 scavenge pump – Similar assembly for turbine lubrication

Turbos:
Twin KKK units and waste gate units

Intercooling:
2 air to water intercoolers

Weight:
180kg with starter motor clutch and turbos

Index